BirthMarks

II0631124

Sandra Patton

BirthMarks

Transracial Adoption in
Contemporary America

New York University Press

New York and London

NEW YORK UNIVERSITY PRESS
New York and London

Library of Congress Cataloging-in-Publication Data
Patton, Sandra Lee.
BirthMarks : Transracial adoption in contemporary America /
Sandra Patton.
p.   cm.
Includes bibliographical references and index.
ISBN 0-8147-6681-1 (cloth : alk. paper) —
ISBN 0-8147-6682-X (pbk. : alk. paper)
1. Interracial adoption—United States. 2. Adoptees—United States—
Interviews. 3. Afro-Americans—Race identity. 4. Adoption—
Government policy—United States. I. Title: Birth marks.
II. Adoption—Government policy—United States. II. Title.
HV875.64 .P37 2000
362.73'4'0973—dc21   00-010141

New York University Press books are printed on acid-free paper,
and their binding materials are chosen for strength and durability.

Manufactured in the United States of America

10 9 8 7 6 5 4 3 2 1

*In memory of
my father, my friend,
Robert Bleakney Patton,
who instilled in me a passion for social justice,
and taught me to know a good story when I heard one.*

CONTENTS

ACKNOWLEDGMENTS

This study would not have been possible without the generosity of time, insight, and emotion of the adoptees and social workers I interviewed. I wish to thank the social workers I spoke with for teaching me what the adoption world looks like from their perspective, as well as for the enormous help many of them provided me in my search for adoptees to interview. I am particularly indebted to the twenty-two transracial adoptees who shared their narratives about their lives and identities with me. For many of them, and certainly for myself, these interviews were profound, intense encounters that not only shaped this research, but also our sense of self as adoptees. I am deeply grateful to them for the stories they shared with me.

I would like to thank my teachers and mentors at the University of Maryland, College Park, for their generous support and wise counsel throughout the research and writing of this study. I am particularly indebted to my dissertation advisor, John L. Caughey, whose thoughtful and meditative guidance, reflective questions, and generous insights into questions of identity, culture, and consciousness were invaluable. I am deeply grateful to Bonnie Thornton Dill for her thoughtful engagement in and incisive perspective on the issues of families, children, women, and race that we are both so committed to, as well as her graceful example as a politically engaged scholar-activist. I must thank Deborah S. Rosenfelt for initially suggesting adoption as a dissertation topic. Our common personal connections to the subject have fueled provocative and fruitful discussions during the course of this research, and her generous insights and unflagging support have contributed immeasurably to its completion. In addition, Claire Moses, Michael Agar, Myron Lounsbury, and Rhonda Williams have contributed enormously to this study.

I am indebted to Rickie Solinger for her profoundly helpful comments and critiques. Her research on single pregnancy and her suggestions when I was revising my dissertation for publication were invaluable. I also thank Lisa Disch for her cogent suggestions and valuable criticism. I am deeply grateful to the critical acumen and unwavering support of my friends Dabrina Taylor, Eva George, Lillie Ransom, Psyche Williams, Sharon Kirkland, Debra DeRuyver, Laine Snowman, Kerry Brooks, Sara Dorow, Mark McCandless, S. P. Udayakumar, and Miranda Rosenfelt. I thank Jennifer Holt for her research assistance.

I am enormously grateful to my family, whose support as well as personal reflections and insights on their experiences with adoption enriched this study. I am indebted to my mother Lois Patton, my sister Nancy Patton, my birth mother, who wishes to remain anonymous, and particularly my sister Diane Hollingsworth. Diane listened endlessly to my reflections and questions about what it means to be adopted, and her perspectives were invaluable. I also thank Josh and Casey Hollingsworth.

I am grateful to the American Association of University Women for awarding me an American Fellowship that allowed me to devote a full year to writing. I would like to thank the University of Maryland's Africa and Africa in the Americas Project for a travel grant to conduct fieldwork. I am grateful to the American Studies Association for Annette K. Baxter Travel Grants that provided travel expenses to two conferences where I presented papers based on this work. I thank the University of Maryland, College Park, for awarding me a Jacob K. Goldhaber Travel Grant that also facilitated travel to a conference where I presented a paper based on this research. I thank the Institute on Race and Poverty at the University of Minnesota Law School for their support during my postdoctoral fellowship there.

I am deeply grateful to my partner, M. Imani, for enormous patience, support, and belief in me; for reading drafts so many times the words blurred together; and for critical engagement in our seemingly endless dialogues on adoption, gender, race, and identity.

BirthMarks

Narratives of Adoption, Roots, and Identity

> It's hard being adopted, in many ways. . . . I mean, when I was in fourth grade—this is something that stays with me today because my father is getting into it again—we had to do family trees. And I refused. And the teacher said, "Well, go home and do the assignment at home." And I remember being—I mean there are very few moments I remember being upset about school because I loved school, but I was upset about this homework assignment. And my mom said to me, "Well, we're your family now." And I said, "But that's not my *real* family." [with anger] I mean I had this definite idea to have a family tree you had to know—I mean, I had an idea of *roots*, that you had to be able to trace it *biologically*. I mean, I *knew* *that* even at whatever age you are in fourth grade, at age nine.
>
> —Lynn Praeger, twenty-nine-year-old transracial adoptee

Lynn's story about *roots* and *family trees* raises the question: What makes us who we are? How do we, lacking knowledge of our birth families, claim a history, a heritage, an ancestry in a social context that largely defines "real" kinship through "bloodlines"? The metaphor of *roots* resonates beyond the lives of adoptees. It assumes that identity—who we are—is shaped at least in part by who our ancestors were, whether we define that identity through *blood, genes, culture, nature, biology,* or *nurture.* The idea of roots is a powerful metaphor for connections between genealogy, history, family, race, and identity. Cultural studies scholar Julia Watson explains: "Genealogy specifies *origin*. Its fundamental assumption is categorical: Humans are defined by who and where we are 'from'—in terms such as *stock, blood, class, race*" (emphasis added) (Watson 1996:297). Lynn and the other transracial adoptees I interviewed struggled with questions of history, origins, and the meaning of adoption as they continually engaged in processes of identity construction and maintenance. Their struggles undermine traditional assumptions surrounding the metaphor of *roots,* challenging us to redefine popular understandings of "genealogy," race, gender, and identity.

This book is about stories—individual, familial, cultural, political, and institutional narratives about the births, lives, and identities of African American and multiracial adults who were adopted and raised by White parents. Race and identity were the central issues that emerged in the life history interviews I conducted with twenty-two transracial adoptees. Their stories raise questions about the social construction of identity, and the connections between identity, race, gender, class, and public policy. My method is ethnographic. While a number of studies of transracial adoption exist, most have focused on the "adjustment" of adoptees and have only addressed racial identity in limited ways. Remarkably little attention has been paid to how Black and multiracial adoptees raised by White parents articulate their own identities. Also glaringly absent from existing research are considerations of how these lives and selves have been shaped by cultural and sociopolitical forces, such as public policies concerning child welfare, the socioeconomic situation of unwed mothers, changing social views of gender and family, and shifting racial politics. The exploration of transracial adoption raises fundamental questions about how social structure affects individual experiences. How does society define which mothers are "fit" and which "unfit"? How does the language of public policies inscribe and shape individual lives? How do social institutions account for differences in age, race, and class when defining gender and motherhood? Although most academic discussions of social policy address people in abstract aggregate terms, the lives of adoptees demonstrate that policy questions often touch them in profoundly individual and personal ways. Indeed, this book argues that the identities of transracial adoptees are socially constructed through the implementation of public policies concerning race, family, gender, poverty, and child welfare.

Transracial adoption first became a controversial issue in the early 1970s. A heated public debate occurred about the transmission of African American cultural identity to Black children adopted into White middle-class families.[1] The central question in these debates was whether or not White parents were capable of teaching their children African American culture and history, and inculcating them with the skills necessary for Blacks to survive in the racially unequal United States. Concerns over the transmission of identity have shaped public opinion and social policies regarding racial matching between children and parents since the 1970s. Transracial adoption became a contentious public issue after the National Association of Black Social Workers (NABSW) released a position paper in 1972 stating their opposition to the practice, citing their concerns about racial identity and survival skills as the basis of their objections (NABSW 1972).

The Black social workers' critique of the ways Black children were treated in the child welfare system was a contestation of state-sanctioned regulations determining which families African American children would become part of, and thus be socialized by. Their protests against transracial adoption were largely motivated by a concern for the futures of African American children and a desire to strengthen Black families, and were often politically grounded in Black nationalism. Policy changes reflecting these concerns gradually occurred at the state, county, and agency levels. While standards varied in different regions, in most areas of the country adoption agencies became committed to the goal of racial matching whenever possible. Many states drew up regulations governing how long agencies could spend searching for same-race placements.

Transracial adoption receded from public debate later in the 1970s, and received very little media attention until the early 1990s when it once again became the subject of fierce public discussion. While arguments against this practice continued to focus on racial identity, the political context of the 1990s had changed. Whereas in the earlier debate attention was focused on the importance of racial matching between children and parents, in the current political climate the debate has led to new federal policies promoting "color-blind" adoptions by prohibiting the consideration of race in the adoptive placement of a child. The public discourse concerning this issue goes beyond the specificity of transracial adoptees' lives. Indeed, this policy dialogue has implications for political struggles over teenage pregnancy, "illegitimacy," and welfare reform.

While the current public dialogue is explicitly concerned with issues of race, the linkage of transracial adoption with welfare reform, tax credits to adoptive parents, and the termination of (birth) parental rights reveals a more implicit agenda focusing on women. In fact, the 1996 law was explicitly designed to combat "illegitimacy" among welfare recipients. In a political context dominated by proponents of traditional "family values" as the solution to the supposed "breakdown of the family," celebrations of adoption as a panacea to the "epidemic of illegitimacy" among "underclass" women and the misfortune of infertility among primarily middle-class heterosexual couples must be viewed critically. This political dialogue sounds disturbingly similar to early-twentieth-century eugenic prescriptions for strengthening the White race by limiting the reproductive capacities of "undesirables"— namely, Black women, immigrant women, "imbeciles," and "immoral" women. In the shifting political alliances and commitments of the 1990s and beyond, adoption has become a curious battleground on which the social meanings of race and identity, gender and family, work and poverty, culture and nation are being constructed, contested, and enforced.

Questions about the relationship between individuals, families, and the state intersect with the shifting and contested meanings of race, gender, and class in this multicultural, racially stratified, postindustrial society. Our struggles for social meaning occur in *narrative* form. While we may not typically associate politics with narratives, when we consider policy debates and dialogues it becomes evident that it is through storytelling that arguments are made. Personalized narratives often carry more weight than statistical analysis. The news media report political events and issues in easily accessible stories. Dramatic narratives provide a "hook" for viewers' and constituents' attention. The intersection of welfare reform and adoption, particularly transracial adoption, has become the site for storied battles over public understandings of social and political change at the nexus of representation and public policy. Issues of identity, family, and race have emerged as powerful discursive lightening rods through which a broad range of social, political, and economic issues are debated. Political conservatives and centrists have successfully promoted narratives of social crisis and decline in which inner-city "welfare mothers" and their "illegitimate" children are cast as responsible for poverty and crime, and thus as a fundamental threat to middle-class security.

Social narratives—in political discourse as well as popular culture—that identify "the breakdown of the family," "illegitimacy," and teenage pregnancy as the most fundamental social problems of the 1990s often find plot resolution in salvation stories of adoption. In the standard formula, White middle-class families are repeatedly cast as the bearers of traditional "family values," the only possible salvation for the "at risk" child—variously signified by neglect, abuse, HIV or AIDS, drug exposure at birth, and frequently racial "otherness." In this view, "political correctness" and "reverse racism" are blamed for creating and enforcing racial matching policies that, it is argued, impede adoption and keep Black children in "foster limbo." This classic racial narrative of the "White man's [family's] burden" of "civilizing the [impoverished urban] native" has been used in political dialogue to justify the dismantling of the U.S. welfare state and prohibit the consideration of race in making adoptive placements.

Most of the existing literature on transracial adoption has relied on quantitative methods or survey questionnaires to study the adjustment of Black children adopted into White families (Grow and Shapiro 1974; McRoy and Zurcher 1983; Simon and Altstein 1977, 1981, 1987, 1992; Simon, Altstein, and Melli 1994). While valid as far as they go, these studies are limited by methodological practices that approach race as a fixed category and limit the scope of inquiry to the individual and familial levels. Virtually no attention is given to the institutional, cultural, social, economic, and political contexts within which such families are constructed and maintained. Such research avoids the issues raised by critics of transracial adoption. The NABSW and other critics are concerned about the transmission of culture within a racially stratified social structure, and their questions are not addressed by positivist research approaches. Indeed, considerations of culture and social structure are outside the purview of such studies because identity is unproblematically viewed as an individual matter.[2]

I employ a narrative analysis, drawing on cultural anthropology, critical race theory, social theory, feminist theory and research, cultural studies, and discourse analysis to explore conflictual versions of truth concerning adoption and race in the United States. In exploring these narratives I link identity, kinship, culture, social institutions, and the political economy in a range of cultural sites including public policy, political discourse, news coverage, popular culture, the perspectives of social workers in the field of adoption, and the life histories of adult transracial adoptees. I interviewed sixteen social workers and directors of public and private adoption agencies in the greater San Francisco Bay area and the Mid-Atlantic region in 1995 and 1996. I also interviewed twenty-two adult transracial adoptees, as well as several White and Black adoptees raised in same-race families on the West Coast and the Mid-Atlantic region between 1994 and 1996. In 1998 and 1999 I conducted follow-up interviews with several key informants. The primary focus of this study is the period from 1993 to 1996, when transracial adoption reemerged as a controversial issue in public policy and popular culture. The contentious public dialogue that converged in this social issue fundamentally concerned the futures of low-income women and their children, and other children who, for a variety of reasons, could not be raised by their birth families. I contend, however, that this dialogue can also be read as a broader discourse involving questions that touch the lives of all people living in the United States at the turn of the century.

Adoptee as *Native Ethnographer* and *Ethnographer Gone Native* as Adoptee

Lynn Praeger, whom we met at the beginning of this chapter, was a twenty-nine-year-old biracial woman raised by White parents at the time of our interviews. She recognized, like many adoptees (myself included), that we occupy a particular social location that gives rise to a commonly held set of assumptions about identity, race, ethnicity, and kinship. Indeed, at times the sense of difference adoption typically fosters makes many of us feel that we constitute our own race or ethnicity, or even that we belong to a separate ontological category of humans. Symbolically, we are not part of humanity's great chain of being. Rather, we often feel like extraneous links hanging off to the side, disconnected from primary streams of lineage, from *legitimate* lines of descent. Our identities are forged without genealogical patterns, without biological histories beyond our embodied selves. By their very absence, these mysteries of heritage construct our selves as much as our known families do, for the sense of being without a "true" family history and identity—in a society that defines familial "truth" through biology—shapes our vision of our selves and our place in our families and in society. For while we may at times seem to belong in our families or our social groups, we know that we are different, that we came from somewhere else. We live our lives at the margins of difference—perpetually crossing borders, we are both insiders and outsiders, both natives and foreigners.

The situation of adoption—regardless of whether we know our birth families or not—locates adoptees in a curious position in relation to assumptions about kinship, culture, and where one belongs. In a sense, we are like ethnographers "gone native." Our origins are somewhere else, but we have so thoroughly "adopted" the kin system and culture we are in that the lines of demarcation between our original and adopted cultures have been blurred. We don't so much belong to one family or the other, as to both our "native" and our "foreign" cultures. Yet our lives elude traditional definitions of self, family, and culture. *Which family and culture are native? Which are foreign—birth or adoptive?*

Anthropologist Renato Rosaldo discusses "going native" as follows:

> Cautionary tales that circulate among field-workers warn against going too far in identifying with the so-called natives. . . . Moral: don't go native. "Going native" is said to mean the end of scientific knowledge. . . . [T]his view asserts that the optimal field-worker should dance on the edge of a paradox by simultaneously becoming "one of the people" and remaining an academic. The term *participant-observation* reflects even as it shapes the field-worker's double persona. (Rosaldo 1993:179–80)

When I first began learning ethnographic methods I found myself feeling *at home* in a curious way. While other graduate students sometimes struggled with the notion of being both a participant and an observer of the cultural scene being researched, I experienced a sense of validation of a part of myself I had never quite been able to articulate: my insider-outsider sense of being in the world. I was not learning a way of perceiving cultural reality so much as discovering a set of practices that drew on my daily mode of social interaction. As a White adoptee in a White family, I have spent my life looking like an insider while feeling I was *really* an outsider. In fact, I was both an insider and an outsider; the "double persona" Rosaldo attributes to ethnographers captures an aspect of adoptive identities as well. We are our outward, apparent selves, while carrying within us the shadow selves we might have been, often feeling we aren't "authentically" anyone. I have often felt that I've spent my life "passing"—as a real member of my family, as a real person, in a sense.

One of the ways that I, like many adoptees I've spoken with, learned to cope with the sense that I didn't really belong anywhere, was to develop techniques for appearing to fit in everywhere—my own set of ethnographic tools for learning the cultures of whatever groups I encountered. These techniques of cultural observation and analysis provided me both with avenues of entry into a broad range of social groups and with a way of perceiving and understanding myself as participating in, but not fully a part of either my family or the social groups I joined. Like a number of people I interviewed, my imagined other selves provided different subjectivities, alternate social locations from which I viewed my adoptive self and family. While most children, at some point, imagine they were adopted and come from somewhere else, for adoptees this mysterious alternate possibility is real. It is based on the facts and secrets of our life stories. We did come from somewhere else. We do have other families.

In effect, many of us become like native ethnographers in our own families and social worlds. Like anthropologists who turn a critical eye on their own cultures, adoptees are observers and participants in "our own" cultural worlds. At the same time we are like ethnographers "gone native," in the sense that we have come into these cultures and families from unknown origins and have in varying degrees accepted them as "our own." Our lives—particularly those of transracial adoptees—deconstruct and denaturalize the category "native." In a sense, we are never natives, never "authentic" members of any tribe or clan. For even when we are (re)united with our birth families we are foreigners who have been raised and socialized in other families. We write our identities through the trope of difference; within ourselves we are only "authentically" other.

Many of us find our "home" at the margins, learning to adapt by learning to blend in with whatever groups we choose to interact with. As I explained above, I am "at home" as an ethnographer, continually engaging in the process of learning other people's lives and cultures.

In interviewing adoptees there was none of the traditional "danger" for me of *going native,* because, as I learned, I was already "one of the people," though, true to form, also always an outsider, also an academic. An interesting connection often developed between myself and those I spoke with. We often discovered and rediscovered that it was only with other adoptees that we were in any sense natives. While there are drawbacks to such close identification with one's informants, I believe the benefits of an insider perspective far outweigh the disadvantages. While I was an outsider with regard to racial identity, the commonalities we discovered as adoptees gave me an insight into and understanding of my informants' experiences that a nonadopted person would probably not have had. In the following excerpt from an interview, Gabrielle Michaels, a self-defined Afro-Latina and "out" bisexual woman, explained how, for her, being able to move among different social groups was central to her sense of self as an adoptee. It also demonstrates the benefit of my insider status as an adoptee, for had I not identified with Gabrielle's description of self, I may well have overlooked something that eventually emerged as a central theme in the lives of the adoptees I interviewed.

Sandi: And then, did that change as you went along—your sense of what the primary issues were? Are you still in therapy?

Gabrielle: Yeah, different therapist, but—It pretty much focused right down to adoption.

[Both of us laugh.]

Sandi: I know what you're saying!

Gabrielle: Pretty fast, you know. I mean, I think that that is pretty core to me. I don't think of myself as you know, this *lesbian-whatever* [sarcastically]. Or I don't think of myself as like *Latina fighter,* you know. I don't think of myself in those terms so much. I sort of—I can kind of blend and move between circles pretty easily, but as far as like primary identity, I think that it comes back to adoption.

Sandi: I feel the same way. You said you move through circles pretty easily. That really strikes a chord with me. Can you say more about that?

Gabrielle: Yeah.

Sandi: A sense of belonging and identity . . .

Gabrielle: Well, I feel like—and this is the positive, up side of being
   adopted, I guess, or at least maybe just my identity and who I
   am—that, you know, I can go to Mexico and I can like fit in. I
   can hang out with African American people and fit in. I can hang
   out with straight people and fit in. I hang out with gay people.
   You know, I can work in the financial district, or I can go slum-
   ming in the Haight, or wherever. You know? And I can kind of
   just totally slide through these worlds pretty easily. And they're
   really, sometimes pretty opposite. You know?

This ability to interact with different groups and cultures with ease
emerged repeatedly in my interviews; in fact, I would characterize it as
one of the foremost survival skills my informants learned to use in navigating through their complex lives. This is what James Clifford calls a
"modern 'ethnography' of conjunctures, constantly moving *between* cultures" (Clifford 1988:9). As Gabrielle made clear, movement across
boundaries is not the sole province of ethnographers; in this study the
borders are necessarily blurred between "ethnographers" and "natives."
The adoptees I spoke with had a heightened awareness of crossing cultural boundaries, for they were in "a state of being in culture while looking at culture" (Clifford 1988:9).

   The interviews I conducted were moments in the continual process of
identity construction and discovery for both those I interviewed and myself. Many of the interviews were powerful interactions for myself as well
as my informants. Often these were a source of understanding and connection over issues that are misunderstood and misrepresented by people who were not adopted. My own identity was part of this process in
ways that I hadn't fully anticipated. My informants often wanted to hear
my story after they had shared their own with me. Spending several
hours in intimate discussion about our struggles over our identities, our
families, our childhood fantasies, our need for or aversion to the search
for our birth parents, was not only cathartic and validating; it was also an
occasion of self-definition, a moment when we narrated our lives to
someone who identified with what is often experienced as a fundamental sense of *difference*.

"Multicultural" Identities

As Black children raised by White parents in a racially stratified society, transracial adoptees have access to a variety of often conflictual systems of cultural meaning about race and African American identity in the contemporary United States. Black children of White parents are exposed to a different range of racial meanings and narratives of self than Black children raised by African American parents. Demographic and cultural factors such as the racial composition of the neighborhood and community, and the racial assumptions of parents and other family members fundamentally shape the cultural systems of racial meaning that are made available to these children.

Consistent with the hegemony of race in the contemporary United States, the identities of adoptees are often discussed in monolithic terms in the public discourse about transracial adoption, as if they develop either a White *or* a Black cultural identity. In an interview in a popular magazine targeted at women, Judy Turner, a White foster parent who struggled to adopt a Black toddler and eventually succeeded, explained that the private adoption agency "steadfastly maintained that if Jordan were raised by us, he would grow to hate both whites and blacks—presumably because he'd feel he didn't fit in with either race" (Turner 1992:140). However, the human construction of a meaningful sense of self is rarely played out in such simple, neatly divided categories. People construct their identities in terms of the cultural meaning systems available to them in particular social contexts. Anthropologist John L. Caughey defines culture as "a conceptual system of beliefs, rules, and values that lies behind different ways of behaving" (Caughey 1984:9). This approach allows us to see all human beings as *multicultural;* that is, all humans are exposed to, and in turn utilize a broad range of cultural meaning systems in everyday life. The central question concerning the formation of racial identity among transracial adoptees is not which cultural group—Black or White—the adoptee belongs to, but rather how his or her identity is informed by the particular versions of African American and White cultural meaning systems he or she encounters.

As the focus on survival skills in the debate about transracial adoption suggests, African Americans have developed particular cognitive strategies of survival and resistance as members of an oppressed group in a racist society. In a *Washington Post* article Damon Hersh, a twenty-five-year-old African American who was adopted by White parents when he was three, explains: "The biggest thing would be to tell a black adopted child there's nothing wrong with being black, that in fact it's a very good thing, though society is going to tell the child otherwise" (Evans 1993:B5). Hersh points to a central issue, namely, the negative ideological messages Black children growing up in the United States receive about themselves through popular culture, educational materials, and social interaction. African Americans need to learn how to deconstruct and delegitimate racial stereotypes and racist treatment.

Elisa Jacob, a twenty-six-year-old transracial adoptee who was raised in a nearly all-White community in northern California, discussed the pain and difficulty of facing racist incidents without the survival skills to respond:

> *Elisa:* You know, I hated high school. And the memories that I have are just . . . I mean I was in art class and these two "red-necks" were—They drew pictures of Black people in nooses and they pinned them up around the classroom. And the teacher, I remember, you know, she took them down, but she didn't say anything. But I was always taught by my parents—it pisses me off now—I was always supposed to ignore stuff, because if you ignore stuff they'll see it doesn't bother you and they'll stop. So when things like that happened I didn't—I would—I saw them drawing it, and I saw them put it up and stuff. But I didn't want to call attention to myself and make a big deal about it. And when the teacher was looking at me to see my reaction I would just look away. You know when people would say things . . . You know my best friend in high school was White and you know, she would stick up for me sometimes, but I wouldn't do it myself. I think one, because of what my parents always taught me, and two, I had no sense of identity, so I really didn't know what to say. I think high school is when it all came to [a] head.

While such an encounter would be difficult for many people, the pain and confusion were magnified for Elisa by the fact that she had no coping mechanisms to explain or deal with it, beyond her parents' advice that she ignore such behavior.

Survival skills can involve cultural knowledge as well as particular ways of seeing; indeed, the sense of a "double-consciousness" written about by W. E. B. Du Bois is still socially relevant nearly a century later (Du Bois 1903). Sociologist Howard Winant explains: "Today we can see that dual consciousness is an immensely significant phenomenon. It can be theorized as resistance and subversion, as ambivalence, as standpoint and critique" (Winant 1993:179). From the perspective of cultural anthropology, survival skills are part of a system of cultural meaning, a mental map that individuals use to navigate the routes of their lives. The crucial question for transracial adoptees is whether White parents, whose unmarked racial identity is continually reinforced as the social norm, are capable of teaching their Black children how to resist and undercut potentially devastating and ubiquitous racial stereotypes and racist ideology.

The experiences of African American adoptees raised in White families are often similar to those of international adoptees raised by White parents. While the parents of some adoptees are conscientious about exposing their children to their cultures of origin, others see these concerns as irrelevant. Whether raised with such awareness or not, international and African American adoptees often feel compelled as adults to explore the cultural meaning systems associated with their ethnic origins. Both international and African American adoptees report a disjuncture between the ways they experience themselves in their families and the racist treatment to which they are subjected in public. Indeed, such experiences are often the catalyst for their cultural explorations as adults. Transracial and transcultural adoptees are "multicultural," in that they draw on a repertoire of cultural meaning systems in charting their course through life. However, despite such similarities at an experiential level, the public policy issues surrounding the adoption of African American children in the United States differ significantly from those surrounding international adoptions. While U.S. social policy is concerned about the reproductive behavior of poor women in other countries, the state's level of involvement in the regulation of women's reproductive "choices" in the United States is significantly higher. As I have discussed, in the 1990s Congress was deeply concerned with issues of reproduction among low-income women of color in the United States.

Most of the transracial adoptees I interviewed had birth parents of two different races and/or ethnicities. Their lives often paralleled the experiences of children of mixed-race couples in interesting ways. As with transracial adoptees, the "presence of racially mixed persons defies" commonsense understandings of racial boundaries and challenges "long-held notions about the biological, moral, and social meaning of race" (Root 1992:3). Transracial adoptees further disrupt dualistic and monolithic conceptions of the U.S. racial order; their lives have separated the organizational categories of biology and culture. They are not easily classified as either White or Black. In fact, their identities argue for a recognition of the hybridity of identity. Andrea Bailey, a twenty-five-year-old transracial adoptee, explained her sense of herself with regard to rigid racial categories as follows:

> *Andrea:* I fit in with people that are marginalized. You know? That's something that has helped me. My mom has helped me a lot. But yeah. I don't have any one particular group that I fully identify with, and that's a problem I think for me. Feeling like you don't really have that place, so you find other people that also don't necessarily fit in.

Transracial adoptees are indeed multiply defined, multicultural selves; this must be acknowledged to understand their lives and identities. Yet this insight has wider ramifications beyond their specific circumstances. Philip Tajitsu Nash argues: "Those of us with parents of two distinct 'racial' backgrounds are a visible reminder that *everyone* is multicultural and deserves to be treated as a multifaceted individual" (Nash 1992). In our postmodern, postindustrial, global political economy, we would do well to concede that all identities are multiple, all individuals are cultural hybrids.

Roots and Routes

As an adoptee myself, I have spent my life struggling with issues of identity—who I am in relation to my family, my birth family, my unknown ancestors, and the messages that my social interactions with other people and media representations send me regarding the roots of my "true" self. The metaphor of roots is variously invoked to describe both biology—typically in discussions of searches and reunions—and culture, usually in relation to African American culture. As a White adoptee raised by White parents I have often felt the absence of roots, in that I did not know my biological ancestors, as well as social pressure to search for my birth parents. While many of the transracial adoptees I interviewed also had these experiences, most of them also longed for a sense of connection with their African American cultural roots.

All the adoptees I have spoken with, including those I interviewed formally, those I know personally, and the countless people I have spoken with more casually, are familiar with the dominant public narratives concerning adoption and identity—that searching for our birth parents (more often mothers) is the only way we can know who we "really" are. Some embrace this view, while others are more critical. While search and reunion narratives typically lean toward the nature side of the nature-nurture divide, some people stress the importance of culture and environment, particularly in the controversy over transracial adoption. Public discussions of racial identity usually highlight the socialization of transracial adoptees through African American culture as an issue for White parents raising Black and multiracial children.

While there are diverse opinions on these issues, the mainstream public discussion is framed by the tension between biological and cultural explanations of race and identity, that is, by the nature-nurture debate. Little attention is accorded to the possibility that other social forces, such as public policy and social institutions, fundamentally shape the lives adoptees lead. This oversight obscures a crucial force of identity formation: social structure. Indeed, in my view, the nature-nurture polarity masks the power relations involved in the construction and maintenance of selves in contemporary society. For while biology and culture clearly contribute in multiple and unquantifiable ways to who we become, ideology, social institutions, and structures also define us, shape us, and regulate the boundaries of our lives. The categories of biology and culture that are usually used as organizational frames in considering such questions are necessarily separated among adoptees, and the role of social structure in shaping selves stands out clearly. We are not defined solely by either our genetic heritage, nor by our culture and environment. Rather, like everyone else living in the complex, globalized, and socially stratified United States today, adoptees' identities are intricately constructed and reconstructed by our biological histories, the various cultural meaning systems we encounter, and our interaction with public policies and social institutions. Nevertheless, the ambiguities and complexities of identity, race, adoption, and *roots* are rarely discussed in public discourse.

The voices and experiences of those I interviewed provide a counternarrative—an alternative story of identity—to the public view that transracially adoptive people are solely defined by birth ties, whether cast as biological or cultural. Drawing on the life stories of those I interviewed, I would like to offer an alternative theoretical understanding of the social construction of identity, including racial identities. The life stories of the adoptees I interviewed point to a "genealogy" of identity that moves beyond the limitations of the biology-culture tension to include the forces of ideology and social structure. Transracial adoption is a particularly rich site for exploring contemporary U.S. understandings of race, identity, gender, class, and family. Indeed, in my view transracial adoption has emerged as a highly charged social issue at this historical moment precisely because it embodies the ambiguities of race, identity, gender, and family that characterize the lives of so many people living in the United States at the turn of the century.

Cultural studies theorist Stuart Hall argues that the contemporary moment of race relations is characterized by "the end of the innocent notion of the essential black subject" (Hall 1996:443). The truth of this is borne out in the life stories of transracial adoptees. By virtue of their socialization by White parents, often in predominantly White communities, the question of African American identity is highlighted and problematized. Transracial adoptees recognize "the extraordinary diversity of subjective positions, social experiences and cultural identities which compose the category 'black'"; and know that "Blackness . . . has no guarantees in nature" (Hall 1996:443).

Indeed, most adoptees are keenly aware that their families and identities were *literally* socially constructed by the child welfare system. They are not easily classified as either Black or White. In fact, their life stories argue for recognition of the hybridity of identity and the fluidity of racial categories. Their lives disrupt dualistic, immutable conceptions of the contemporary racial order, and complicate our understandings of racial identity by emphasizing the multiplicity of racialized experience. The idea of race and identity as "socially constructed" is frequently alluded to by academics, but rarely do we question what this *means.*

Public discourse represents transracial adoption as a question of culture, focusing on the way Black children raised in White families will acquire survival skills and a positive sense of African American *cultural* identity. However, as Mary Helen Washington argues: "personal cross-cultural experiences only become comprehensible and liberatory when they are connected to a relevant institutional history" (Washington 1998:13). The "cultural" issues that face transracially adoptive families have been constructed and configured by the child welfare system, the labor market, social welfare policy, and the widespread segregation of housing and education, among other things. Indeed, as one of the transracial adoptees I interviewed explained, transracial adoption is only an issue because we live in a racist world. As she put it bluntly: "It should be okay, but society is screwed."

Yet this public focus on African American culture on the one hand and biological ties on the other, obscures the racialized gender and class politics involved in transracial adoption. Public discourse has typically asked: Should White parents be allowed to adopt Black children? In light of the intersecting issues of gender, poverty, and race we must broaden the question to ask: How do so many Black children become available for adoption? What social circumstances lead them to be removed from their families? And why is transracial adoption offered as a solution to both "illegitimacy" and the large number of children of color in the foster care system? Public policy concerning transracial adoption has been explicitly linked with welfare reform in ways that suggest that the reproductive behavior of poor women of color has been targeted as a means of reducing poverty.[3] While the socializing practices of adoptive families undoubtedly contribute to adoptees' constructions of racial identity, we must move beyond this focus on culture to understand how transracial adoptees' lives have been shaped by the race, gender, and poverty politics that caused them to be separated from their families of origin in the first place.

Thus, it is not enough to recognize the multiplicity and hybridity of racial identity, or to simply consider the ways in which transracial adoptees' parents have dealt with African American culture. Sociologist John Gabriel proposes that we think of "routes" rather than "roots" to understand the "ethnic configurations" produced by "cross-cultural fertilisation" (Gabriel 1998:1–2). Doing so takes us beyond an exclusive focus on biology and culture as signifiers of racial identity to the metaphor of roads, paths, intersections, borders, bridges, boundaries, and diasporic histories. Such images may be used to link individual lives to the institutional and structural forces that shape us to become who we are. As Paul Gilroy puts it, we are all "rooted in and routed through" the powerful social structures of society (Gilroy 1993).

In this framework individual genealogies go beyond tracking ancestors to encompass the multiple paths through which people's lives are formed. Indeed, anthropologist James Clifford suggests that identities are constructed through a dialectic between roots and routes (Clifford 1997). This is particularly evident among transracial adoptees; their sense of self is fundamentally shaped by a sense of displacement, or travel from, their familial "roots." When we recast genealogy as routes, that is, as paths of travel and paths of institutional knowledge, it becomes apparent that race is not the only social force that shapes the identities and families of adoptees. Complete genealogical exposure of their lives requires an exploration of the politics of gender and class as well. Adoptees' identities are shaped by the race, gender, ethnicity, and class histories of our birth and adoptive families, as well as by our own and our parents' multiple relationships to the social institutions regulating the social reproduction of families.

With an issue as highly charged as transracial adoption one is usually expected to "pick a side" in the public debate. I am not arguing "for" or "against" this social practice, but rather for a redefinition of the terms of the dialogue and the scope of inquiry. However, my contextual, interdisciplinary research has led me to resist the dominant public narrative that presents transracial adoption as a simple solution to the problems in the foster care system and the so-called "epidemic" of "illegitimacy." Although I am not "against" transracial adoption, I do feel the need to counter the dominant public version of the issue with a more complex and nuanced view that includes the voices of many of the people involved whose stories have not been heard. The perspectives of transracial adoptees as well as those of social workers in the adoption field complicate the widely available popular story.

BirthMarks

In narrating this piece of her life, Thorley Richardson, a White woman adopted into a White family who was thirty-one when I interviewed her, revealed several ideological principles embedded in the U.S. adoption system:

> *Thorley:* I don't really know where I got this idea, but it seems to me that when I was born in 1965 they tried to pick babies that would fit in physically with the family that was adopting them. And I remember someone telling me that they actually took a picture of my family—my adoptive family—and matched it up to the babies in the room, and I sort of got put with them based on looking like them—skin tone, hair color, that kind of thing. Which is ridiculous because that all changes when you're a baby anyway. So this idea of it just being so easy to pick me out of one place and put me down in another, and just having me fit in without any seams seems strange to me. Finding out that—I think that babies adopted in that time frame—The most oft-adopted children in that time were babies without any marks or physical problems. So I think that made me feel that kind of the absence of a *birthmark*—made it kind of easy for me to just be transplanted into another family or another surrounding and not having anyone know. No one would ever actually *know* that I could be different or have a whole different set of everything—that I could so easily be picked up and matched with a picture of another family, and plausibly grow up never knowing that I was adopted until somebody slips one year at Christmas, or something crazy like that. And of course that wasn't my situation. But the idea that I didn't have any distinguishing marks, that there wasn't anything distinguishable about *me* physically always bothered me.

Thorley's story conveys the power of being *marked*, and the multiple meanings attached to that term. She begins with an explanation of the matching principle in adoption. The practice of racial matching that I have discussed grew out of the kind of matching that Thorley describes. Between the end of World War II and the late 1960s, when the system began to change, there were enough White children available for adoption for agencies to be able to place children in families that closely matched their physical features and ethnic makeup. The underlying ideology was rooted in naturalizing and normalizing the state's reproduction of White nuclear families. The goal was to have adopted children look *as if* they had been born into their families. This was a means of making the sexual deviance of White unwed mothers and infertile White couples invisible. The U.S. postwar adoption system largely functioned on behalf of infertile White middle-class couples (Ladner 1977; Solinger 1992). This led to the development of a system in which resources were devoted toward placing healthy White infants, largely disregarding Black children's needs for adoptive families. Thus, while ostensibly "color blind," the system was driven by racial ideology. Within this framework to be Black was to be *marked.*

Thorley's view of being marked was directly rooted in the politics of disability as well; to have health problems or to be disabled was to be *marked* as "unadoptable," along with Black and mixed-race children. Conversely, to be a healthy White infant—a "blue-ribbon baby," as they were called—was to be effaced, to have no identity, to be a blank slate ready, in Thorley's words, to be "transplanted into another family or another surrounding and not having anyone know." Clearly Whiteness functioned as the *unmarked* category in adoption, as it does more generally in U.S. society. And thus, for Thorley, as for many adoptees raised in same-race families, the birthmarks of difference stemming from adoption were only internal, yet deeply felt.

The Social Construction of Identity: Adoption and Public Policy

My interest in the social construction of identities began with my own experiences as an adoptee. I first began considering questions of identity and adoption in light of the racial and ethnic match between myself and my White parents. When I was adopted in the mid-1960s there were still enough White infants available for agencies to match children and parents closely enough to create the desired illusion of birth ties between them. Yet the invisibility of adoption and difference that this process was meant to ensure did not spare adoptees the pain of struggling with identity issues. In a society that defines *real* families through biological ties, those of us with origin narratives beginning in a public agency rather than a human body could not help but struggle with questions of who we "really" were, who we might have been, and how our identities had been constructed.

From a cultural studies perspective, all human identities are socially constructed; this is often an assumption made by adoptees as well. Adoption is the *literal* social construction of families, and thus of identities. Those of us who were adopted into our families—whether across or within a racial category—often go through life acutely aware that our identities have been put in place by outside forces, that who we are is not "natural." Not only are adoptees often aware that we would have been fundamentally different people had we been raised by our birth parents, but our sense of identity as constructed yet somehow arbitrary, is heightened by the feeling that there are other lives we could have lived, other people we could have been, had some small circumstance surrounding our birth or adoption been different. The knowledge that the choice of which family is allowed to adopt which child is made by a social worker according to the policies and practices guiding the agency erases all sense of identity as "natural," that is, as being acquired by birth. The range of possible selves a child may become is dramatically multiplied when the social construction of identity begins in the files of the U.S. child welfare system.

The genealogy of an adoptee's identity, then, must move beyond the family tree, to the discursive roots and routes of race, gender, and class politics embedded in the public policies and social institutions governing this means of social reproduction. Racial identity is the explicitly contested terrain in this social dialogue. Yet, when we examine the public policies on transracial adoption of the 1990s, gender and poverty emerge as important considerations as well.

Adoption makes apparent the ways in which "state institutions organize and enforce the racial politics of everyday life" (Omi and Winant 1986:76). In the case of transracial adoption, both racial matching and "color-blind" policies directly organize racial identities by legislating which families—Black or White—children are placed with. This determination significantly shapes the cultural meanings of race that are available to Black children in constructing their identities. Although the development of subjectivity occurs at the personal level, the range of cultural meanings of race available to individuals is structured systemically through racial matching policies and practices, as well as child welfare policies which, while not explicitly racial, nonetheless serve in practice to track Black and White children through different channels of the adoption and foster care system.

While federal adoption policies passed in 1996 prohibiting any consideration of children's or prospective parents' races were ostensibly meant to remove racial considerations from the adoption process—to make the system "color-blind"—in practice these policies enforce a very rigid definition of race. A "color-blind" view of race denies both the existence of systemic racism and the salience of racial and cultural difference in a racially stratified society, while claiming the moral high ground of racial "neutrality." As sociologist Howard Winant explains, contemporary arguments for a "color-blind" approach to race in the United States suggest "a strictly limited role for the state in racial policy," contributing to the maintenance of "the structure of racial inequality" (Winant 1994:5).

The state organization of racial identities in adoption underwent a fundamental restructuring between 1993 and 1996. During that period a series of public policies were proposed, argued, repealed, and passed regulating the use of race in making adoptive placements. In 1993 Senator Howard Metzenbaum introduced the "Multiethnic Placement Act" (MEPA), a bill designed to remove barriers to transracial placements in order to eliminate delays in the adoption of Black children. It was signed into law in March 1994 after a number of changes had been made to its language, and implemented in January 1996. However, dissatisfaction with the final bill led those in favor of increasing the number of transracial placements to argue for its repeal.[4]

In 1994 the new Republican congressional majority introduced the "Personal Responsibility Act" in their *Contract with America*. It was a conservative bill designed to reformulate, and effectively dismantle, the U.S. social welfare system by revoking federal entitlement to benefits through the allocation of block grants to individual states. In an attempt to correct what many legislators and advocates saw as the flawed Multiethnic Placement Act, this version of welfare reform legislated the removal of all restrictions on transracial placements and prohibited the use of race in considering the placement of a child for adoption.

What did this seemingly unrelated bill have to do with welfare reform? After all, adoption was not part of the public debate about welfare reform. Remarkably, adoption policy was included in Congress's early drafts of the Personal Responsibility Act. In fact, up until the final version of the welfare reform bill, the legislation removing all restrictions on transracial adoption was part of the Personal Responsibility Act, located in the section called "Reducing Illegitimacy" (Title I, March 22, 1995 version). Up until its penultimate version, this bill paired adoption with welfare reform as a means of relocating "illegitimate" children in "legitimate"—two parent, heterosexual—families. Conservative and centrist policy thinkers argued that "illegitimacy" contributed to poverty, and that it could (and should) be corrected by welfare legislation. The "Personal Responsibility and Work Reconciliation Opportunity Act of 1996"—welfare reform—accepted that premise. Section 101 of the bill, entitled "Findings," addressed "illegitimacy" (in its language, "out-of-wedlock births") by enumerating a long list of "negative consequences of out-of-wedlock birth on the mother, the child, the family, and society." This section included such statements as: "Young women who have children before finishing high school are more likely to receive welfare assistance for a longer period of time." And, "children of teenage single parents have lower cognitive scores, lower educational aspirations, and a greater likelihood of becoming teenage parents themselves." Also, "areas with higher percentages of single-parent households have higher rates of violent crime." The legislators framed welfare reform as the answer to this crisis.

Through the long legislative battle over the Personal Responsibility Act," including two presidential vetoes, some of the proposed limitations on welfare benefits were removed. Nonetheless, the net result was to dismantle the U.S. social welfare system. The version of the bill President Clinton eventually signed into law placed a five-year lifetime limit on benefits, required able-bodied adults to work after two years, required minors to be enrolled in school and living at home or with a responsible adult, required unwed mothers to cooperate in identifying paternity, and disallowed support to anyone convicted of a felony drug charge. The section of the Personal Responsibility Act dealing with adoption and race was removed just prior to the bill's passage, and, along with legislation that provided a $5,000 to $6,000 tax credit to adopting families, was amended to H.R. 3448, the "Small Business Job Protection Act of 1996" (most commonly known as the minimum wage bill). During the week of August 19, 1996 President Clinton signed this bill, which repealed the Multiethnic Placement Act, and the Personal Responsibility and Work Opportunity Reconciliation Act of 1996 into law. Together, these two pieces of legislation reduced the social safety net for low-income mothers, removed all racial restrictions on adoption, and provided a financial incentive for adoption. In effect, the legislation made it more difficult for poor women to keep their families together, while making it easier for middle-class people to adopt the children removed from their mothers. Policymakers' explicit removal of racial barriers to adoption revealed their desire to regulate the reproductive behavior of women of color and White women who "cross[ed] the color line" and gave birth to multiracial children.

The historic changes in social welfare policy effected in 1996—dismantling the federal Aid to Families with Dependent Children (AFDC) program and prohibiting the consideration of race in adoptive placements—were rationalized in part by the belief that the future economic viability of the United States in the global marketplace was dependent upon the transformation of the next generation of inner-city children (read Black) from potential teenage mothers and criminal gang members—"super-predators"—into "productive citizens."[5] As anthropologist Sharon Stephens argues, the question of "state-controlled socialization" of children escalates in importance during an era of widespread political change. Concerns about the inability of particular mothers to properly socialize their children "legitimize new state-supported interventions into families" (Stephens 1995:28). This explains the linkage of adoption and welfare reform in political discourse and the concern with socialization and identity.

This is a very old story. As the work of feminist scholars Angela Davis (1981), Bonnie Thornton Dill (1988), Rickie Solinger (1992), and Dorothy Roberts (1997) demonstrates, the reproductive capacities—childbearing and child rearing—of Black women have historically been subjected to coercion and control by the social welfare system and the labor market. Employment discrimination against African American women and men has contributed to the presence of a high proportion of Black women and their children in the social welfare system, placing them under greater scrutiny and control. Their children have disproportionately been labeled "at risk." However, let us be clear that the well-being of children is jeopardized when their mothers' lives are unstable and "at risk."

The lives and identities of transracial adoptees have been shaped by these social narratives and material circumstances in profound ways. While it is clear that public policies governing the practice of adoption agencies regulate which children will become part of which families, this discourse shapes adoptees' identities in more subtle ways as well. Thus, I am concerned not simply with the concrete ways in which racial considerations influence adoption decisions as to which children become wards of the state and which ones are relinquished for adoption to particular families. As they grow and develop a sense of self, adoptees not only internalize overt familial and institutional norms but also actively construct their identities through the social narratives and cultural meaning systems available to them. Social allegory accessible through television, film, music, literature, and political commentary provides explanations and definitions of race, gender, class, poverty, family, "illegitimacy," adoption, personhood, citizenship, and so on that come to represent the "forms of truth by which we have come to know ourselves and others" (Dean 1996:220).

The forms of truth in the discourse about transracial adoption are contentious on account of disagreements in three primary and interrelated areas: (1) tensions between "nature" and "nurture" or "biology" and "culture" in considerations of identity; (2) tensions between the racial meaning systems of essentialist racism, "color blindness," and "race cognizance";[6] and (3) social definitions of legitimate and "illegitimate" personhood and citizenship. These concerns were evident in the cultural dialogue about the appropriateness of transracial adoption that emerged in 1993 and dominated popular and political discourse until the welfare reform bill was passed in August 1996. This period was characterized by heated public dialogue regarding "legitimate" citizenship, social anxiety over the meanings and salience of racial difference, and contentious debate over how racial-ethnic[7] diversity and social inequality were to be accounted for, whether as the result of cultural tradition and/or structural inequality or through what Troy Duster has called the "prism of heritability" (Duster 1996). The narratives about transracial adoption that emerged in numerous discursive sites are a rich source for an exploration of the contested meanings of some of the most salient sociopolitical issues of the late twentieth century.

Conclusion

I encountered many competing social narratives about transracial adoption in my interviews with adoptees and social workers, as well as public sources: news coverage, editorials, congressional dialogues, and federal legislation. I am concerned with the way these different forms of social dialogue relate to each other. Thus, I attempt to map out the discursive patterns in the production of social knowledge that shape the lives of some of this country's most vulnerable citizens, namely, mothers and children in the child welfare system. In this book I explore the social construction of identity through a genealogy of adoptive selves, and hope thereby to contribute to a broader understanding of the complex relationships between individuals, families, culture, and society. Questions about how such relationships are constituted and maintained are central to my research.

In chapter 1, I address the origin narratives of adoptees along with a history of transracial adoption in the post–World War II United States, paying particular attention to the social and political context in which the cultural controversy of the 1970s developed. Chapter 2 focuses on the life histories of twenty-two adult transracial adoptees, based on ethnographic interviews I conducted on the West Coast and the Mid-Atlantic region between 1994 and 1999. While the subject of this study is identity construction among transracial adoptees, I also conducted several formal interviews and had countless informal conversations with Blacks and Whites who had been adopted into same-race families. I focus on the question of survival skills and racial identity, considering the life stories of adoptees who were primarily Black-identified, White-identified, or who defined themselves as bi- or multiracial. In chapter 3, I address adoptees' search narratives and imaginings about their birth parents, and discuss the social, economic, and political climate for Black and White unwed mothers in the 1960s and 1970s. I demonstrate that full genealogical exposure of adoptees' origin narratives demands attention to the public policies and social institutions regulating unwed mothers' reproductive "choices." In chapter 4 I consider the public discourse about adoption and welfare reform between 1993 and 1996. I explore the dominant public narrative that emerged in popular culture and political discourse in news coverage, editorials, political commentary, the Congressional Record, supportive legislative documents, and actual legislation. I then offer the counternarrative that surfaced in my ethnographic interviews and in participant-observation with social workers in public and private adoption agencies in the greater San Francisco Bay area and the Mid-Atlantic region. In the Conclusion I discuss the "discursive map" that emerged in this study while I considered the various competing and complementary forms of social knowledge concerning the adoption of Black children into White families. I consider the broader impact of the patterns of race and identity, family and culture, gender and work, citizenship and nation revealed in these narratives, which reach beyond the lives of adoptees and their families. I consider how such social allegories respond and speak to some of the most provocative and challenging social issues in the United States in the late twentieth century.

| ONE |

Origin Narratives

When I was a child I had a book called *The Chosen Baby* (Wasson, 1950). Originally written in 1939 by Valentina Wasson, the edition I was given had been revised and updated in 1950. My adoptive parents gave me the book to help me understand adoption—my origins. It told the story of Mr. and Mrs. Brown, who had everything they could ask for, except one thing: they needed a baby to make their happiness complete.

> One day Mr. and Mrs. Brown said to each other: "Let us adopt a baby and bring him up as our very own." So the next day they called up the lady who helps people to adopt babies and babies to adopt parents, and said to her: "Mrs. White, we wish so much to find a baby who would like to have a mother and father and who could be our very own. Will you help us find one?"
>
> Mrs. White said: "It will not be easy. Many, many people wish to adopt babies, and you may have to wait a long time. But come and see me and let's talk it over." (Wasson 1950:8)

So the Browns went down to the friendly government agency where they met the nice caseworker, who began searching for just the right baby for them. After an anxious wait (probably about nine months), Mrs. White finally called with wonderful news. She had a beautiful baby boy for them to come and see. They went to the adoption agency the next day, and of course fell in love with him instantly and took him home the very next day. Their family and friends were so happy for them.

When Peter was a little older Mr. and Mrs. Brown decided they wanted to adopt a girl.

> So the next day Mrs. Brown called up Mrs. White and said: "We wish to find a baby sister for Peter." And Mrs. White said: "We shall gladly try and

find a sister for Peter, but you may have to wait a long time. More and more people wish to adopt babies." (Wasson 1950:34)

After waiting about a year they brought home a little sister for Peter, whom they named Mary. The last page of the book shows them several years later, the ideal nuclear family: the two children lie on the floor in front of the fireplace with their dog and cat, while their parents read and sew in their "family room."

I was adopted as an infant in 1965, and this was the story I, like many adoptees, was given to help me understand how I came to be part of my family. It is a public origin narrative about adoption. *The Chosen Baby* was one of the two best known versions of the dominant adoption story between 1945 and 1965. It was often recommended by social workers as a way of explaining adoption to children. In fact, in the foreword, Sophie Van S. Theis, Secretary of the Committee on Child Placing and Adoption declares that it is "the story of every adopted child," and suggests that it "be used by parents to supplement their own explanation to their children of the fact of adoption" (Wasson 1950:6).

I begin with this story because it is a useful means of understanding how adoption was constructed and practiced during this period. Through it we can study some of the ideological assumptions underlying the social reproduction of families through adoption in the post–World War II United States. First of all, Mr. and Mrs. Brown are a nondisabled, White, middle-class, heterosexual married couple, and it is no accident that their caseworker's name is Mrs. White. In fact, everyone in the story is White and middle class. The presence of a social worker is significant in adoption stories—she approves the adoptive parents and "finds" the baby. She represents the state's definition of good parents.

This book tells a culturally and historically specific story. Yet perhaps even more revealing are the absences—the stories that it doesn't tell. Can we imagine this story with a Black family? How about a working-class family? Think about the images it conjures in your mind. What if the child were Asian, Black, Native American, or multiracial and the parents were White? Where are the birth parents in this story? What is made invisible by their exclusion? What assumptions about class are hidden? According to *The Chosen Baby*, Peter and Mary Brown were never "born"—they came from a government agency!

In this chapter I consider the origin stories of adoptees as they move between what we traditionally think of as public and private domains. I discuss the historical development of the adoption system in the post–World War II United States and argue that an understanding of adoptees' identities must move beyond the individual and familial levels. Adoption must be viewed in the context of changing notions of gender, race, and class since World War II. In the following pages, I examine the development of transracial adoption and the public controversy surrounding it in light of race, gender, and class politics in the United States.

Reconsidering Kinship

Anthropologists Sylvia Yanagisako and Carol Delaney, drawing on Malinowski, explain the importance of studying origin narratives as follows:

> Origin stories are a prime locus for a society's notion of itself—its identity, its world view, and social organization. Anthropologists often include origin stories of the people they study, recognizing, after Malinowski, that "an intimate connection exits [*sic*] between the word, mythos, the sacred tales of a tribe, on the one hand, and their ritual acts, their moral deeds, their social organization, and even their practical activities, on the other." (Malinowski 1954:96; Yanagisako and Delaney 1995b:2)

As Yanagisako and Delaney point out, people in all cultures tell stories to explain the beginnings of life—of the cosmos, of the earth, of human beings, of animals and plants, and of their own society.

Adoption stories in the United States reflect the basic Western assumption that identity is structured through tensions between biology and culture. Likewise, kinship is also defined in light of Western views of "culture" and "biology" as mutually exclusive categories. Consequently, adoptees view their birth and adoptive parents in exclusive terms as well. "Kinship, who one is related to, is established in the popular American view by the prenatal act of conception. By the time one is born, in fact at the moment of conception, it is established who one's 'real' kin are" (Meigs 1989:36). In the United States few people born into their families question the "naturalness" of such biological kinship bonds or the tacit cultural assumption that conception is a biological and genetic process that establishes the basic "truth" of individual identity. This assumption is based in turn on the idea that genetic codes and markers of personhood and family are basically unchanging.

While such ideas about conception, birth, identity, and family are a taken-for-granted "truth" in the United States, an examination of kinship and reproduction in a non-Western society provides valuable perspective on the "mythos, the sacred tales . . . and social organization" (Malinowski 1954:96) of adoption, identity, and family in America. Adoption is an extremely variable practice worldwide. In fact, this diversity reflects cultural variations in social definitions and practices of kinship and personhood.

Among the Hua of the New Guinea Highlands reproduction is not defined solely as a biological, genetic process that terminates at birth, but is conceived as continuing throughout the child's life through the sharing of *nu*. *Nu*, which can be understood as "vital essence," is basic to the Hua construction of personhood. Anthropologist Anna Meigs explains:

> Nu is basic to life and growth. The fetus is created prenatally out of the semen nu of the father and menstrual blood nu of the mother and then nourished postnatally by nu in all its many forms: breast milk, blood (let from veins and fed growing children), sweat (rubbed from real and classificatory parents onto the skin of growing children), and, of course, food (understood to promote growth and health by virtue of the nu it contains). Nu is the quintessential substance and basis of all nurture. (Meigs 1989:34–35)

In Hua culture, "individuals develop and change throughout their lives in accordance with the same processes by which they were created prenatally," and kinship and gender identities are seen as "unfinished" and changeable throughout their lives (Meigs 1989:35–36). Whereas in the United States reproduction is defined solely as the discreet, physiological process of prenatal development and birth, and thus "real," biological kinship is attributed solely to the birth parents, in New Guinea, where the "physiological relationship of kinship can be produced, reinforced, or weakened through postnatal transactions, foremost among which are food exchanges," adoptive parents are considered part of the reproductive process together with birth parents (Meigs 1989:36). Indeed, because the *nu* of parents is transferred to food through the processes of production and preparation, and other cultural rituals are enacted which nurture the bodies of adoptive children with the *nu* (in the form of bodily fluids) of their adoptive parents, adoptive children are seen as *physical* extensions of their adoptive parents.

This view of adoption contrasts sharply with Western perspectives, in which kinship ties based on *nurture* are devalued and seen in binary opposition to *nature*, which is associated with the biological, the real. In the United States, following World War II these tacit assumptions linking "real" kinship with biological, genetic ties underlay the development of an adoption system based on silence, secrecy, and the principle of "matching" parents with racially, ethnically, and physiologically similar children. These policies were intended to reproduce, through adoption, families who would appear to be "real" in the sense of being biologically constructed.

I would like to take a conceptual turn here. The "mythos [and] sacred tales of a tribe" that Malinowski described reside in the public space of a culture; but in the postmodern global information economy of the late twentieth century the boundaries between public and private have blurred. Individual lives are constructed and maintained in interaction with public discourse, and in a world of opinion polls and confessional talk shows individual lives inform public space as well. Feminist cultural critics Sidonie Smith and Julia Watson explain:

> If we are not telling our stories, we are consuming other people's lives. Consuming personal narratives on an everyday basis, we imbibe the heterogeneous "lives" authorized by and authenticated in the institutions through which we negotiate daily existence. Media, for instance, offer a dazzling display of possible lives through daytime television, the movies, and the news. The news frames its selected fragments of autobiographies of political candidates that are shaped by the institutions of official politics as permissible life stories. (Smith and Watson 1996:3)

Media representations of adoptees' identities suggest that finding our birth mothers (and occasionally fathers) is the key to our "true" identities (Wegar 1997). The prevalence of this belief contributes to the fact that origin narratives typically carry more weight among adoptees than they among people raised by their birth parents. Indeed, adoptees often cite the lack of a birth story as one of the core issues in their struggles over identity, and a prime motivation for initiating a search for their birth parents. However, from an anthropological perspective, adoptees' lack of factual birth histories does not mean we have no origin stories. Although adoptees who don't know their birth parents, don't have tales of being born—of physical birth—this is only one aspect of our origins.

The issue of *origins* follows most adoptees through our lives; the stories we are told about our births and beginnings often continue to change throughout the courses of our lives, depending on the inclinations of parents and social workers, the discovery of hidden identity documents, and/or finding or being found by birth parents. Thus, our origin stories are told and retold, constructed and reconstructed as we continue to come into being.

Adoptees' origins seem at times more discursive than physical; many of our narratives begin with an anonymous infant written into being by a social worker in a secret file—our "sealed records"—that are forbidden to us. The omniscient creator in our stories is the social worker as an agent of the state; she is the only person granted the power of *legitimacy*, the power to make the weighty decisions regarding who these anonymous infants will become and what families will transform them from *illegitimate to legitimate* citizens. She is the only person in possession of the complete stories of birth and origin; she is the state's guardian of knowledge, the keeper of our "truths."

Reproducing "the Family"

The tension in the 1990s over the increasing number of children of color, older children, and children with health problems and/or disabilities in the foster care system, and the concomitant demand for healthy White infants on the U.S. mainstream and underground adoption markets have roots in the cultural, economic, political, and institutional construction of the adoption system in the post–World War II era. While cultural mythology may still present visions of an adoption system dedicated to "the best interests of the child," in fact, as Joyce Ladner (1977) demonstrates, the social practice of adoption was largely institutionalized following World War II in response to an unprecedented increase in adoption requests for healthy White infants from infertile White, middle-class, heterosexual, married couples. "[A]doption policies and practices were formulated and functioned in behalf of this small clientele" (Ladner 1977:56).

Following World War II, White suburban family life, and the gender-, race-, and class-specific characteristics associated with it, came to be seen as the "normal" and "natural" choices for American adults. Historian Elaine Tyler May argues that "Procreation in the cold war era took on almost mythic proportions" (1988:135). May continues:

> Along with the baby boom came an intense and widespread endorsement of pronatalism—the belief in the positive value of having children. A major study conducted in 1957 found that most Americans believed that parenthood was the route to happiness. Childlessness was considered deviant, selfish, and pitiable. (May 1988:137)

The postwar increase in demand for healthy White infants occurred in the above context. A narrowly drawn White, middle class, Christian, suburban, nuclear family came to be seen as the ideal and only "legitimate" form of family (Ladner 1977:56). This suburban family ideal was not only a cultural construct, but was also fundamentally rooted in economic access to home ownership, the means to acquire a wide range of consumer products, and a man's ability to financially support his wife and children. Clearly, this middle-class, patriarchal family model was not equally accessible to Whites and Blacks; the discrimination against African Americans in the U.S. labor force limited most Black men to low-wage jobs and required a large number of Black women to participate in the labor market in order to sustain their families.

This ideological, race-specific definition of the family implied that other cultural forms were deviant, and marginalized the historically diverse kinship patterns and experiences of racial-ethnic groups and working-class cultures, as well as other family forms among European American groups. This narrowly defined family ideal became embedded in the policies and practices of an adoption agency structure that systematically disregarded children of color, those beyond infancy, and children with health problems and/or disabilities (Ladner 1977; Day 1979; Cole and Donley 1990; Solinger 1992). It also discouraged and discriminated against most prospective adoptive couples who were not able-bodied, married, White, heterosexual, and middle class. Adoptive parents were usually required to own a home with a separate bedroom for the child, to demonstrate their ability to provide an education for the child, and to have a modest amount of savings. Furthermore, the family was required to meet these financial criteria through one person's paycheck—adoptive mothers were not allowed to be employed (Ladner 1977:57).

One of the women I interviewed was adopted into just this sort of 1950s "ideal" suburban White middle-class family in 1956. Yet her story was not typical. Samantha (Sam) Bennett was born at a time when little attention was given to the needs of African American and "mixed-race" children in the U.S. adoption system, and the movement for transracial placements had not yet begun. Sam's placement in a White family was almost certainly due to the uncertainty of her racial identity, both in terms of doubts about the identity of her birth father and the relative lightness of her skin. The connection between racial identity, cultural knowledge, and social institutions is explicit in the origin narrative of Sam Bennett, a biracial woman raised in a White family in a small town in central California. At the time of the interviews she was thirty-nine years old, married to a White man, and living in a racially diverse city in northern California with her husband and their three-year-old daughter.

Sandi: Why don't we start by you just telling me your story?

Sam: Well, I was five and a half months when I was adopted. And I was living in San Francisco. I was born in San Francisco, and I was in foster care. It was apparently a very bad foster care. They didn't pick me up ever. I suppose they picked me up to change my diapers. I don't know, but my mother said that was the story. They never picked me up. I was very pale and kind of washed out, and very stiff when they got me. Anyway, I was the second child that was adopted. My parents adopted a child through a private adoption three years prior to adopting me. [interruption]

Sandi: So your parents are White.

Sam: My parents are White.

Sandi: What about the first adoptee?

Sam: White. My parents are—my mother was German, grew up in Montana, and my father is I think German and English. So I'm half German, so they matched the German part up. And tried to fake the rest of the part. I was a county adoption.

Sandi: Did your parents know when they got you that you were mixed?

Sam: Well, they knew—They were lied to. They were told by the adoption agency that there was a possibility that I was half Black. It's really a ridiculous story. Let's see. My mother was German, and her husband was German, and they had come to San Francisco to study. They were both in the medical profession. They separated. She had an affair. She had an affair with a Black serviceman from Louisiana. And on the papers she states that she doesn't know who the father is. And you get this little printout—you can after you're twenty-one.

Sandi: Nonidentifying information?

Sam: Yeah.

Sandi: I haven't done that, but people keep talking about it, so I'm going to have to do it.

Sam: Well, actually you don't get much. I'll show you mine. I should show you some pictures!

Sandi: Yeah.

Sam: I'll show you some pictures of my family. Anyway, what they tell you is the age of the parents, the physical description, education. I don't think there was age, but I'll look at it. And that's it. Then of course, the place of birth or something. The two potential fathers actually were very similar in looks. It was you know, the coloring. Her natural—her real husband was dark with frizzy hair. He was Jewish, she was not. About five foot seven or something. And the man she had an affair with was light-skinned from Louisiana, and about the same height. So, but I'm way too dark to be all German. But anyway, the adoption agency chose to tell my parents that there was a possibility—that they had had these tests done, these anthropological tests, bone tests to determine if I was part Black.

Sandi: What year was this?

Sam: Fifty-six. In those days you're matching White babies with White parents, and that's it. And nobody had wanted to adopt me because I was biracial. And because, if I had been all White, they had this long list, and they would have placed me right away. I don't know if I was turned down by a lot of parents once they saw me. I just know I wasn't being adopted, and maybe I was deemed "unadoptable." I'm sure the ladies of the county are long gone by now, so it's too late to find out.

In 1956 "adoptable" children were healthy White infants—"blue-ribbon babies." Sam's belief that her racial identity initially marked her as "unadoptable" was probably correct. In placing her with White parents the agency stressed only that there was a *possibility* that she was "half Black." Sam found out when she was in her twenties and received her "nonidentifying information"—the set of facts the state is legally obliged to provide to adult adoptees, if they request it—that her birth mother had blond hair and blue eyes, making it almost certain that the "Black serviceman from Louisiana" was her birth father. As she observed, "I'm way too dark to be all German."

The description of these two possible fathers demonstrates the power of language in enforcing racial categories. Each man was unproblematically considered Black or White, and once this had been established the categories were maintained through the adjectives chosen to describe the two men, who looked alike. The German—read White—man was "dark with frizzy hair" and the Black man was "light-skinned." In a society structured by a different racial order these two men might have been be considered members of the same race, but in the United States the "one drop rule" is still largely enforced, both socially and juridically.
Sam continued:

> *Sam:* I'm trying to think. When I requisitioned my papers, which is all you have to do—this is only if you're a county adoption. If you're private it's totally sealed, and I don't think they have to come forth with anything. [interruption]
>
> *Sam:* They called me and they said, "We're going to send the information, but because there's some sensitive information we're going to send it to the local adoption agency, the social services, in Oakland and a worker will meet with you and discuss the material."
>
> *Sandi:* That's kind of ominous.
>
> *Sam:* Well, I mean, part of the strangeness of my story is that my parents didn't tell me about my racial identity until I was twenty.

Sandi: Oh my.

Sam: Well.

Sandi: You wonder how they got away with that.

Sam: It wasn't hard. Anyway, so, but at that point I didn't know that I was half—Well, I guess my dad had told me at that point, because I was twenty-four when I got the stuff. And he'd said there was a possibility. So of course, that sealed it for me. And then when they told me that I thought oh well, you know. But I didn't realize it was the racial stuff that was sensitive. So I went down there and I met with this woman, and that's what it was. And she said, "My, you're taking this so well." And I thought what does she think? That I've been looking in the mirror, thinking I was blond and blue-eyed all these years, and all of a sudden? It's like, "No, lady, this is just confirming." You know, it's always—when you don't exactly know, there's always this shade of doubt. You know, especially when these fathers looked alike. But in my rational mind I know that I'm not all German, so I have to be biracial.

Sam's origin narrative powerfully demonstrates how directly her racial identity was socially constructed. It was particularly striking that her parents followed the lead of the adoption agency in hiding the stigmatized, *marked* elements of her racial identity from her. In 1956 the United States was a racially segregated society, and her parents felt it necessary to do their best to erase the non-White history of their daughter. They were able to do this because Sam was not, nor had been as a child, easily classified in terms of race. With her tan skin, long, curly, and somewhat frizzy dark brown hair, and brown eyes she could be identified with various racial-ethnic groups. She grew up in a nearly all-White agricultural town in central California where there were very few African American families and a small population of Mexican migrant workers.

She always looked different from everyone else she knew, and was often teased about her difference. The only racial-ethnic category other kids were able to affiliate her with was Mexican, and in that town at that time, this was not a positive association. She would often cry to her parents about this, and they would comfort her with assurances that they loved her and that looking different didn't mean she wasn't a good person. But they always insisted that they didn't know what her racial-ethnic background was. Their eventual confession to her when she was twenty that there was a possibility she was "half Black" was prompted by the fact that she was dating an African American man. Her mother told her at the time that her father had sworn her to secrecy because he didn't want Sam's life to be any harder than it already was. Clearly, her parents loved her and did what they believed was best for her. Their approach to race was consistent with the times—in their eyes, to be "half Black" was a stigma that would damage one's self-esteem. This sentiment was also evident in the way she was handled by the adoption system when she received her "nonidentifying information."

Though race had sometimes been a painful issue for Sam, at the time of our interview she was quite definitely a woman who knew who she was. She defined herself as biracial, lived in a racially diverse area, and had a diverse group of friends and colleagues. Her parents raised her in a very humanistic atmosphere, which ultimately worked for her. There were times in her life when she felt compelled to locate herself racially, and situations in which others pushed her toward disclosure. Though she had struggled with the issues of race and adoption, particularly in her midtwenties, she had not felt the need to search for her birth parents and had not experienced her adoption as a problematic aspect of her life. In considering the tensions between nature and nurture, she drew primarily on a cultural framework to understand who she was and how she came to be. Thus, she focused on the experiences that had shaped her rather than the biological facts that had eluded her. Yet she was clear that her identity had been fundamentally shaped through her interactions with the U.S. child welfare system and their attempts to erase her "Blackness."

Had Sam been born in the late 1960s or early 1970s she might have become part of her family through an explicitly transracial placement. If she had been born after the late 1970s social workers might have considered placing her with either an African American family or a biracial couple. But in the 1950s few Black couples met the stringent policy requirements for adoption eligibility. Dawn Day (1979) demonstrates that through the early 1970s most adoption agencies enforced criteria that were inappropriate for most Black families. A large number of prospective Black adopters were turned away from agencies for failing to meet such requirements as economic stability, home ownership (with a separate bedroom for the child), and a full-time wife and mother. Additionally, Day's study shows that many Black couples withdrew from the adoption screening process at each stage of evaluation in response to numerous forms of institutional discrimination and a sense of social distance from predominantly White social workers. The resulting difficulties in placing children of color, older children, and those with disabilities in adoptive homes led these children to be labeled "unadoptable." In turn, agency resources focused on placing what were commonly referred to as "blue-ribbon babies," that is, healthy White infants.

While White infants were the most desired commodity in the adoption market, children of color were seen as an administrative and financial strain on the system. Historian Rickie Solinger's (1992) important study of out-of-wedlock pregnancy before the legalization of abortion demonstrates that social resources for young pregnant women were largely allocated by race and class, and that these decisions were linked with those determining the life courses of their children.

The social support services available to single pregnant women were completely different for White women and Black women. For young White women, the stigma of pregnancy was often hidden through their seclusion in all-White maternity homes. Stories of semesters in Europe or summers with a faraway aunt often sheltered "deviant" young White women from middle-class judgments against unwed pregnancy. In the 1950s and 1960s maternity homes were typically segregated, and very few Black maternity homes existed.

The social meanings of White and Black unwed pregnancy differed significantly. Solinger demonstrates that: "The meaning assigned to the child's existence shaped public policies that distinguished between unwed mothers by race, as socially productive or socially unproductive breeders" (1992:39–40). By producing a White baby a woman was reproducing a White, middle-class, two parent "ideal" family, and thus the evidence of her sexual deviance—the child—disappeared. Birth mothers, babies, and adoptive parents were, in a sense, "redeemed." White women were heavily counseled in maternity homes that their only socially acceptable "choice" was to relinquish their babies for adoption; the desire to keep their children was interpreted as evidence of their psychological instability. This process constituted an elaborate system of social control that effectively coerced countless young White pregnant women to relinquish their babies to the state (Solinger 1992). White women produced children who, upon adoptive placement, reproduced a "normal," White, middle-class, nuclear family by transforming an infertile—and thus, "deviant"—couple into an ideologically defined "legitimate" family. Thus, for White birth parents, infants, and adoptive parents, the stigma of "illegitimacy" and infertility was rendered invisible through social policies and practices such as all-White maternity homes, the matching of physical characteristics and ethnic origins between adoptive parents and children, and mandatory sealed adoption records. Conversely, the needs of Black birth mothers and their children fell outside the purview of such social services; indeed, Day found that some adoption agencies actually had regulations *against* Black adoptions. Because these institutions were not designed with the needs of Black children in mind and there was virtually no "market" for them, unmarried pregnant Black women were frequently turned away from adoption agencies and pushed toward welfare agencies.

"Whitewashing" Ethnicity

Sam Bennett's story exemplifies the institutional imperative to reproduce the post–World War II White, suburban, middle-class "American" family ideal. While many children of color remained in foster care in the 1950s, the uncertainty of Sam's racial identity—her ability to "pass" as racially ambiguous, if not White—motivated social workers to place her in a White family before transracial adoptions became common practice in the late 1960s. My own origin narrative sheds light on the institutional reproduction of White middle-class Christian suburban families as well.

The question I was most commonly asked by both the adoptees and the social workers I interviewed was whether or not I had searched for my birth parents (and frequently, there was an implicit "yet" attached to the inquiry). I explained that I hadn't and that at this time in my life I didn't feel compelled to search. Unlike many of the people I talked with, I resist the idea that I can't know who I "really" am until I know my birth parents. To those who continued probing I revealed that there had been times, particularly during my teen years, when I had felt that need, but that, curious though I've always been, the drive had dissipated in my early twenties. I never ruled out the possibility that I might, at some time in the future, embark on such a quest. I usually concluded my little "search narrative" with the quip that I had to agree with one of my mentors, who always said that my academic research was my "search." I had no idea how true that observation was to become.

In January 1996, while concluding my interviews in California, I found myself, through a series of connections between area agencies, sitting in the lobby of the agency through which I had been adopted, waiting to interview a social worker. I couldn't help thinking: *I came from here. This is the place where it was determined who I was to become. And somewhere in this building is the file holding my sealed adoption records— my identity papers, those magical, ominous keys to the story of my birth, my beginnings, my possibilities, the original shadows of a self I might have become.* I've never talked to an adoptee whose records were sealed for whom this mythical, elusive *file* does not stir both longing and fear. What narratives of truth might those government forms and clinical observations reveal?

As social worker Gail Frank and I settled into a conference room for our interview I could not help but tell her that I had been adopted through her agency. Her excitement was evident as she asked, "You've signed one of our waivers, haven't you?" I didn't know what she meant, so she explained that in the state of California if both the adoptee and one or both birth parent(s) signed waivers to their rights of confidentiality the agency could facilitate a reunion. She went on to ask me questions about my birth and explained that birth mothers who relinquished children of my generation often came back to the agency hoping for information about or contact with the child. Somehow, that seemed unlikely to me.

After our interview we turned to the practicalities of adoption records. I was interested in receiving the nonidentifying information that adoptees are legally entitled to, and Gail was happy to oblige. I didn't think much about signing the waiver. She put it in front of me and I signed it, anticipating that it would simply collect dust in some file. As I left, Gail assured me that I would receive information in the mail soon after I returned to Maryland. I remember thinking as I walked to my car, "Wouldn't it be something if my birth mother was searching for me?" It was a heady thought, but one I quickly dismissed as thoroughly implausible.

A few weeks later, on January 17, 1996—just a few days before my thirty-first birthday—I received the letter that threw me into a sort of existential vertigo. My birth mother had signed a waiver in 1990. She had come back for me. Within the sense of falling-into-being, within the surreal oceanic whirlpool I had slipped into, just one reaction was decipherable. I felt an overwhelming sense of redemption.

My birth mother, it turned out, had been searching for me for thirteen years, since I had turned eighteen. The first few days and weeks of letters and email provoked a revolution in my sense of self and family and history. I had spent a lifetime constructing and maintaining a life history that relied on *culture* as the only accessible source of truth about identity and kin; *biology* had no tangible meaning for me. In the language of adoption, *biology* and *birth* signify the realm of the unknown and unknowable. I was suddenly overwhelmed with new "relatives"—how do I refer to my birth father's sister, my birth mother's stepfather, my three new "half birth" siblings? What do "blood" ties mean when divorced from emotional, familial, and cultural meaning? The stories they told me about themselves, their families, and their ancestors didn't fit into any organizational framework in my head. This was not simply new information about my family. It was a *fundamentally new kind of information*, a new category of meaning—biological kinship—about which I had no experiential or tangible knowledge. What does it, can it, should it mean to a thirty-one-year-old woman who was raised as a WASP-ish Lutheran and now leans toward Eastern thought to learn she is "biologically half Jewish"? What "is" my ethnicity when I "am" by birth Jewish, but haven't been raised with the cultural knowledge telling me what that means? The shadow identity that has haunted me—a self I might have been—now has a name. How does Sandra Patton incorporate a spectral self named Nicole Goldberg?

The problematics of being and meaning are not the sole province of adoptees. The shifting narratives of self we adoptees fashion throughout our lives speak beyond the specificities of our familial experiences. Our lives point to the contingency of identity, the tenuousness of coherence, and the fictional character of all human life stories. We are not the only people asking, "Who am I really?" We are not alone in receiving conflicting stories about who we are and how we should be. Adoptees are not the only ones who must construct a sense of self through partial familial "truths" and convoluted cultural "lies."

We all write and rewrite ourselves into being as we continually construct and refine our life stories throughout the course of our lives. Yet, as the identities of adoptees make apparent, the scripts we are given are not solely our own:

> *On a daily basis, then, personal narrators assume the role of the* bricoleur *who takes up bits and pieces of the identities and narrative forms available and, by disjoining and joining them in excessive ways, creates a history of the subject at a precise point in time and space.* (emphasis in original) (Smith and Watson 1996:14)

We make sense of our lives not only through the familial and cultural narratives we collect from our families, our communities, and the media, but also through our interactions with social institutions. My own experience revealed the power of a governmental agency and its application of ideological definitions of family, ethnicity, gender, and class. The single, handwritten sheet of information my parents were given about my birth parents and their families provided such information as the height, weight, hair and eye color, skin tone, age ranges (teens), occupations, and ethnicities of my birth parents, as well as the occupations, ages, and brief medical histories of their families.

However, this documentation of my birth family history did not match the story told in my case file. Most of the information was accurate, but the inconsistencies were revealing. Anything that may have signaled "deviance" from the "mainstream" White nuclear family ideal prevalent in 1965 was either left out or changed. The most glaring omission concerned ethnicity. I was told that one birth parent was Irish, Scottish, and English, and the other was German and Polish. The information that my birth father was Jewish was left out. My birth mother was told that because I was a White infant I would be placed immediately, yet I remained in foster care for almost four months before I was adopted. Did the agency spend those months trying to match me with a Jewish family? By the time I was a few months old it was evident that with my red hair and fair skin I didn't "look Jewish," and so I was "matched" with my adoptive parents, who were Irish, English, and Scottish, and German and Swedish. In 1965, when adoption records were supposed to be irrevocably sealed, I assume my caseworker thought no one would ever detect the omission.

Information that might have indicated that my birth parents' families deviated from mainstream middle-class gender identities was changed as well. My birth mother's mother was listed as a housewife. The case file reveals that she was a waitress and a seasonal cannery worker. Even information about the minor disability of my birth father—one arm was slightly deformed at birth—was left out. I was quite literally "whitewashed" and "rewritten"—symbolically born anew—through the selective discourse of the social welfare system. As cultural studies scholars Sidonie Smith and Julia Watson explain, interacting with social institutions engenders engagement with "their already provided narratives of identity, their already mapped-out subject positions" (Smith and Watson 1996:11). The child welfare system operated in accordance with a particular narrative about family and identity that both drew on and enacted cultural assumptions regarding what kinds of families and citizens should be reinforced and reproduced. These social narratives were based on particular definitions of race, ethnicity, class, gender, and disability.

The absence of information that my birth father was Jewish demonstrates that the policies and practices of the social welfare system defined Whiteness-as-norm as Anglo-Saxon and Protestant, and thus, perhaps tacitly defined Jewish as non-White. In this context and in the historical moment of 1965, to be Jewish was to be *marked* with a non-White/non-normative racial-ethnic identity; it was the absence of the information that I was "half Jewish" that marked it as significant. Indeed, as Karen Brodkin Sacks explains, prior to World War II Jews were not legally defined as White on government census forms and official documents, anti-Semitism was open and rampant, and Whiteness was defined as Nordic or Anglo-Saxon (Sacks 1996). These social definitions of Whiteness and racial-ethnic identity slowly began to change after World War II; clearly this legacy had not been fully erased by 1965. My Jewish racial-ethnic identity was made to discursively disappear only because I could *pass* as "purely" White.

Contested Meanings: Race, Identity, Culture, and Kin

The situation in the 1990s, in which there were more children of color waiting in foster care than there were African American families who qualified for adoption, developed as a result of the state's valorization of

White, middle-class, nuclear families. This ideological definition of the family was reflected in public policy as also in the marginalization of racial-ethnic families and children. While there have been reforms in the system since the 1960s and 1970s, the fates of Black and White children are still determined differently by the state. Indeed, how the state defines and uses racial categories of identity remains one of the most salient and contentious issues in the current policy debate.

In the late 1950s and early 1960s social workers as well as the broader public began to become aware of the urgent need for adoptive homes for children of color. Transracial and transcultural adoptions began in the 1950s and first involved Korean and Native American children.[1] The civil rights movement raised public awareness of the large number of African American children relegated to foster homes, and the integrationist spirit of the movement made transracial adoption a new consideration for many social workers and prospective White parents.

Subsequently, toward the end of the 1950s several agencies and organizations were formed with the goal of promoting the adoption of those children who, because of the enormous demand for healthy White infants, had previously been classified as "unadoptable"—particularly children of color, older children, and those with health problems and disabilities.[2] While some agencies began actively recruiting White couples willing to adopt children of color, others only began making transracial placements when an increasing number of White applicants expressed interest in adopting "hard to place" children (Sellers 1969:355). They often did so because they faced waiting periods of several years for healthy White children. The introduction of birth control pills in 1960, changing cultural patterns of White teen-age sexuality in the 1960s and 1970s, changing social attitudes regarding single parenting, and the legalization of abortion in 1973, all contributed to the decline of White infants surrendered for adoption. These factors contributed to an increase in transracial placements in the late 1960s and early 1970s.

As I discussed in the previous section, race was the primary determinant of the relationship between pregnant teenagers and the social welfare system. Young White women were frequently coerced into relinquishing their babies for adoption, while Black women were often turned away from adoption agencies because there was no "market" for their children. Solinger explains the role of race prior to the advent of transracial adoption:

> Race, in the end, was the most accurate predictor of an unwed mother's parents' response to her pregnancy; of society's reaction to her plight; of where and how she would spend the months of her pregnancy; and most important, the most accurate predictor of what she would do with the "fatherless" child she bore, and of how being mother to such a child would affect the rest of her life. (Solinger 1992:18)

This understanding held true in a slightly different way for young White women in the 1960s and 1970s. Not only was the mother's race determinant, but as more and more young, unwed, White women gave birth to biracial babies, the race of their children often determined whether or not they kept their children.

I now turn to the origin story of Elisa Jacob, a transracial adoptee who was raised in a nearly all-White community on the West Coast. She told me the version of her beginnings made available to her through her adoption agency and her (adoptive) parents.

Elisa: Let's see. I was three weeks old when I was adopted. I was born in Chicago, White mother, Black father. From what I know my mother's parents didn't want her to have this interracial kid, and so they made her put it up for adoption. So when I was three weeks I got placed with my parents in foster care.

Sandi: Did they live in Chicago then?

Elisa: They lived in DeKalb County. Maybe Springfield or something like that. So I went there. I still have the article actually that my mom gave about why she adopted me. She was saying she had read an article about interracial adoption, and it sounded interesting. It just seems kind of strange to me, but they just thought it was an interesting thing, and that there were these kids that people weren't really looking for. So they had actually sought out interracial adoption.

Sandi: What year was this?

Elisa: 1969.

Elisa's story begins with the view of race as stigma. There were various reasons the parents of an unwed young woman in 1969 might have strongly pushed her toward adoption, most notably because she was not married. Her "*mother's parents didn't want her to have this interracial kid.*" To be Black was to be marked. Elisa became part of her family in 1969 because her mother had read an article about the need for adoptive homes for Black children. The narrative that emerges here is of an unwanted (at least by her grandparents), "illegitimate" mixed-race child who was rescued or saved from the fate of perpetual foster care through adoption into a White family. This story clearly fits its moment; interracial relationships were on the rise in 1969, and the campaign for adoptive homes for Black children was in full swing. It was also one of the peak years in the number of transracial adoptive placements.

As the number of Black children adopted by Whites increased in the late 1960s, transracial adoption became an issue in public discourse, including social welfare journals, newspapers, and popular magazines. Ladner summarizes the two contending positions on transracial adoption:

> Transracial adoption became a social problem when, on the one hand, adoptive parents and adoption agencies and, on the other, black social workers and black nationalists enunciated two fundamentally different sets of values. The values in conflict are racial integration, espoused by the adoptive families, and black autonomy, a preliminary step to the development of cultural pluralism, advocated by black social workers and their allies. (Ladner 1977:73)

At the heart of the debate between those for and against transracial adoptions was the concern that transracial adoption would undermine African American cultural identity and the transmission of survival skills among children of color in a racially oppressive society. Underlying these perspectives were conflicting definitions of race.

Ladner indicates that parental motivations were often related to a liberal, integrationist view of the future. "They acknowledge that, although transracial adoption will have but a small impact on creating their idealized integrated society, it is, nevertheless, an expression of their commitment to the philosophy of the 'brotherhood of man'" (Ladner 1977:92). In attempting to teach the values of a society where people are judged on merit rather than skin color, in their interaction with their children they often used language and behaviors that downplayed the importance of race. Indeed, McRoy and Zurcher found that 60 percent of their sample of transracially adoptive parents approached the issue of race from a "color-blind" perspective (1983:130).

This construction of race is not as innocuous as it may appear. The cultural discourse of "color blindness" is informed by a liberal humanist stance in its construction of race as a characteristic added on to an essential human sameness. Anthropologist Ruth Frankenberg argues that within this framework "people of color are 'good' only insofar as their 'coloredness' can be bracketed and ignored" and that in effect, this "preserves the power structure inherent in essentialist racism" (Frankenberg 1993:147). Indeed, the majority of adoptees I interviewed stressed the problems with this denial of race. Chelsea Wald, a twenty-five-year-old transracial adoptee who was raised on the East Coast explained the importance of raising children with an awareness of race:

> *Chelsea:* I am for adoption across races and everything. That does not bother me. But I think you need to be a little bit aware. Um . . . it's ignorant. It's just . . . I mean, we do not live in a society that's "color blind." We just don't. And as nice as it would be, we need to accept reality especially when you're raising a child. Because they're gonna be subjected to things that you might shelter them from.

A "color-blind" view of race is rife with contradictions. While "color blindness" has frequently been embraced as antiracist, it has also been shown to be an *evasion* of race that situates Whiteness as the "norm" and denies the salience of racial difference (Frankenberg 1993).

While many White parents saw this approach to race as a positive means of affirming their children's identities, their perspective was not shared by everyone in African American communities.[3] In an influential article, Edmund D. Jones, Assistant Director of Family and Children's Services in the city of Baltimore, stated:

> My basic premise, in opposing placement of black children in white homes, is that being black in the United States is a special state of being. At a time of intense racial polarity, recognition of this fact is crucial to sur-

vival. I question the ability of white parents—no matter how deeply im-
bued with good will—to grasp the totality of the problem of being black
in this society. I question their ability to create what I believe is crucial in
these youngsters—a black identity. I suggest that creation of a black identity is a problem for many black parents also; the difference, perhaps, is one
of degree. (Jones 1972:157).

At issue here are questions of identity and survival; indeed, Jones defines
"Black identity" as a *state of being* that, by definition, White parents cannot have experienced, and thus cannot convey to their children. The National Association of Black Social Workers, who in 1972 took center
stage in fighting against transracial adoption, argued that White parents
are incapable of providing a child with a positive sense of African American cultural identity or the survival skills necessary in this society to con-
front the racism that the child would inevitably encounter. The NABSW
argued that positive individual and community identity can only develop
if children learn "their own" cultural traditions and history. In a 1972
position paper the association stated:

> Black children should be placed only with Black families whether in
> foster care or for adoption. Black children belong physically, psycho-
> logically, culturally in Black families in order that they receive the total
> sense of themselves and develop a sound projection of their future.
> Human beings are products of their environment and develop their
> sense of values, attitudes and self concept within their family struc-
> tures. Black children in white homes are cut off from the healthy de-
> velopment of themselves as Black people. (National Association of
> Black Social Workers 1972)

Along with the concern over African American identity, some Black nationalists labeled the adoption of Black children by Whites an act of cultural genocide. Clearly, there was more at stake in these exchanges than
the well-being of particular children; these arguments were grounded in
integrationist versus nationalist visions of the future.

A number of people I interviewed mentioned this controversy in
the 1970s as part of their life stories. Ahmad Grant and his twin
brother were adopted in Chicago in 1972, the very year the NABSW

issued their statement against transracial adoption. He knew that he and his twin were biracial, but was unsure about which birth parent was White and which was Black. Their adoption speaks to the racial issues discussed here. Their parents had just become members of the Bahai faith when they decided to adopt Ahmad and his brother. He explained that "part of the faith is to believe in like unity and not like segregating anybody or whatever," and that his parents' belief in integration shaped the way they lived their lives and raised their children. Ahmad was clear in his mind that racial politics were an issue when they were adopted.

Sandi: Do you know why they decided to adopt transracially?

Ahmad: Not really. Except for my mom is . . . I think it was more my mom's decision as far as her having like a dream that we were gonna be adopted. And then uh . . . she said she . . . I don't know if she wanted to adopt twins or if she wanted to adopt like racially mixed twins or what the situation was. But uh . . . she said that if we weren't gonna be adopted by her we were gonna be separated too.

Sandi: Oh.

Ahmad: I don't know if that made 'em jump on the decision at that time . . . or whatever. But . . . yeah . . . we were gonna be . . . Like we were already set to go into different families. So . . . maybe that's what made her adopt us . . . rather than waiting another month or whatever.

Sandi: Yeah.

Ahmad: I think they were in the adopted . . . adoption process for awhile. Like . . . it took 'em awhile to find . . . for like people to get back to them. And then uh . . . they did have problems from like different racial groups or whatever who were against us being adopted for whatever reason.

Sandi: What kind of problems?

Ahmad: Uh . . . just like phone calls . . . people just being against it. No one like harassing us or anything like that. Uh . . . more like, just people against it. Just feeling it whatever way they did. Mostly by like phone calls.

The Politics of Race and Identity

The nationalist political perspective is rooted in a nation-based racial paradigm, which has historically understood racial dynamics as products of colonialism, and thus, in resistance, has emphasized "collective identity, community, and a sense of peoplehood" (Omi and Winant 1986:42). And while some defenders of transracial adoption have argued that separatist political ideologies should not stand in the way of serving "the best interests of the child," particularly in light of the generally positive findings in the research on transracial adoptees, the nationalists' criticisms are rooted in the historical and present-day material reality of life for African Americans in a racially stratified society. The sharing of culture and survival skills is tied to a particular tradition of parenting in African American families that developed historically in response to the systematic assault that they endured under the system of slavery (Dill 1988; 1994). Evelyn Brooks Higginbotham has shown how, "Through a range of shifting, even contradictory meanings and accentuations expressed at the level of individual and group consciousness, blacks fashioned race into a cultural identity that resisted white hegemonic discourses" (1992:267).

Questions of cultural identity raised by Black nationalists in the debate about transracially adopted individuals are inseparable from power relations. Black nationalists view the rearing of Black children in White families as a form of colonization; conversely, they see the raising of Black children with a strong sense of African American identity and a sense of belonging to a people and a history as a process of resistance to hegemonic racial meanings.

While the research shows that overall most transracial adoptees have adjusted positively, it also suggests that concerns about the construction of a "double-consciousness," considered necessary for the cultural survival of African Americans,[4] are well founded. Central to the question of cultural survival for African Americans is "the ambiguity and marginality of living simultaneously in two worlds—the world of the Black community and the world of mainstream society, a phenomenon unique to Blacks" (Peters 1988:233).

In a comparative study of Blacks adopted into European American families and Blacks adopted into African American families, McRoy and

Zurcher concluded that the "major distinction" between the two populations of adolescent adoptees "stemmed from their socialization concerning ethnicity."[5] The transracial adoptees tended to be more White-identified. The differences were attributed to the "social psychological contexts" in which their racial identities were constructed. Most of the Black transracial adoptees (87 percent) studied were raised in predominantly White communities, and subsequently had limited social contact with African Americans. The researchers found that while these adoptees acknowledged "their racial group memberships," they tended to develop "negative or indifferent" attitudes to their classification as African Americans, a preference for White friends and dates, and a "problematic ambiguity about racial identity" (McRoy and Zurcher 1983:140). McRoy and Zurcher found a difference in the sense of African American identity between those transracial adoptees raised in predominantly White communities and those raised in integrated areas: "Adolescent adoptees who had the opportunity to relate to blacks and whites tended to internalize the duality of character, or functional cultural paranoia that so often is necessary for survival in a racist society" (McRoy and Zurcher 1983: 140). Despite many White adoptive parents' professed belief in an integrated future, McRoy and Zurcher found that "only a few of the white adoptive families behaviorally responded to the necessity of equipping the child to become bicultural and to realistically perceive the historical and current black-white relations in American society" (1983:140).

This social debate must be understood in the context of a broader political discourse about the cultural construction of racial meanings—specifically, contested definitions of African American cultural identity following World War II. The movements for change that emerged in the postwar era are themselves evidence of the contested nature of race (as well as gender) as a category of social identity. Higginbotham explains: "Black nationalism itself has been a heteroglot conception, categorized variously as revolutionary, bourgeois reformist, cultural, religious, economic, or emigrationist. Race as the sign of cultural identity has been neither a coherent nor static concept among African-Americans" (1992:270).

Similarly, integrationism has been a "heteroglot" political perspective, embraced differently by Blacks and Whites. The politics of the civil rights movement and Black nationalist movements were not only concerned with legislative and structural changes in U.S. society, but also addressed questions of *identity*. Indeed, Omi and Winant argue that a defining feature of the "new" social movements following World War II was a "'politics of identity' which spilled over into arenas not traditionally defined as 'political'" (Omi and Winant 1986:146). The cultural debate about the appropriateness of transracial adoption is a political contestation of African American cultural identity, rooted in integrationist versus nationalist paradigms of racial meaning.

Ambiguous Identities

Gabrielle's story was distinctly different from the origin narratives of the other adoptees I interviewed. I include it not because it represents a widely shared experience, but rather to consider an extreme situation that grew out of some common circumstances. At the time of the interview she was a twenty-eight-year-old, single "out" bisexual woman, living with her grandmother, and working in the financial district. She was born in 1967 in San Francisco, where she was living when I interviewed her. Her birth mother was Mexican; her birth father was Creole.

> *Gabrielle:* Well, it's funny. My story again, is a little bit different in that when I—even though I'm Mexican and Creole I was born with blond hair. You know, and um [pause] [She shows me a picture of herself as a toddler.]
> *Sandi:* That's a great picture.
> *Gabrielle:* Yeah, my dad's a photographer. And so um, the whole race thing with me, I think, um, initially I—I can't help but to think that my birth mother was like, "Oh my God. Not only was this kid not mine, but it's of another race than my other kids."
> *Sandi:* Do you have any idea what your birth father looks like?
> *Gabrielle:* Light-skinned African American, olive skin. I think he was very, very light, but he probably had kinky hair. That's all I know. And so there's that whole sense. And then the thing with my adoptive parents was [pause] a really kind of [inaudible] thing, that is that some of the sixties idealism that was flying around during those times, was, I'd have to say, their main emphasis towards adopting a difficult-to-place child.

Sandi: So where would you put them on a spectrum?

Gabrielle: Of politics?

Sandi: Yeah, 'cause there was a lot of stuff going on.

Gabrielle: Well, they were liberal. But, so I feel like I got adopted only as a symbol [slowly and deliberately] to show the world [pause] that *they* were cool and p.c. and blahblahblah.

Sandi: Now, did they know about the fact that your birth father was Creole?

Gabrielle: Yeah.

Sandi: So they knew you were technically biracial. So was that part of it or was this just about a poor "hard-to-place" child?

Gabrielle: They wanted a Black child. Or, yeah, I think they really wanted a Black child, or maybe Mexican, as long as it really *looked dark.*

Sandi: How does that make you feel?

Gabrielle: It sucks. I mean, and I didn't learn it until like the last four years. I don't know when—I'm not great with dates. But um, you know, that was the final trip when I got the truth. I never knew that was what my truth was until, you know, I was like twenty-four or twenty-five. So, I mean, it's something—It's like reverse racism. It's really contorted. I can't—I don't really know anything like it. My mom even said to me when we finally had this conversation, "If you had been Black there's not a doubt in my mind that I would've been able to love you."

Sandi: What does that mean?!

Gabrielle: It means that they're all wrong, and that they're [screwed] up, and that um . . .

Sandi: Does that mean that she wasn't able to love you because you're not Black?

Gabrielle: Yeah, that's what she was saying.

Sandi: Oh, I'm so sorry. What a horrible thing to have to take in.

Gabrielle: Yeah, thank God I was like twenty-five.

Sandi: Yeah, at least you weren't twelve or something like that. So say more about that. I still—I don't get that.

Gabrielle: Yeah, I don't get it really either. But I really—She's twisted it in some way that she feels she was lied to by the adoption agency and dadadadada. Um, because there were all these difficult-to-place children—which is like a euphemism for Black, Hispanic, you know, whatever else—and you know, they call it like matching. She didn't want to have matching go on. She didn't want like a White child to be with a White family. It's like, this is her twisted analysis.

Sandi: So she didn't want someone who looks White.

Gabrielle: Right. So it was all benefitting her. Like "I am the good White person."

Sandi: Okay, I gotcha. Because if it's invisible then nobody knows that she'd done this good thing about taking in a "hard-to-place" child.

Gabrielle: Yeah. Yeah. So—

Sandi: I'm sorry but—So she didn't want a child she wanted a symbol.

Gabrielle: Yeah.

Sandi: Oh, I'm so sorry.

Gabrielle: So surprise, surprise. Along I come with blond hair and light skin—a genetic anomaly. It's just like twisted.

Gabrielle's mother was unable to bond with her adopted child, and attributed this to Gabrielle's blond hair and light skin. When Gabrielle was four years old her parents told her that her mother was sick and couldn't take care of her any more. They deposited her with her grandparents, and abdicated all responsibility for her. While her mother was apparently too "sick" to take care of her, she was well enough to take care of their birth son. Gabrielle grew up knowing her parents in a distanced way, as she put it, like an aunt and uncle.

Gabrielle saw herself as having been abandoned by both her birth mother and her adoptive mother, and saw both losses as rooted in racial issues. As she understood it, one of the primary reasons her birth mother had relinquished her—in addition to the financial difficulties she faced as a single mother of two other children—was that she was "half Black," while the other two children were Mexican. Her adoptive mother's sense of race was more convoluted. Gabrielle was adopted, at seven months old, during the wave of transracial placements that took place in the late 1960s and early 1970s. A great deal of public attention was given to the need for adoptive homes for children of color. The public discourse about transracial adoption was dominated by narratives of salvation, as is apparent in Gabrielle's account of her parents' actions and motivations. In the excerpt quoted below, she discussed the reasons behind her abandonment when she was four:

> *Gabrielle:* It was about *me*. It was about the whole decision. It was about the race issue, the class issue, about symbolizing. . . .
> *Sandi:* How does class fit into it?
> *Gabrielle:* I think that they were—they were—again, I think that they view themselves as [long pause] you know, you know sort of at least having power, even if they didn't have a lot of money. They had knowledge, and they had White skin and they had the ability to rescue, you know.

Adoption has not always been cast as rescue. Indeed, this narrative contrasts sharply with the social understandings of adoption in the 1950s that shaped the circumstances of Sam's adoption. While White infants were adopted in the 1950s largely because infertile couples needed a baby to make their lives complete, the 1960s impetus toward the placement of "hard-to-place" children—most prominently children of color—drew on racialized stories of salvation and rescue. Cultural studies scholar Leslie Roman suggests that such redemptive discourses provided Whites with "a kind of *premature* and *undeserved absolution*" for their complicity in receiving the benefits of White privilege (emphasis in original) (Roman 1997:274). In Gabrielle's story, her adoptive mother wanted to adopt—to *save*—a child of color because the "racial otherness" of her child would signify to people in her social world that she was a "good White liberal." The presence of such a symbolic child would have absolved her of responsibility for her participation in the maintenance of a racially stratified society.

Racial-ethnic identity had always been an issue in Gabrielle's life. With her olive skin and dark, curly, kinky hair, her appearance was racially ambiguous, and like Sam, her understanding of her racial-ethnic identity had changed in significant ways throughout her life.

> *Gabrielle:* I remember taking like African American Studies classes and feeling like I did not belong in these classes.

Sandi: Really?

Gabrielle: Yeah. And like, oh my God, what if someone asks me why I'm in here. You know, just felt really bad about it, like I was being intrusive and I wasn't giving them their space to have you know, an all-Black class.

Sandi: So would you be the quote only "non-Black" in the class?

Gabrielle: That's what I would feel like.

Sandi: But was that in actuality true?

Gabrielle: Yeah. But, I guess in looking at, and eventually under-standing what Creole really is, and then getting papers that say "White/Negro child" under my name, it's like I have entitlement.

Sandi: When did you find that out?

Gabrielle: Um, a couple years ago.

Sandi: Oh, that's interesting. So you didn't know all those years?

Gabrielle: Well, I knew that I was Creole, but I really—Creole is so vague that I really didn't have a handle on what that—it's like this is what Creole is: it's French, American Indian, and [whispering] Black, sometimes.

Sandi: So what was your motivation for taking African American Studies?

Gabrielle: I think that I actually, somewhat do have an affinity, or a drive to Black folk. There's just something more warmer, and there's like the whole jivin', and all this stuff that I like and like didn't get in my family. And so [pause] there's a lot that's differ-ent, and just a survivor—a survivor edge to it, of having gone through something and gone—And this is heavy imagery, but sometimes I've felt like a commodity or like a bought symbol or something, and the parallels between African American struggle and my life are pretty heavy.

At twenty-eight Gabrielle still struggled with questions of who she was racially, and where she "belonged." She had always felt like a "racial other," though she was uncertain as to the specifics of her identity des-ignation. In the passage quoted above, she discussed her sense of affin-ity with African American culture and history and her discovery that she was "entitled" to that identity. For her, one of the effects of her adoption and sense of racial ambiguity was that she felt she did not belong anywhere. She eventually transformed that feeling into an insider-outsider mode of being that allowed her to interact with different groups with ease—in a sense, belonging anywhere. Still, seeing her state-defined racial identity—"White/Negro"—spelled out in her "nonidentifying information" gave her a sense of profound *legitimacy*. It gave her a sense of legitimate belonging to a particular racial-ethnic group. While she had always known she was of Mexican descent, and had studied Spanish and traveled to Mexico as part of her undergraduate education, she had never been able to feel like an "insider" in Latino culture. She had found African American communities significantly more open and inclusive of her biracial identity. She defined herself as Afro-Latina, and continued to explore her identity. At the time of our interview she was engaged in a search for her birth parents.

There is a certain irony in the fact that the only information about our identities that adoptees in closed adoptions are legally entitled to is officially designated as "*nonidentifying* information." Indeed, these official papers do not identify the names or other traceable information about our birth parents and their families, but they *identify us* in terms of race and ethnicity, and often provide us with the first narrative of our births and biological histories we have ever had. These papers say to us, "*You were born.*" They resolutely state in typewritten words on official forms, "You are . . ." Black, White, French, Negro, Mexican, Jewish, Irish, Indian, German, Creole. . . . Sam discussed her "papers":

> *Sam:* It's funny 'cause I was telling someone about this—a woman who is trying to adopt. And she said, "Oh they lie on those." I went, "What?!" I mean I had never heard that, ever! I just went, "Are you kidding? That's the only truth I have!"

In adopted lives of secrecy and uncertain identity this state-sanctioned *truth of the self* has the potential to cut through years of internal questioning with coveted origin narratives, peopled with nameless characters whose past choices so profoundly shaped who we are. Such storied truths compel us to believe. But what do such disclosures mean for who we are?

There are a number of ways of defining racial-ethnic identity. While the legacy of nineteenth-century scientific racism has not completely disappeared, contemporary scientists stress the meaninglessness of race in terms of biological and genetic understanding.[6] However, such understandings do not dismantle the racial foundation of the legal and political infrastructure of the United States. Racial categorizations have been inscribed in our identities and institutionalized in the state-regulated discourse of birth certificates and "nonidentifying information," school records, and census forms. Cultural understandings of race and racial difference shape our perceptions of ourselves and those in our social worlds.

When we consider the lives of these two women we must ask: *What does race mean?* Are you "really Black" if your physical features do not identify you as Black—your skin is light and your hair is curly and frizzy, but not "kinky"? For many African Americans the answer is, "Yes, because I was raised in a Black family as part of African American culture and community." We know that skin color and hair texture are not the determinants of Black identity. But what if you were adopted by a White family and grew up in a predominantly White community? For several of my informants, this combination of factors contributed to lifelong struggles around issues of racial identity; however, because they knew that at least one birth parent was Black, they were aware that African American history and culture were part of their heritage, and thus could seek it out if and when they desired. But Sam and Gabrielle didn't know. Legal scholar Judy Scales-Trent writes:

> Not only do I know black people who are not brown, I also know black people who did not know they were black until they found out by accident in their later years. . . . So tell me: how can you and I be sure when the players themselves do not know? The most we can know for sure is that black does not equal brown. Brown is in our eyes; "black" is in our mind. (Scales-Trent 1995:89)

Such questions cut to the heart of the social construction of race. Sam and Gabrielle had lived somewhat unusual lives with regard to this issue, but their experiences question the "commonsense" foundations for the construction of race and identity and their configuration at the individual, familial, institutional, and discursive levels. Their identities and changing origin narratives show how directly social institutions and the policies and practices which govern them shape adoptive families and selves. The differences and commonalities in Sam's and Gabrielle's experiences demonstrate the links between the development of individual families and identities, social policy, public discourse, and race ideology, and attest to the importance of considering adoptees' lives in context.

The most striking commonalities in the origin narratives I have discussed center on the role of social institutions in the construction of identity and family. Social welfare agencies and the judicial system implement and enforce ideological definitions of identity, race, ethnicity, gender, (dis)ability, class, and family. The narratives of Sam and Gabrielle particularly illustrate the way in which social institutions construct racialized identities and families. Their origin stories can be read as allegories of racially specific births regulated through the bureaucratic arm of the state.

While the "naturalness" of a child's birth into its original family is often taken for granted in our society, the role of social institutions in the lives of adoptees should lead us to question how natural and unfettered a process creating a family really is for most people. The bonds that develop between parents and the children born into their families are no more *natural* than the relationships adoptive families develop. As anthropologist Kath Weston explains, in light of critiques of kinship raised in the past twenty years "*all* kinship ties (indeed, all social ties) could be characterized as fictive" (Weston 1995:88). Though a child is born to a couple, the tenor and substance of the relationships that develop between family members are fictive in the sense that they are filtered through cultural definitions of and prescriptions for families. While people who give birth to children are not required to go through the kind of screening process that adoptive parents endure, and their children's identities are not largely determined by social work practices, nonadoptive families nevertheless interact with social institutions that enforce social rules, define social identities, regulate familial behavior, and shape the identities of their children throughout their lives. The policies and practices of educational institutions, social service agencies, and governmental agencies, among others, regulate an individual's relationships to society. Issues of race, gender, class, (dis)ability, sexual orientation, age, and citizenship are defined, made relevant, and used by social institutions to determine and direct the allocation of social resources and privileges to particular individuals and deny those resources to others.

| T W O |

Navigating Racial Routes

Elisa: So like when I got to college that's when it was like
such a huge culture shock. It's like suddenly realizing
you're Black, but not knowing what that meant. Or having to interact with other Black people. It was really really hard. And that's where a lot of the anger came from,
'cause I suddenly was faced with everything I missed out
by being with White people and not knowing who I was
or having cultural identity. It's like even now, as much as
I've grown it's something I'll never be able to get back.
And I think, you know, I go back and forth about this.
Obviously I'm grateful for them giving me a home. And
I'm successful and I wouldn't be here, most likely if I was
bounced around in foster homes. That's what my mom
always says. [inaudible] I definitely believe Black kids
should be adopted by Black parents. I mean, there's just
such a huge hole. And there's just so much—no matter
how much I read or learn or study I'll never get it back.
And I just hate that.

Sandi: What things were a culture shock to you?

Elisa: You know, the way people talk, the way people acted.
It's hard to explain. It's just like this confidence—I don't
even know if confidence is the right word. . . . Like I'm real
shy and reserved, whereas my friends and my boyfriend
they just don't—there's like an inner strength. I'm missing
that I think for a lot of reasons.

Culture shock is a term used to describe the bewilderment and distress
individuals often experience upon traveling to a foreign land. It occurs
when a person's assumptions and expectations about self, others, and

reality fail to provide the information necessary for cultural interaction and survival. Elisa experienced this sort of disorientation on several levels. The assumptions she had learned to make about herself while living in a White family and community were inconsistent with others' social expectations of her as a Black woman in her new college setting. There was a dissonance between her social expectations—"the way people talk, the way people acted"—and the skills she needed to comfortably interact with the Black community at her college. She felt like a foreigner, an outsider in the cultural group to which she was supposed to belong. This sense of dislocation stemmed from her rather unique social location as the Black child of White parents. Transracial adoption violates what we typically think of as the normal familial channels of socialization and enculturation.

What does it mean to have a racial identity? What cultural skills and cognitive maps does a person need to successfully navigate through contemporary U.S. society as an African American? How is identity—one's conception of self—connected to cultural knowledge and social policy? What does Elisa's sense of culture shock say about the way race is constructed in the United States? Culture shock points to the sense of displacement at the heart of transracial adoptees' identities. Their existence as African Americans in White families disrupts mainstream assumptions about race, family, and identity. Their self-definitions often challenge the way other people classify them with regard to racial identity. Indeed, their sense of self testifies to the hybridity of identity.

In this chapter I consider the identities of transracial adoptees in light of the social controversy over this issue: the development of a positive sense of racial identity and the acquisition of survival skills for dealing with racism. However, important as these questions are in considering the effects of adoption and welfare policies in the lives of children, the lives of Black children raised in White families are profoundly significant in broader ways as well. I argue that, though the social locations of transracial adoptees are somewhat unique, their life stories raise challenging and intriguing questions about how race is structured, how social policy shapes individual identities, the way kinship is socially structured and made meaningful, as well as how individuals—whether adopted or not—construct a meaningful sense of self in a swiftly changing society rife with contradictory prescriptions for self-definition and presentation. I argue that everyone navigating life in the contemporary United States needs to learn survival skills to cope with cultural diversity, oppression, and power inequalities; all contemporary "American" identities are multicultural; all our identities—whether adopted or nonadopted—are constructed and maintained in interaction with social institutions and public policies; and finally, who we are is the result of a complex process involving continual social construction and cultural negotiation that cannot be neatly labeled to fit the categories on census forms or social science surveys. To be sure, the struggle for identity is often more difficult and painful for members of racial-ethnic minorities in the racially stratified United States. The process of navigating through life is highly variable, depending on one's social location in the power structure. In arguing that everyone needs survival skills to navigate the contemporary racial terrain, I am proposing that such skills vary widely according to the specificities of identity—race, gender, class, age, disability, and sexual orientation. In fact, the nature of the struggle, the need for survival skills, and the ways one uses these skills vary with one's location in the power structure.

The life stories chosen here are drawn from interviews with twenty-two transracial adoptees—Black and mixed-race children adopted by White parents—conducted between 1994 and 1996. I conducted follow-up interviews in 1998 and 1999. Twelve of the interviewees lived on the West Coast, and ten resided in the Mid-Atlantic region of the United States.[1] All of them were eighteen years or older at the time of the interview, with the majority between twenty-two and thirty. Five of the twenty-two interviewees were men, while seventeen were women. With the exception of one man, who was a senior in high school at the time, all my informants were employed, and all but two had attended college for some period of time. I interviewed each adoptee at least once for at least one hour; most of the interviews ranged from one and a half to two hours, though a few ran as long as three hours. I conducted follow-up interviews with several key informants, and interviewed the parents of seven adoptees. I draw on interviews with key informants to illuminate the central issues that emerged from their lives, and on the broader sample to illustrate the range of experiences represented by the people I spoke with. The names of the adoptees have been changed, as have other identifying facts.

As we will see in this chapter, the experiences of the twenty-two people I interviewed varied widely in some ways, and were profoundly consistent in others. Clearly, one cannot hope to assemble twenty-two people who "represent" the experiences of all transracial adoptees in the United States. This was not my goal. I did, however, seek to interview people whose lives represented a broad range of experiences as African Americans raised by White parents. My goal has been to explore in depth the lives and identities of those I interviewed, focusing on the processes by which they constructed and maintained a meaningful sense of self. In approaching their lives in cultural, social, and political contexts I have sought to understand the dynamic interplay of identity, family, culture, and social structure. I begin with a discussion of survival skills and cultural knowledge, and continue with a consideration of adoptees' identities as multiply defined and multiracial. Finally, I consider the processes by which the adoptees I interviewed constructed a meaningful sense of self.

Survival Skills and Cultural Knowledge

The question of whether or not White parents can and/or do impart survival skills to deal with racism to their Black children has been central in public debates regarding the appropriateness of transracial adoption. This issue also speaks to broader questions about the maintenance of ideology at the level of individual experience, and the ways in which individuals are able to resist power-infused social narratives of subordination. The work of W. E. B. Du Bois is a useful place to start in considering questions about race, oppression, and consciousness. In 1903 Du Bois wrote that the American of African descent was:

> born with a veil, and gifted with second-sight in this American world,—a world which yields him no true self-consciousness, but only lets him see himself through the revelation of the other world. It is a peculiar sensation, this double-consciousness, this sense of always looking at one's self through the eyes of others, of measuring one's soul by the tape of a world that looks on in amused contempt and pity. One ever feels his twoness,—an American, a Negro; two souls, two thoughts, two unreconciled strivings; two warring ideals in one dark body, whose dogged strength alone keeps it from being torn asunder. (1903:5)

Du Bois's concept of "double-consciousness" addresses a central aspect of contemporary scholars' questions about the way oppressive systems of cultural meaning are both maintained and resisted at the individual level. Du Bois articulated both the negative and positive effects of this state of being. Seeing oneself and the world through the eyes of one's oppressor, he wrote, led to an internalization of the negative cultural messages that justified inequality and an alienation from self. Du Bois characterized the positive effects as the gift of "second sight," an ability to recognize the inconsistencies of racial ideology. Contemporary scholars have interpreted this second sight as a necessary "survival skill" for members of racially oppressed groups living in a racially stratified society. Examples of such survival skills include the methods of deconstructing and delegitimating racial stereotypes and racist treatment, resistance and subversion, the ability to deal with a variety of cultural settings, and the ability to anticipate and read cultural signals, as in the behavior of police.

In a discussion of parenting in Black families, Marie Ferguson Peters explains that:

> Black families encourage the development of the skills, abilities, and behaviors necessary to survive as competent adults in a racially oppressive society, and a number of studies have investigated the characteristic, often culture-specific, child-rearing behaviors and survival mechanisms which enable Black parents to cope with everyday exigencies or with crisis situations. (Peters 1988:233)

The central questions in the public debate have been whether or not White parents can raise Black children with a positive sense of African American identity, and teach their children the survival skills they will need although they themselves had never experienced racism personally. The majority of people I interviewed felt that the socialization they had received from their parents was often inadequate when they experienced a racist incident. While they acknowledged that their parents had done their best and given them whatever cultural knowledge they were *able* to give, most of my interviewees had found it necessary to learn and incorporate their own survival skills to navigate the contemporary multicultural landscape. While everyone I talked to had struggled with this issue in varying degrees, most had acquired satisfactory methods of coping.

Brian Scott, a twenty-five-year-old transracial adoptee at the time of our interview who was raised in the diverse community of Berkeley, California, directly addressed the question of whether or not White parents could impart such coping mechanisms to their Black children:

Sandi: Do you feel like they gave you any of those skills?

Brian: Nope. I don't think they could, 'cause they've never been there. And a White person will never be there. I mean, White people go to Africa and they're in charge! I don't know how that happened. [wryly]

Sandi: That is really well-put.

Brian: You know? You can see it and you can talk about it, and you can—like my dad went to the "I Had a Dream" March in the Civil Rights . . . and he got whupped by the police in Alabama. Stupid ass strayed from the Civil Rights bus, and said, "I'm gonna go look at Alabama" by himself. They beat him up and said, "We're gonna throw you in the river with some cement if we ever catch you again." But he'll never have walked into a store and be treated like they treat a Black person—watched, you know, handed a bill before you eat—"pay now." You know? He just never will go through that. He can see it all he wants. He can't tell me how to deal with it; he couldn't and he didn't tell me how to deal with it. You know? Here in Berkeley I went to a store—New West—a couple years back when those were just coming in, and I had to go get something. My grandpa took me to New West to get some jeans. You know. Paying for 'em with a credit card, and the lady's taking a helluva long [time] to process the credit card. What the hell is she doing? It's fifteen minutes, and you gotta punch a number. And I'm sittin' here—Gramps is loaded [rich]—I know it's not his credit card. The police show up. She was like I held my grandpa hostage. And you know, my dad will never go through something like that because he's White. You know what I'm saying? It just doesn't happen. When police pull him over they don't pull their guns on him. They talk to him like a respectable person. So he couldn't teach me that. And I don't think he wanted to even *see* what he couldn't teach me, and *needed* to teach me. I mean, I think that's the hardest thing for White people, is they—the good people—they don't want to have to think it's really like that. You know? I mean, they really don't. And they want to believe that the police aren't like that.

Brian's story demonstrates the powerful role of media images and public narratives in the social construction of race and identity, and conveys the embodied aspects of racial identity. A Black male body carries a different social message than does a White male body. These racial codes of social identity are conveyed and understood through public narratives of race that shape the way people are seen and treated in everyday social interactions. A Black man has to deal with such encounters, which often involve police, throughout his lifetime. Thus, of necessity his sense of self is constructed and maintained in interaction with public narratives which define Black males through crime, unemployment, drug addiction, and gang violence.

Brian was not alone in having to define himself against and through such social narratives. All Black men living in the contemporary United States are, in varying degrees, affected by such stereotypical images. Yet his situation was complicated by the fact that he was raised in a White family, and thus grew up with a White man as his familial role model. As he so vividly illustrated, his father couldn't teach him what he had never experienced or even learned to see himself: "When police pull him over they don't pull their guns on him. They talk to him like a respectable person." Brian was tacitly and unconsciously taught to walk through the world as if he had the privilege of White skin and its attendant social meanings. Although Brian was also a respectable person, he had learned through encounters like the one he described that he must constantly navigate the distance between his sense of self as a respectable person and the dangerous images others often had of him. In popular narratives Black skin is not a signifier of respectability.

Popular ideological narratives often locate the meaning of "authentic Blackness" in images of inner-city gangsters and teenage mothers. In her analysis of the Anita Hill-Clarence Thomas controversy, cultural studies scholar Wahneema Lubiano discusses racial narratives in relation to perceptions of social reality. Though she specifically addresses Black women, her observations apply equally to Black men:

Categories like "black woman," "black women," or particular subsets of those categories, like "welfare mother/queen," are not simply social taxonomies, they are also recognized by the national public as stories that describe the world in particular and politically loaded ways—and that is exactly why they are constructed, reconstructed, manipulated, and contested. They are, like so many other social narratives and taxonomic social categories, part of the building blocks of "reality" for many people; they suggest something about the world; they provide simple, uncomplicated, and often wildly (and politically damaging) inaccurate information about what is "wrong" with some people, with the political economy of the United States. (Lubiano 1992:330–31)

Transracial adoptees must interact with this racial narrative in constructing a meaningful sense of self. Most of the adoptees I interviewed had, at various moments in their lives, found it necessary to question their own sense of themselves as African Americans in relation to such dominant media images. A number of them cited television images of Blacks as their primary exposure to African American people and culture as they were growing up. One woman explained that because most of her childhood ideas about African Americans came from television, she thought all Blacks were poor and uneducated. As a child she thought she had better marry a White man to make sure she didn't live in poverty. Feminist cultural critic bell hooks discusses White viewers of Black images on television as follows:

Many white folks who never have intimate contact with black folks now feel that they know what we are like because television has brought us into their homes. Whites may well believe that our presence on the screen and in their intimate living spaces means that the racial apartheid that keeps neighborhoods and schools segregated is the false reflection and that what we see on television represents the real. (hooks 1995:112)

hooks points out that televised views of Black life likely shape the racial perspectives of many Whites who have little or no social interaction with Black folks. If this is true for Whites, perhaps it is true for many transracial adoptees as well. How do you construct a positive sense of African American identity if your family is White, the community you live in is predominantly White, and many of the media images you are exposed to equate Blackness with poverty, crime, drug addiction, gang violence, and single-parent families? In such a situation one of the survival skills a Black adoptee needs is a critical consciousness that will help him or her deconstruct such racial representations and the power relations embedded within them. Transracial adoptees must not only learn to say, "That is not me," but also, "That is not 'authentic' Blackness."

In their discussion of Black families, socialization, and identity development, Jackson, McCullough, and Gurin explain:

> The minority family is the important agent of socialization, for it is within the family context that the individual first becomes aware of and begins to grapple with the significance of racism and discrimination. The intrafamilial socialization of group and personal identity has considerable bearing upon personal functioning in a society that cultivates negative conceptions of minority group members through direct interaction, the media, and institutional barriers. (Jackson, McCullough, and Gurin 1988:244–45)

This is not to suggest that White parents are *incapable* of teaching such survival skills. However, we must acknowledge that a critical consciousness about race and racism has to be learned. It is possible, and is indeed quite common, for White people to grow up in the United States with little or no contact with people of color, no suggestion that social reality is perceived differently from social locations other than their own, and/or no awareness that racism still operates at multiple levels in contemporary society. In fact, many of the messages aimed at Whites in mainstream public discourse support and foster the view that racial inequality was eradicated by the civil rights movement, and that the United States is a "color-blind" society. There are countless channels through which Whites can and do bring a critical perspective to bear on race relations and media representations of racial-ethnic minorities. When transracially adoptive parents take the opportunity to educate themselves and their children, to (re)locate their families to racially diverse communities, and to grapple with the sticky, often painful, issues that arise in multiracial families their children benefit tremendously. Indeed, this is a critical factor for transracial adoptees.

Thirteen of the twenty-two people I interviewed were raised in predominantly White communities in families that made little or no effort to diversify their social world. The levels of struggle and pain my informants experienced around issues of racial identity and racist treatment were related to their parents' attitudes and awareness about racial issues and the racial makeup of the communities in which they lived. All the adoptees I spoke with experienced their sense of identity as an "issue" that had to be dealt with, yet their responses to this varied. These findings are consistent with those of McRoy, Zurcher, Lauderdale, and Anderson in their studies of transracially adopted children (1982, 1984). They found that:

> The children whose families were residing in integrated areas, who attended racially integrated schools, and who had parents who acknowledged their children's racial identity, tended to perceive themselves as black persons and to feel positively about it. Those children who had little, if any, contacts with blacks tended to develop stereotyped impressions of blacks and were likely to feel they were "better off" in a white adoptive family than in a black adoptive family. . . . Such children were likely to act as similarly as possible to their white peers and white family members and to renounce any similarities or allegiances to blacks. (McRoy et al. 1984:39)

It is difficult to separate the intertwined issues of racial identity and survival skills. Adoptees who had been surrounded by Whites all their lives and had never learned to critically appraise representations of African Americans in the mass media, books, toys, and social attitudes tended to be the most White-identified and most accepting of negative, stereotypical views of Blacks. Their coping mechanisms to survive the onslaught of racist attitudes, treatment, and representations they encountered involved distancing themselves from Blackness and embracing Whiteness—they largely accepted representations of African Americans as truth and posited themselves as "exceptions" who were "different" from other Blacks. On the other hand, those who acquired a critical perspective to deal with racial representations and racism as a systemic issue developed survival skills that both allowed them to question and criticize racist images and narratives *and* to define positive, healthy views of themselves as African American and/or biracial people.

Kristin Rhineholt and her three transracially adopted brothers (none related biologically) were raised in a nearly all-White community in Pennsylvania. Kristin and her older brother Nicholas were strongly

White-identified. Nicholas, the only Black member of the police force in a small East Coast town, saw racism as a learned condition taught in Black families that was used as an excuse for thinking "*they*" were inferior or explaining why "*they*" hadn't succeeded. Kristin unquestioningly accepted stereotypes associating African Americans with poverty, lack of education, and the enjoyment of particular kinds of foods—watermelon, fried chicken, collard greens, and orange soda. There was a seven-year gap between Kristin and her two eighteen-year-old brothers, and my interview with one of them, Steve, indicated that the family had dealt with racial issues differently with the two younger siblings. Steve was significantly more comfortable with himself as an African American. However, the following excerpt from an interview with Kristin illustrated the connections between race, representation, and the formation of her White-identified consciousness:

> *Sandi:* What about like books and toys, things like that?
> *Kristin:* We had both.
> Sandi: Black dolls?
> *Kristin:* Um hmm. But then again, people are appalled at *Little Black Sambo.* She read that to us.
> *Sandi:* Really?
> *Kristin:* Oh yeah. I like it. And I don't see what other people see.
> *Sandi:* I don't think I've ever actually read the story. I've just heard a lot about it.
> *Kristin:* Really? It's a good book. And she used to do voices to Brer Rabbit. Ya know. It was never an issue of "Oh, this shouldn't be read." You know, stuff like that.

Little Black Sambo has been held up as an intolerably racist children's book. "Sambo" is a caricature of Blacks as buffoons whose roots lie in the nineteenth-century racist theater tradition of minstrelsy. The thrust of the plot is that Sambo is stupid enough to allow tigers to repeatedly trick him out of the new clothes his mother has just given him. The Sambo character in the children's story also represents the racist stereotype of the "pickaninny," typically a scantily clad, unkempt, wild-looking, animal-like Black child. Kristin was clearly aware that the book had been criticized, but emphasized that she liked it. The key phrase here was: "*I don't see what other people see.*" Her parents did not teach her to recognize racist stereotypes.

Kristin's and Nicholas's experience represented one end of the spectrum. While a number of other families did little to teach their children critical race skills, most of the adoptees went searching for their own racial enculturation at different points in their lives. Only four of the twenty-two people I interviewed were primarily White-identified and had not felt the need to learn more about Black culture and become more comfortable with themselves as African Americans. Eight of the adoptees I interviewed were raised in diverse communities; of these, the parents of five were aware of the need to teach their children survival skills and to engage the family in multiracial groups and activities. However, these five only represented three sets of parents—there were two sets of siblings among them. Andrea and Erika Bailey were both adopted from Africa and were raised in Los Angeles. Both their parents were academics whose specializations focused on Africa, and both had been deeply committed to movements for social justice in the United States. While Andrea and Erika had not been immune to struggles over identity issues, they had been given a solid foundation that included an understanding of racism and oppression, as well as an appreciation of African and African American cultures. Andrea explained:

Andrea: Do I have the survival skills to respond to racism? Oh yeah.
Sandi: So how did your parents deal with racism? Can you think of the ways that they taught you about it?
Andrea: These are hard questions.
Sandi: I know. Sorry.
Andrea: It's just they're large in scope. Well, to answer the first question—Have I been able to deal with the survival skills?—I'd say most definitely, because I consider myself well-educated from a very progressive family, so I know issues that are out there. I know how to defend myself. I know that I have resources. Which I might not feel like I had if I was in a different environment, and if I didn't watch and learn from the ways my parents handled different situations. You know? So yes, I can survive. In terms of how they've dealt with racism, racism in the small, as how it affects our family or racism in the broader spectrum?

Sandi: However you have felt it.

Andrea: Well, my parents have actively fought against that, just being the progressives that they are. They actively wanted to—I don't know. In their literature, in their readings, I may not have necessarily always understood what they were talking about at dinner time and stuff like that but you know, it was always about social causes, trying to get me and my sister to immerse ourselves in those causes as well. So it wasn't just E.R.A. and Women's Rights and stuff that we were a part of. I remember once I was in junior high I think. I was in this young people's theater company, and we were putting on this play. I forget the name of the play, but I got this really big part, but it was the part of a servant. But it wasn't stereotypically designated for African Americans role. It was actually an Irish part, but you know, I got this part and my parents told me I couldn't do it. They told me I couldn't be in the play if I did it. And I didn't understand it. And I was like—

Sandi: Oh wow.

Andrea: You know, it's just any part. It's not anything racial. And I remember we got into big fights about it, so I never—I didn't take the part. But I remember that was—I remember that was one of the first times I remember really race and racial issues really affecting myself.

Sandi: Did you understand why?

Andrea: At the time I didn't. At the time I just thought they were being extreme, and they didn't understand that the part was just a part. But you know, I can understand why.

Sandi: Looking back on it now, do you think they made the right decision?

Andrea: Uh, yeah, sure. Um, I think yeah.

Andrea's parents were clearly aware of the history of Black representation in the American media. For many years the only roles available to African Americans in film and television were as servants. Even now one of the most prevalent roles available to Black actors is a variation on the mammy/servant stereotype whose primary concern is the well-being of

White folks.[2] Andrea was also confident about dealing with racist attitudes and treatment. Importantly, she was raised with an understanding of race and inequality as *systemic* issues. In contrast to many of my informants, this provided her with an explanatory system that did not blame and stigmatize African Americans for being poor and having access to fewer social resources. Unlike explanatory systems that locate racism in the ignorance of individuals, her racial analysis was grounded in a critique of social structure. This gave her a way of understanding racial difference and inequality without requiring her to define herself as "not Black" in order to maintain a positive sense of self.

Transracial adoptees are not alone in needing to learn survival skills. We all construct our sense of self and others through interaction with public discourse about identity and "difference." As I noted at the start of this chapter, such critical skills for "reading" and deconstructing racial representations are invaluable for members of all racial and ethnic groups in the racially stratified United States. As the work of multiracial feminists and race relations theorists has demonstrated, questions of power are relational; we all exist in complex webs of power relations that vary according to our multiple identities and social locations. Racial-ethnic identities are not monolithic, but are experienced differently on account of differences in gender, class, sexual orientation, age, and disability. Sociologist Howard Winant explains that:

> Nearly a century ago Du Bois analyzed "double consciousness" as a basic tension in black identity produced by the painful but ineluctable presence within black subjectivity of white attitudes and prejudices. Today we may reasonably extend this insight to propose the existence of a "multiple consciousness" through which most North Americans necessarily experience their racial identities. (Winant 1994:53–54)

In my view, learning to untangle ideological narratives of "difference" from the actual diverse range of identities we embody and encounter in others is a necessary survival skill for all of us living in the United States. Whites need to learn how to decenter Whiteness as normal, as generically human, and above all, as innocent. Indeed, the acquisition of such deconstructive skills would likely contribute to the survival of our society and to all of us living in it.

Black/White/Biracial: Multiply Defined Identities

Sam: but because I was so clearly unidentified—I mean, even now nobody ever thinks I'm Black. I'm at my darkest now because I hung out at the beach all summer—well, not all summer, two weeks. [We both laugh.] . . . So in the winter when I'm much lighter, you know, I'm taken either for Jewish or French or Hispanic. I'm taken for East Indian a lot. I have a lot of East Indian friends, so when I'm with them. Whenever we travel, no matter where we go, if we're in Mexico I'm Mexican. If we're in Guatemala I'm Guatemalan. If we're in Equador I'm Ecuadorian. So, um, in some ways it's been—once I passed out of adolescence and I felt more of a whole person, just in general, then it became something I could play with. I don't ever say I'm anything but what I am, but it's something that has become more—it's just more comfortable than having to defend—not defend myself, but just being questioned all the time. Whenever I went to a new town—I jumped around from college to college for a couple years—I would get questioned. You know, people would come up to me in like a bank line and ask me what my identity was. I'm serious. You know, it was³ just like it was constant for a while.

The changeling quality of Sam Bennett's racial identity was shared by a number of the adoptees I interviewed. Yet, even among those who were more easily categorized as Black, many had developed multiply defined selves. Many people who do not live on the "color line" view race and racial identity as biological or even cultural givens. However, as I have discussed, the lives of transracial adoptees problematize such assumptions.

There are different approaches to studying racial identity. Perhaps the most widely known is the psychological research of Cross (1991), Helms (1990), and Parham (1989), who track the development of racial identity through a stage model.³ Though some of my informants narrated their identity progression through a similar set of stages, I was struck by the depth and diversity of their experiences. I take a life-history approach that focuses on the insider's view—the ways in which people experience themselves in relation to family, community, culture, and society. This perspective allows me to consider the multiplicity of identities each person assumes by exploring the various systems of cultural meaning they draw on in the course of their lives. A number of cultural anthropologists have used this "person-centered" approach to ethnography, in which, as Caughey explains:

> we see that we need to attend to the fact that it is not only modern communities but modern individuals that are multicultural. That is, contemporary Americans are likely to think about themselves and their worlds in terms of several different cultural models and also to play multiple social roles which are associated with and require operating with diverse and often contradictory systems of meanings. (Caughey 1994:129)

This approach is particularly relevant to a consideration of transracial adoptees, whose lives have been structured by multiple systems of cultural meaning. With a few exceptions, most of my informants actively sought out African American cultures and communities in their struggle for self-understanding and social survival. As anthropologist Ward Goodenough explains: "A person may not only attribute different systems of standards to different sets of others, he may also be competent in more than one of them—be competent, that is, in more than one culture" (Goodenough 1981:99).

My informants' social location as Black children of White parents placed them in the rather unique position of having, as many of them expressed it, "insider" access to both African American and White cultures in the cultural and historical era following the civil rights movement. Even Kristin Rhineholt, the most White-identified among them, said that though most comfortable in the company of White people and most conversant in that cultural meaning system, as a person with brown skin she was typically treated like other African Americans, and thus felt she was "sitting on the fence."

Transracial adoption in the late 1960s occurred alongside another social change with regard to race and family. The landmark Supreme Court ruling in *Loving v. State of Virginia* in 1967 removed the last legal barriers to interracial marriages, and the first generation of children from these marriages had come of age at the same time as the largest cohort of transracial adoptees. Though the number of multiracial births in the United States was only 3.4 percent of all births in 1989, for the first time in history the rate of bi- and multiracial births was increasing at a greater rate (260 percent) than that of single-race births (15 percent) (Root 1996:xiv). Along with these demographic shifts has come a new wave of scholarship, autobiography, and movements for the recognition of multiply defined people and families.[4] G. Reginald Daniel discusses multiracial individuals as follows:

> The psychosocial configuration of their identity is premised instead on a style of self-consciousness that involves a continuous process of "incorporating here, discarding there, responding situationally." Because the contemporary blended individuals maintain no rigid boundaries between themselves and the various contexts within which they operate, their identity has no fixed or predictable parameters. They are liminal individuals whose identity has multiple points of reference and, yet, has no circumference, due to the fact that it manifests itself *on* the boundary. (Daniel 1996:134)

Daniel's description suggests that like transracial adoptees, multiracial individuals juggle a diverse repertoire of cultural meaning systems during the course of their lives. This sense of liminality, or as Anzaldua puts it, "mestizo" identity (Anzaldua 1987), was evident in most of my informants' life stories. Of the twenty-two adoptees I interviewed, sixteen had birth parents of different races; only six had two Black birth parents. While there are parallels between multiracial individuals raised in their birth families and transracial adoptees, there are significant differences as well. While both multiracial individuals and adoptees such as my informants occupy a space on the social "boundary," their experiences differ, often in profound ways, because nonadopted people are usually raised with their birth families. The identity issues are complicated for adoptees by the absence not only of their birth families, but also by the absence of any significant biological or medical history (except in the case of one informant, whose adoption was open). Also, transracial adoptees lack a familial socialization in African American culture.

The people I interviewed responded to these circumstances in a variety of ways, constructing and defining complex, multifaceted senses of self. While their racial identity was fluid and contextual, their primary self-definitions frequently diverged from the official definition of race by adoption agencies, based on the races of their birth parents. Of the six adoptees with two Black birth parents, two were primarily White-identi-fied. Among the group of sixteen whose birth parents were of different races, two were principally White-identified. The remaining four with two Black birth parents were Black-identified. Five adoptees whose birth parents were not of the same race were Black-identified. These adoptees explicitly defined themselves as Black, often reasoning that they were seen and treated as Black, regardless of the race of their birth or adoptive parents. This sense of identification was usually articulated as a conscious choice to learn about and participate in African American cultural tradi-tions, to celebrate African and Black American history, and to resist White cultural ideology. The remaining eight, all of whom had birth par-ents of different races, defined themselves as mixed or biracial. Thus, of the twenty-two people I interviewed four were primarily White-identi-fied, nine were Black-identified, and nine saw themselves as multiracial. Significantly, all of them recognized the "constructedness" of such racial categories and were clear that their self-definitions were based on cultural *choice* rather than unproblematically given. These configurations clearly revealed the separation of biological and cultural factors in assigning racial identity; indeed, the force most evident in the construction of the identities of adoptees was *social structure*—adoption agencies and the public policies which governed their practice.

In recent years ethnographers, feminists, and other cultural studies scholars have emphasized the contextual and relational character of iden-tity. With regard to ethnographic method, increasing attention has been paid to the ethnographer's presence in shaping the self-narratives of the people being interviewed. Renato Rosaldo explains:

> The study of differences, formerly defined in opposition to an invisible (ethnographic, authorial) "self," now becomes the play of similarities and differences relative to socially explicit identities. How do "they" see "us"? Who are "we" looking at "them"? Social analysis thus becomes a relational form of understanding in which both parties actively engage in "the inter-pretation of cultures." (Rosaldo 1993:206–7)

Indeed, my interviews were contextual, relational, interactive moments of identity construction and definition for both my interviewees and my-self. Not only did I provide my interviewees an occasion for self-reflec-tion and the articulation of self, but my identity as an adoptee gave them a listener and questioner who was an "insider." The sense of validation was powerful for me as well, as each of us participated in a unique dialogue in which another person "got it"—an "insider's view" of adoption. Certainly, there were profound differences among the group of people I spoke with, but some foundational assumptions seemed present in almost every encounter. All of us carried the stigma of having been "given up" or "relinquished" or "abandoned." For all of us, biology was absent from the experience of kinship and thus fully separated from our cultural, emotional, and experiential understandings of family. We each had a sense that our identities were not "natural," but rather, contingent and constructed. We knew that we could easily have grown up in other families, and thus have been entirely different from the selves we now knew.

The relational definition of self was particularly interesting with regard to my interviewees' understandings and articulations of the "constructedness" of racial categories. One subject that came up repeatedly with the women I interviewed was the "hair issue." Many of them described the problems their mothers had in caring for their hair—"Black hair" often demands a different kind of care than "White hair." Some of their mothers learned, while others took them to hairdressers or family friends. The majority of the women I spoke with had one White birth parent, and thus many of them had what has often problematically been referred to as "good hair," curly and/or frizzy as opposed to "kinky."[5] We often bonded over hair issues. Many of the women and I had similar curl-frizz ratios, and this was frequently commented on. However, such comments were not casual but deliberately made, to illustrate the arbitrary social distinctions drawn between racial groups. Skin color became another point of comparison used to highlight the gaps between actual skin tone and the constructed categories of Black and White. Many of those I interviewed had such light skin that the differences between us were very slight. (I have very pale skin.) They often pointed this out, or sometimes would refer to my skin color in describing a sibling. One woman showed me both color and black and white photos taken throughout her life to demonstrate that unless she was tanned, it was very difficult to tell she was African American.

I will now turn to excerpts from interviews with four women who defined and discussed their identities in distinct ways. Andrea Bailey addressed the difficulties she had had in dealing with identity issues. Cat

Benton discussed her identity as a biracial woman. Karinne Randolph emphasized the importance to her of defining herself as Black. Finally, Kristin Rhineholt articulated a White-identified sense of self.

Andrea was a twenty-five-year-old woman who had been adopted into her family at the age of two. She and her older sister Erika (not biologically related) were adopted from an orphanage in Africa, and were raised in the Los Angeles area. As I discussed earlier, their parents, academics whose work focused on Africa, made great efforts to raise them in a racially diverse community with an awareness and understanding of their African heritage and racial issues in the United States. What was striking about Andrea's experiences was that though her parents did "all the right things" with regard to race, she still struggled over her racial identity and the sense that she did not belong anywhere socially. She emphasized: "I don't fit in right now. I don't fit in anywhere really." In the following excerpt, she discussed the enormity of racial issues in her life:

Sandi: Do you ever think about how it would have been if you had been adopted by a Black family?

Andrea: Umhm.

Sandi: What do you imagine?

Andrea: Life would be easier.

Sandi: Really?

Andrea: Sometimes. The identity problems I'm having would not exist, I don't think. They might. But I'd feel, I guess, like I belonged a lot more than I do now.

Sandi: Do you have any sense of what is about race and what is about adoption?

Andrea: I think for me, I'd say that about 95 percent of it is about race. I feel like . . . It's contradicting because I feel like I have this perfect life in terms of a stable family that loves me and would do anything for me and I would do anything for them. And that if I compare my life with that of my friends who have not had the same situations, or life events that I've had, I'd say that I have one of the more stable families, more open and communicative. And parents with good politics and all that kind of stuff. And I think that—I don't think it's an adoption thing. I think it's a transracial adoption thing, because the feelings that I've had

| 81 |

towards my family have been mostly—well, up until I was able to notice or truly understand the profound differences, the issues surrounding transracial adoptions—it really was normalcy for me. So normal that it would anger my sister, because I would treat them—I would take them for granted. I think if I was older when I was adopted issues of adoption might be more profound.

Andrea's sense of the stability of her family in contrast with her angst over her racial identity spoke to the pervasiveness and perhaps, the inevitability of such struggles among transracial adoptees. All twenty-two adoptees discussed race and racial identity as issues that demanded their attention. While some, like Andrea, were contending with their sense of self as racial beings at the time of the interview, others felt they had passed through their most tumultuous years and had come to some kind of self-understanding and definition.

Cat Benton was a twenty-three-year-old biracial woman who was adopted into her White family—her father, mother, and their birth son—as an infant. She was raised in the multiracial city of Oakland, California, where she was residing when I interviewed her. More than any other informant, she grew up immersed in both Black and White cultures. She discussed her sense of self as biracial in the following passage:

Sandi: So when you think about your identity, how do you define your identity? Not necessarily in terms of race, but let me ask you about who you are.

Cat: A few years ago I would have been—well, you would've had to figure out—if you asked me on this day I would say something different, but because of the exposure and the experiences and the people I've been around I have to say that being Black and White—of some Black and some White—whatever that is, biracial, having one parent one, one parent the other is a unique background, is its own background, its own culture. I don't mean biracial period—Black and Hispanic, White and something—I mean Black and White is a separate background. And I consider myself biracial, Black and White.

Sandi: So what does that give you and not give you? What does it lack and what does it have?

Cat: Um, it has an understanding that no other culture can understand. There's no other culture that can truly understand and feel at home being around two different—being around these two groups of people. It lacks a lot because you never feel like—you never totally fit in anywhere unless you're with other mixed people. And it does work in other mixes. When you come across that Black and White person it's like "What's up? You know me and I know you. Don't try to front, ya know." And most mixed people try to identify one way or the other. There are not very many people who I know who identify as a mixed person, biracial Black and White person. More and more I come across that, especially in Berkeley. Yeah, no matter where you were raised, I mean, depending on the color of your skin and maybe if you're thinking of yourself as all this or all this, if you are in tune with the fact that you are biracial and are strong on both sides, you're never gonna feel all the way comfortable here and you're never gonna feel all the way comfortable there. And that's what it lacks. And society craves that, society—"Label yourself! What are you?"

Sandi: Check that box!

Cat: Other!

Cat enjoyed playing with traditional racial categories and mixing them up. This discussion was notable for her engagement with questions of *culture,* though there was an interesting slippage between her biological definition as biracial—having one Black and one White birth parent—and the cultural familiarity with both groups that she acquired as a member of a White family living in a racially diverse neighborhood. She defined being biracial as having "its own background, its own culture." Thus, she identified three cultural meaning systems in her life: biracial, Black, and White. She was exposed to these systems of meaning in the family and community she was raised in; as she intimated, biracial culture was alive and well in Berkeley, California. These meaning systems, along with others she drew on, constituted her own repertoire of cultural tools for navigating the borderlands she inhabited. Rosaldo discusses the crossing of cultural demarcations as follows: "The result is not identity confusion but play that operates within, even as it remakes, a diverse cultural repertoire. Creative processes of transculturation center themselves along literal and figurative borders where the 'person' is crisscrossed by multiple identities" (Rosaldo 1993:216).

Adoptees who defined themselves as mixed or biracial did so on the basis of the racial identifications of their birth parents. However, they were also biracial or multicultural in terms of their engagement with various systems of cultural meaning. All of them were raised to be culturally proficient in "mainstream" White cultures, yet they had all sought out some exposure to Black communities and cultures. Such exploration was minimal for a few, but more substantial for others. For some, the experience of going away to college provided new social opportunities in more diverse settings than those in which they had been raised. Some searched for their birth parents as a means of establishing a connection with their Black families.

Eight of the people I interviewed defined themselves as Black, a number of them reasoning that as they were seen as Black by others, it was important that they take an affirmative stand regarding Black identity. Karinne Randolph, the child of an interracial relationship, was adopted into a large family with other transracial adoptees at eighteen months of age. She was raised in a racially diverse city in Pennsylvania, where she lived and worked as a social worker when I interviewed her. Her parents had raised her and her siblings in a mixed neighborhood, where they attended diverse schools. The parents' social group included both Whites and African Americans, and they encouraged their children to explore Black culture as much as they wished. In the excerpt below, Karinne discussed the importance of defining herself as African American:

Sandi: So when did you come to this decision or this understanding of yourself as African American rather than mixed?
Karinne: In high school. I know I did that in high school, but I became more serious about it in college. I think lots of people do that in college. They really go there to try and find themselves, so to say. I think we're just a bunch of big babies trying to define ourselves. And part of it's that and part of it's that I'm an adult now. I can't be wishy-washy about this for the rest of my life. I have to make a firm decision. I believe in you know, identifying what the problem is and dealing with it head-on, and taking care of it. It's kind of hard to say that about something so

deep like this, but I made a conscious decision probably in eighth grade to really try to focus on that. I think it went back and forth for a lot of years depending on what the circumstances were at the time. Whether I was liking someone specific at the time or whatever. Because of the way I [inaudible] I felt I really needed to make a decision. And I think that with adult African American adoptees, if you live with White parents you either make the decision that it doesn't matter, and you end up with someone who's White. Or you make a decision that it does matter, and that your generations are going to be affected because of the decisions that you make, that you really go the way that you feel in your heart. Like if you really feel that you're African American and you're proud of that, that's just what you do. That's the decision I made for me. I can't talk for anybody else. That's just what I perceive in them.

This definition of self shaped different aspects of her life. For example, it was important to her that she raise her daughter with a strong sense of African American culture. She was engaged in a continual process of education, from history and culture to cooking practices. She was very involved in the Black church she belonged to, and worked in a predominantly Black social service agency. She emphasized that she was comfortable and familiar with White culture as well, but drew her strength from the cultural traditions of African Americans.

The lives of transracial adoptees raise interesting questions about how racialized meanings of self are constructed, disseminated, and maintained through social institutions and public policies. The adoption system in the United States is geared toward the reproduction of normalized, naturalized nuclear families. In fact, historically it has developed as a means of reproducing White middle-class families headed by heterosexual married couples. It is useful therefore to ask what kinds of identities are being socially constructed through the placement of Black children in these families. Thus far, in this section I have discussed the lives of adoptees whose parents were conscientious about raising them in a racially diverse community and gave them the opportunity to become familiar with African American cultures. Now I turn to the experiences of a woman who did not have such social options.

Kristin Rhineholt, a twenty-five-year-old transracial adoptee, was the birth child of two African Americans. She was raised, along with her three transracially adopted brothers, by White parents in a nearly all-White Pennsylvania community. In the following excerpt, she discussed her racial identity in these terms:

Kristin: And people have said to me, they're like "You talk funny." I'm like "What do you mean I talk funny? I talk properly." And, I mean, that was one thing I hated my parents for—you couldn't have a sentence at the table without them saying, "It's Nicholas and *I.*" You know, things like that. I'm like, "God Mom, Nicholas and *me!*" You know? I want to say whatever I want to say, but my command of the English language is pretty good. And I don't have the typical Black slang and accent and whatever. And I guess maybe I'd have that [if raised in a Black family]. And my friends laugh at me when I try and do it, just to mess around. They're like, "Kristin, please stop." Or like when Blacks talk to me sometimes I'll be like, "What? In English? I don't know what you're saying." And so I think about—would I have talked like that?

Sandi: So do people tell you you "sound White?"

Kristin: Oh yeah. Like I don't think anybody ever would ever mistake me for being Black if they never saw me. Never. Never in a million years.

Sandi: Huh. That's interesting though, the way you put that—"mistake" you for being Black. Like you're not really—

Kristin: That's true.

Sandi: That's interesting. A little slippage there.

Kristin: Yeah. Okay, rewind.

Sandi: Well, so, play with that a little bit. I mean *what are you?* Like if—I don't know I just came from interview—

Kristin: Shelley?

Sandi: Yeah. And she said people all the time—because she's very light-skinned—ask, "What are you?" If somebody asked you that—

Kristin: No, no. [meaning no one would ask that, because of her dark skin]

Sandi: Well, I'm asking you. "How do you self-identify?"

Kristin: Well. [pause]

Sandi: Or who are you?

Kristin: [pause] I would probably say I'm White with very, very dark skin.

Sandi: Really?

Kristin: Yeah. I think that for the most part that's the only part of me that I feel—I mean, obviously everyone knows, 'cause they look at me. But I think yeah, that would be the only way you'd know.

Sandi: That's a really powerful statement. So in a sense, you're saying you're making a real distinction between skin color and the way you see the world.

Kristin: Uh. [pause] Um. I don't know.

Sandi: Well, so like what does it mean to be *really Black* in that perspective?

Kristin: Well, I mean, I think—I guess there's a lot—but I think of stereotypes. And that's a very—I mean, to me stereotypes come to be because they're very prevalent in an area. And that's, I mean I think of the stereotypical [pause]—I mean I think it's [pause]—I don't think—I don't know what my life would've been like. I don't. But I don't—A lot of time I don't think I would have been as—not as smart—[pause] but as intelligent, I guess. I mean, that's weird, but . . .

This story can be read through a number of frames. In terms of Du Bois's schema, Kristin had internalized oppression. She accepted stereotypical representations of Blacks as true, and was thus alienated from, or had not developed, that part of herself. In the late twentieth century this alienation from self—the negative aspect of Du Bois's concept of double-consciousness—emerged through the inscription of the language and knowledge of Whiteness through the media, public policy, social institutions, social interactions, and familial socialization. Racial hegemony is maintained through the interaction of individual consciousness with cultural meaning systems, public knowledge, and media representations.

From an anthropological perspective, Kristin's social location in a White family and community had provided her with a set of cultural meaning systems that are usually only available to Whites. To her, these mainstream systems of cultural meaning seemed *natural*; indeed, she explained that she often *forgot* she was Black until someone else reminded her. She experienced a gap between the identity she had constructed through the cultural meaning systems available to her and the way she was seen and treated by the world.

This sense of disjuncture between identity and culture is felt and articulated *linguistically*. Kristin was referring to the racialization of language in her discussion of sounding White because she spoke "properly." In social interaction language indicates one's race and class—people "sound White" or "sound Black," depending on the cadence and accent of the speech and the relative use of "proper" English versus "slang." Kristin made an explicit connection between language, race, and identity when she said: "Oh yeah. Like I don't think anybody ever would ever mistake me for being Black if they never saw me. Never. Never in a million years." The use and understanding of language define insider versus outsider status in different class and racial-ethnic groups. Kristin's command of standard English and her inability to "sound Black" located her linguistically as White and middle class, while her inability to understand the English of some Blacks defined them as other in relation to herself.

This connection between self, language, and culture was explicit in Kristin's discussion of both sounding White and defining herself as "White with very, very dark skin." Mark Poster discusses language and identity as follows: "The individual wrestles with self-constitution through the manipulation of symbols, through carefully elaborated and systematized rules of formation, enunciative statements, and so forth" (1993:79). Kristin's construction of self had been inscribed with the language of Whiteness. The symbols and statements that defined and made meaningful her perceptions of herself and her world taught her to see the world from the perspective of White power, privilege, and innocence. Her *subjectivity* saw Whiteness as self, and Blackness as other. Her views of African Americans had been primarily shaped through media stereotypes, and in fact she said there were times when she found herself thinking racist thoughts about other African Americans. She had learned to view herself as unconsciously White; this *natural and normal* self-concept as White was facilitated by the widespread representation of Whiteness as generic humanness. In her own consciousness she belonged to the unmarked category of humanity. She articulated her sense of racial identity in the following excerpt:

> *Kristin:* Uh. Well, I think it comes back to, you see talk shows where you've got transvestites or where men have said, "I am a woman in a man's body." And I feel like I've been conditioned White, and I am White in a Black body.

Kristin's experience points to the profoundly *racial* character of contemporary prescriptions for identity, through the marking of her difference and the gap between her self-knowledge and the ways she was perceived and treated.

> *Sandi:* You said, when you started on this little stream, that you have your troubles. Do you mean in terms of racial identity or—?
> *Kristin:* Oh yeah, definitely.
> *Sandi:* So how would you express that?
> *Kristin:* You mean like, what do I mean?
> *Sandi:* Yeah.
> *Kristin:* Well, I think I might have said it earlier, but I mean, definitely, I forget. And I mean it's like, it's almost like a *double life*. Because sometimes I can't get away from it. Everyday I look in the mirror there's this brown skin. But at the same time, I forget until someone reminds me, like, "Hey, you're Black. You can't do that."
> *Sandi:* So what are some of the ways you get reminded?
> *Kristin:* When . . . When like people will call me nigger, and I'm like, "Me?" Or like, "Oh yeah. sh-keh [sound meant to signify being hit with something]. But things like that where—or, that's probably the biggest, but, I mean, or the looks you get. I mean, I don't get them as much any more because I think I'm old enough that my mom and I probably look like just friends walking through the mall or something like that. But when I was younger it's like the looks, like, "Who's that Black girl with that blond, blue-eyed woman?" You know, and it's right there. It's a reminder.

Her experiences illustrate how deeply racialized social interactions are in this country. Kristin's physical presence, her Blackness, spoke through the metalanguage of race, disrupting her unconscious sense of White privilege in the nearly all-White settings she found herself in.

This passage calls to mind the works of both W. E. B. Du Bois and Frantz Fanon. The *doubleness* Kristin spoke of was the disjuncture between her internal view of herself as generically and fully human—which in her racial meaning system signified White—and the *otherness* she felt when someone reminded her, "Hey, you're Black. You can't do that." Fanon captured this social *othering* in his phrase, "Look, a Negro!" In *Black Skin, White Masks* he considers the contrasts between his personal sense of himself and his physical presence, and the objectifying "look" of Whites that he calls the "racial epidermal schema" (Fanon 1967:112). By this he means the *racial gaze*—a set of ideological assumptions and narratives that are culturally available to Whites and others for use in affixing meaning to Black bodies. Fanon explains that such visual assaults on his personhood are driven by "legends, stories, history, and above all, *historicity*" that narrate the meanings of Black skin others impose on him (emphasis in original) (1967:112). Robert Gooding-Williams explains:

> Fanon describes the experience of being subjected to the racial epidermal schema as that of being physically fastened or affixed to an image of oneself; one feels as if one had acquired a second epidermis (hence the concept of a racial *epidermal* schema) that had been superimposed on one's body and then come to haunt it like a shadow. (emphasis in original)[6]

For Kristin there was another complexity. She had been socialized with a subjectivity that valued Whiteness and devalued Blackness, and thus had largely internalized the social narratives attributing social dysfunction to African Americans. Thus, the racializing gaze was self-inflicted as well: "Because sometimes I can't get away from it. Everyday I look in the mirror there's this brown skin." As Fanon stressed, what that brown skin means is culturally and historically specific, and is powerfully and painfully conveyed through social narratives. This is evident from the list of characteristics he "discovered" when he turned the racial epidermal schema on himself:

I subjected myself to an objective examination, I discovered my blackness, my ethnic characteristics; and I was battered down by tom-toms, canni-balism, intellectual deficiency, fetishism, racial defects, slave-ships, and above all else, above all: "Sho' good eatin." (Fanon 1967:112)

In describing how she imagined her life might have been either if she had been raised by her birth parents or been adopted by a Black family, Kristin explained that she would probably have liked fried chicken, wa-termelon, collard greens, and orange soda. She thought she would have been less intelligent than she was. She assumed she would have been poor, and thus would not have learned how to play the piano or to swim, or had good educational opportunities. Having grown up surrounded only by Whites, Kristin's views of African Americans were rooted in ide-ological narratives about racial difference available in literature, popular culture, news media, and cultural lore. There was no one in her life to counter such racial fables.

I imagine that some people in favor of "color-blind" adoptions might dismiss these issues. Kristin was a college graduate, was steadily em-ployed, had a close relationship with her family, and led a stable life. Yet race was a major issue for her. Although being White-identified did not present her with insurmountable problems, there were aspects of it that steadily eroded the edges of her self-esteem. Her primary adaptational strategies had involved defining herself as different from most African Americans. However, this tactic was ineffectual in situations in which others "reminded" her she was Black.

Adoption across racial, ethnic, and cultural lines constructs lives that question some of American society's basic assumptions about what constitutes identity. Was Kristin "really Black," if she saw herself as "White with very, very dark skin," was uncomfortable with African Americans, and had no insider knowledge of Black culture? What does race mean in this context? Recently, I found myself in a casual conver-sation with someone about these issues. I had relayed the stories of a few transracial adoptees as well as my own experience of discovering in adulthood that was "half Jewish." I asked rhetorically, "What does it mean then that I'm supposedly half-Jewish, but didn't grow up with that cultural knowledge?" To my surprise, the man I was speaking with answered bluntly, "It means you would have been killed in Nazi Germany." The Third Reich defined a Jew as someone with at least one Jewish grandparent. A contemporary anti-Semitic White supremacist would not care whether or not I *defined* myself as Jewish or not; racial hatred operates on absolutes. Being adopted provides no exemption; such lines are drawn in "blood."

Clearly, transracial adoptees do not have the choice of defining themselves out of the category Black. We live in a social world organized around racial-ethnic categories, and we are seen and treated by others according to the categories we *appear* to fit and the cultural meanings attached to such classifications. While Kristin's story was rather unique with regard to her full identification with Whites and self-distancing from African Americans, her experience was illustrative of my other informants' experiences as well. At some point in their lives they had all felt a jarring sense of disjuncture between their view of themselves and the ways they were seen and treated by people outside their families. Throughout their lives they had had to learn to adapt to a world that recognized the social meanings of racial difference and racism, and often translated those ideologies into actions and utterances.

Routes of Identity

Lynn: I had decided to do a Black Studies minor, but continued to take like all these classes in Black Studies. Because I thought, "At least I better get educated, so I know what this is about." I took an Intro to the Black Woman, or whatever—uh, Black Women in America with this professor that was wonderful. And so I started reading all that literature. And it just didn't add up in my head, that somehow someone had missed my education. Why didn't I know this stuff before? Why was I denied access to the Black community before? So, of course, I blamed my parents.

Lynn described this time in her life as her "radical Black phase," a time when she questioned the racial assumptions she had been raised with, immersed herself in African American culture and history, and became part of the Black community at her school. Her immersion in Black cultures was a search for an understanding of identity.

Like most of the people I interviewed, Lynn found her parents' socialization around issues of race to be inadequate. It is important to contextualize my informants' familial experiences within a broader societal framework. In public discussions of transracial adoption the question of *culture* is too often addressed solely at the individual and familial level. Access to and awareness of Black culture is also a structural issue. Lynn's parents, like most White folks who grew up and were educated in the 1950s and 1960s, lived in predominantly segregated communities and went to schools in which little attention, if any, was paid to African American history or culture.

Indeed, in the 1970s when Lynn and her siblings were growing up, the area in which they lived on the West Coast was still profoundly segregated. When schools were desegregated by busing, the class differences between Lynn and the Black children new to the school seemed so stark that she found herself more comfortable in her already established friendships with Whites. By the time she got to college she knew who Sojourner Truth, Harriett Tubman, and Frederick Douglass were; as she put it, she knew the "biggies," but had little knowledge beyond this of Black culture or history. However, having been raised in a middle-class White family and community, she was well-versed in White culture and history. It was in college that she began to explore African American history and culture, and to question the way she had been raised.

It was often upon leaving home that the transracial adoptees I interviewed first began to grapple with the social and personal meanings of being Black in the contemporary United States. Several of my informants went through a similar process of exploration by dating men their parents tacitly regarded as "too Black"—more in terms of culture and politics than of skin color. One woman became a member of the ballet troupe, the Dance Theater of Harlem. Lynn's story illustrates the power of self-discovery and transformation that is often involved in such a quest. In the following excerpt, she discussed her second semester in college, which she spent in Paris. Just before leaving school for the semester she began dating a South African man.

Lynn: And I had a Black friend, like my [with emphasis] *first Black friend*, who I'm still friends with.

Sandi: God, you gave me chills. I mean, to be a sophomore in

college, or whatever, and to have your first Black friend is really—
that's really powerful.

Lynn: As a freshman in college. Yes. So Amanda Williams, who I'm
still friends with, and who still drives me insane—but we were actually roommates when we were in Paris together. And she gave
me some James Baldwin to read. So I read that and I thought
about it. And she let me read like part of her journal. She kept a
journal and she wrote poetry, and really a lot of it was about what
it was like being Black on an all-White campus, or being Black on
this tour. I mean it was really interesting. She's a really bright
woman. I mean, she's working on her doctorate in chemical engineering. I mean, she's very smart. So I was reading this stuff, and
started thinking, "huh." And then I thought I should read some
stuff about South Africa if I'm going to date this guy, so I started
to buy books. I started to read books about Nelson Mandela
being on Robbens Island. And that started me thinking, "Why
are White people doing this to Black people?" Um, and then I
came back and went back to school. And Louis and I lived together. And Louis—it was interesting too—because he was of
mixed race heritage. They call it "colored" in South Africa. But
he was half Indian. His family had—they were Malay, and from
New Delhi. And then his father was Sutu, so African. So within
their own family they had this dichotomy between races, which in
South Africa, as you can imagine, was really really strong. So
Louis was the most self-righteous Black person I had ever met in
my life. He just really really believed he was Black, and he looked
Indian. So people always said, "Oh you're Indian." And he always
said [with emphasis], "No, I'm *African.*" And that completely,
like changed my frame of mind. And he was—considered himself
a Marxist, to top it off. So he's like espousing Marxist ideology all
the time. This is the guy I got engaged to. And you know we had
an awful marriage, but it completely transformed my identity. I
mean, most of my friends at the university were Africans, so on
some level they did not make that color differentiation. You know
that color stratification within the Black community. Because
Africa, the continent is made up of all sorts of people. And so we
moved—I mean we had friends who were South Africans and

from Nigeria and Ethiopia. So we had this group of African people—and Liberia—who we're buddies with. And they were pretty radical. And then we started to—we used to go down to African Heritage House. I used to go down with him, and then I started going to the meetings. And then they would have sisters meetings, and so I would go to those. And I started taking—I remember, I'm so embarrassed I ever said this. I took this Intro to the Black Novel class in the Black Studies Department. It was the first semester I got back to school after being in Europe. And the teacher said, "Why are you here?" And everybody else had to go around and say—And I said, "Well, I'm here because I want to learn something about my cultural identity." Which you know, in that context was probably a little—they were probably like, "What the hell is she talking about?" Because they didn't know where I was coming from. You know, I started to read, you know, Black writers for the first time. I mean, I knew who Harriett Tubman was and my mother gave me a book on Sojourner—I knew who Sojourner Truth was 'cause my mom gave me a book on her. They were like these isolated—I knew who Frederick Douglass was. I mean, I knew the biggies. . . . So I started you know, Ralph Ellison. And reading this stuff that I didn't even know existed, and reading Black poetry. And it was really powerful.

Sandi: I bet.

Lynn: And so then I became—not to like my White family so much. And it became really hard for me to reconcile being—getting radicalized with this White, upper class, elite—which my family had become by that point—family.

This was how Lynn constructed her roots. She explored the routes of Black culture as they intersected the various pathways she walked. During her "radical Black phase" she explored and claimed an insider view of Black cultures, and since then has also come to embrace the mainstream White cultural meaning systems with which she was raised.

While transracial adoptees deal with specific questions of racial identity, such explorations of and shifts in sense of self are not unusual for nonadoptees in their early adult years. Many people feel compelled to define themselves differently from the way they were raised, and often go through a period of anger at their parents for not fulfilling their needs. In no way do I wish to diminish the importance of the needs of transracial adoptees to live in racially diverse communities, attend diverse schools, and be part of families—of whatever race—that give them some knowledge and a sense of belonging in whatever racial-ethnic groups they are a part of. I simply wish to place the identity quests of my informants in sociocultural context.

Conclusion

It is useful to step back for a moment to consider these allegories of identity in a broader milieu. Adoptees are certainly not alone in feeling that they don't know who they are. Identity politics, coming of age stories, identity crises, coming out stories, midlife crises, and spiritual transformations saturate both the public discourse and private lives.

The stories I have discussed in this chapter indicate the power of social institutions in constructing and shaping individual lives and identities. Transracial adoptees' identities are constructed through the discourse of the child welfare system; such people are written into being as culturally and discursively White, yet are physically viewed as Black. They began as Black infants or young children placed into subject positions mapped out as White and middle class. A few of the adoptees I interviewed had lived in a homogeneous White social world, only moving outside the lines when other people challenged their social status as symbolically White. Some of my informants took it upon themselves to explore and discover their identities as African Americans. Others had parents who had raised them in diverse, multiracial communities.

The disjuncture between the identities prescribed by their social locations and their apparent Blackness demonstrates the constructedness of racial meaning, and suggests the power of social institutions and ideological cultural meaning in guiding and shaping the identities of all individuals in the contemporary United States. For while people who were not adopted cannot point so easily toward the role of the state in determining who they are, I would argue that lives and identities are continually and subtly shaped and constructed in interaction with myriad social institutions that our cultural assumptions about individuality typically prevent us from seeing.

I have addressed the two primary issues in the public dialogue over transracial adoption, namely, survival skills and racial identity. The adoptees I interviewed struggled profoundly with these issues. However, their narratives also show that there are effective ways of dealing with such concerns. I conclude with Cat Benton's perspective on the practice of transracial adoption.

> *Cat:* If I could say one thing—and this is just a message to parents that want to adopt. What is it I want to say? There's no way that you can give that child everything that child needs. Be aware that that child needs a lot more than love. Be aware that that child needs to know where he or she came from. If you can have an open adoption do it. Or at least keep contact with the birth parents so they can find them one day. And [pause] understand that your child is being brought into your home with a dysfunction; they are not a normal child—quote unquote "normal." They are entering your home with a dysfunction.
>
> *Sandi:* Because it's an adoption?
>
> *Cat:* Because it's an adoption. I went to a palm—I didn't go to a palm reader, but there was a palm reader at this party, and there was four adoptees at this party. And she was hired for like three hours to read everybody's palms briefly. And when she got to mine—I was one of the last people—and she said, "God, I keep coming up against this abandonment issue." And she said, "You know you went home with the wrong family from the hospital." And so I really—I believe it's in our bones; it's in our makeup; it's in our lives. There's nothing we can do about it. So, understand that your child needs more than you can give it, and you can never fulfill what your child needs, but do your best to educate your child on where they come from. And think about therapy and groups and people that are like them.
>
> *Sandi:* What about at the policy level? Do you think that they should be made easier for people? Should it stay the same? Should it be made harder?
>
> *Cat:* Adoption?
>
> *Sandi:* Whites adopting Black kids, or children of color.
>
> *Cat:* Oh. Um, I think that it should be made easier, but there

should be some sort of class, or some sort of educational—And there should be some sort of interaction with adoptive—new adoptive parents—to parents that have raised adoptees. You know, some sort of an educational thing going on. When you— you know you have to have a license to drive, you don't have to have a license to be a parent. And I'm not sure what they go through to screen you to be an adoptive parent, but um, it shouldn't be hard in the sense that they're a Black child coming into a Black family. It should be harder in the sense of—Do *you know* what you're getting into? "Oh I want to give love to some child!" Well, that's not enough.

Sandi: So at the same time that you're saying that and that it's deadly to do this, you're saying it should be made easier?

Cat: Umhmm.

Sandi: How do you resolve that?

Cat: Easier in the sense that I don't think that because the family is White—The reasons that I think it's hard now are racist issues, not realistic issues. I think that it should be made easier in the sense of just because this child is Black and just because this family is White it's not okay. That's not what I'm saying. I'm saying it should be okay, but society is screwed. And because of that and because of the adoption issue itself, it should be harder in the sense of [pause] educating those parents and saying, "This is really what you're getting into." And, "Are you capable of that? Are you capable of giving this child what he needs?" Not harder in the sense that you're White and he's Black and shouldn't be with that family. Harder in the sense of really taking a look at it and saying, "This is what this child needs. Are you financially and emotionally prepared to give that to that child?" And if you're not you can't do it.

What seems clear from the lives of those I interviewed is that when transracial adoptions are *necessary* families should be chosen carefully, and should be educated as to the particular needs that child may bring to the family, as well as the way the presence of a person of color will change the family.

THREE

Searching

"I Have a Family with No Blood"

Shelley: I know my father was Black and my mother was White—Italian. Great mix, huh? Um . . . my mother was 17 when she had me. Uh . . . her mother had died when my mother was 15 of, I guess, cancer. When she died my father . . . who would have been my grandfather . . . my mother's father . . . I guess my mother had a lot of brothers and sisters and he couldn't take care of them so my mother was put into foster care and she was kind of a runaway. Uh . . . I'm trying to think. Um . . . . Um . . . my mother kept me for six months. And I don't know if I was taken away or . . . I don't know. I don't know. But . . . I was put into foster care. From what I hear she came and she visited me. Uh . . . put into foster care. I know a year later she had another son. I think she might have gotten married. She might have gotten married. Uh . . . pretty much all I know. She was a runaway.

Shelley was searching for her birth mother. She wanted to know more about her genealogy, about pertinent facts like her medical history. She had had some medical problems, and explained, "You need . . . you need to know. I think it's important." She wanted to see who she looked like. But her frustration with the child welfare system was mounting:

Shelley: Um . . . this lady . . . like . . . Every time I go to do something I get a letter back. . . . Your files aren't here. Your files aren't here. Your files aren't here.

As Shelley's story indicates, adoptees' origin narratives are mediated in multiple ways by social institutions and public policies. What she knew about the circumstances of her birth was narrated to her parents by the social worker who had facilitated her adoption; it was an institutionally authorized story. Her adoptive parents were only given the information the agency and social worker deemed appropriate. Even as an adult, she had had to do battle with the policies and practices of the adoption agency that regulated the information about her origins to which she was allowed access.

Shelley was at least the second generation of her birth family to spend time in foster care. Her birth mother was placed in foster care because her single father had been unable to care for all his children, which suggests that this was probably a family with limited income. Shelley's mother was particularly vulnerable to the scrutiny of the social welfare system when she, a White teenager and a ward of the state, gave birth to Shelley, a biracial baby, in 1975. Shelley was probably correct in guessing that she was removed from her teenaged birth mother. She only knew part of her story: "And I don't know if I was taken away or . . . I don't know. I don't know. But . . . I was put into foster care." What was the role of race in Shelley's removal from her birth mother? What was the role of age? How did class shape this situation? Shelley's story makes evident the role of the social welfare system in determining who she was to become, through the regulation of her birth mother's reproductive behavior.

In popular media narratives about adoption, a person's origins are often simply equated with birth parents. The "search" narrative has become a standard story on television talk shows, sitcoms, dramas, and made-for-TV movies.[1] On television, adoptees struggle with a sense of mystery or confusion about their identity, family, and history, eventually finding their "real" selves when reunited with their birth mothers. Anyone familiar with daytime television talk shows or made-for-television movies could recite the typical search narrative. It is often scripted as an adoptee's identity quest—a search for the "true" self through access to forbidden knowledge, to a previously unknown origin narrative, to a family history, to a genetic and/or medical history, and foremost, to the birth parents. Typically, the message of media representations of search narratives is that biology determines "true" identity (Wegar 1997).

Why have adoption and search narratives become so popular in the contemporary public discourse? Why do adoptees' identity quests carry such currency in media representations? Anthropologist James Clifford suggests that allegory is a useful tool for considering public narratives; it "prompts us to say of any cultural description not 'this represents, or symbolizes, that' but rather, 'this is a (morally charged) *story* about that'" (Clifford 1986:100). Likewise, adoption narratives function as "morally charged" stories about identity, family, race, biology, culture, gender, class, and power. The life stories of adoptees can be read as sociopolitical allegories—stories rooted in the particular that speak beyond themselves, that comment on a broader set of social concerns and themes.[2]

Framing our life stories solely in terms of the tension between biology and culture obscures the power relations involved in the construction of who we are. Popular discussions of searches and reunions are sociopolitical allegories that deny the practice of power by the state in regulating the reproductive behavior of women—particularly women who are young, poor, and of color. On the one hand, ideologies positing biology as deterministic of identity have been used throughout history to justify the oppression of women, people of color, people with disabilities, and gays and lesbians. In light of this history we must ask ourselves why biological explanations of adoptees' identities were so popular in the United States in the 1990s. On the other hand, cultural perspectives on parenting see the environment as determinative of "real" parents. Focusing solely on culture and the environment defines birth mothers as breeders, but not as mothers.

What is generally missing from public discussions of adoption is a structural analysis—attention to the public policies and social institutions that define some women as mothers and some as not-mothers. I contend that complete genealogical exposure of adoptees' identities requires attending to the ways social structure shapes the "choices" birth mothers and fathers make. In this chapter I consider adoptees' desire to search, along with the culture of searching that has developed in the United States. I address the issue of "choice" versus "coercion" for birth mothers, and conclude with a consideration of adoptees' reflections on "reunions."

Grafted Trees: Searching for Family, Race, Roots, and Self

In the 1990s, adoption emerged as a common theme in such media as news coverage, political rhetoric, television talk shows, made-for-TV movies, and cinematic films (Wegar 1997). What do nonadopted viewers find compelling about adoption narratives? Why is the issue of transracial adoption so interesting to the vast number of people whose lives are not affected by this social practice? What is it about search and reunion stories that draws people's interest? Search narratives can be read as sociopolitical allegories about two fundamental concerns: identity and kinship. As sociologist (and adoptee) Katarina Wegar argues:

> The emancipatory discourse of self-discovery [in adoption search narratives] reflects a broader cultural preoccupation with the search for identity or the individual's moral right to embark upon this quest. Ideological or not, the pursuit of "finding oneself" . . . has become not only acceptable but perhaps even normative to the way Americans perceive the quest for identity. (Wegar 1997:81)

For adoptees this quest focuses on family and genealogy. Though there are competing definitions of kinship available in contemporary discourse in the United States, the metaphor of "blood," biologically transmitted, appears to be the most pervasive and tenacious means of defining a family. In a discussion of gay kinship ideologies, anthropologist Kath Weston explains:

> Competing interpretations of "the family" in Western societies draw upon broader themes of voluntarism, permanence, genuineness, and imitation that historically have mediated the conception of kinship as genealogy. . . . The notion of kinship as a biogenetic connection that brings with it diffuse enduring solidarity represents only one among a number of what Arjun Appadurai (1988) has called "ideologies of authenticity." (Weston 1995:90)

The force of this familial ideology is felt by adoptees in multiple ways, from mundane questions about our "real" families to personal feelings of "rootlessness" and cultural ideologies that say that we will never know who we "really" are until we find our birth parents. One of the

adoptees I spoke with, Tanya Randolph, addressed this issue in relation to her siblings:

> *Tanya:* We're all brothers and sisters. I mean you don't have to be
> blood related to be—I mean, that really irritates me when people
> say, "Is that your *real* brother?" That just irritates the living heck
> out of me! Of course he's my real brother! He's not my fake
> brother!

Tanya went on to justify the "authenticity" of her familial ties like many
of my informants did, namely, by redefining the concept of what is "gen-
uine" through love, shared experience, and law. However, even when
adoptees accept that love and law can make a family, just as biology can,
that understanding does not always extend to their view of ancestors.
How do we accept the ancestors of our adoptive families as our own
when we never knew them?

Questions about roots and history were central to Lynn's process of
self-discovery. She and her younger sister Suzanne were born in 1965
and 1966 to a White woman who had had an extramarital affair with a
Black man. For a short period of time the girls lived with their birth
mother. Then they lived in a succession of foster homes and an orphanage. They were adopted by their White parents when they were six and
seven years old, into a family with three birth children and two other
children who had been adopted transracially. They grew up in a predominantly White area on the West Coast. At the time of our interview
Lynn lived on the East Coast and Suzanne lived on the West Coast. Lynn
again discussed family trees:

> *Lynn:* And my father, over the last couple years, well—My father,
> they traced their family—my adoptive father and his family—
> back to the revolutionary war, when like his great, great, great
> grandfather was given land, actually, up near Harper's Ferry,
> which was really *strange*. There's actually quite a few Praegers
> in this area and in the Ohio basin. They were farmers. So like
> when we were growing up there were always like all these family
> pictures, like all on the wall. And I remember just looking at
> these and thinking, "These aren't my people." I mean, I very

consciously knew these were not my relatives. The last couple of years my father has gotten this computer program that is for—that you can use to help trace your family tree. And the Praeger—because it's a relatively small—they have like a whole newsletter of people who are Praegers that is out of Ohio, but it goes to other people. Like the only other person who—Praeger—who moved to our area ended up being like a fifth cousin to my dad. I mean, it was really bizarre. I mean, there's not a lot of Praegers around. And so my dad—I remember a couple summers ago—was like, "Lynn, come look at this really cool family tree program." He was really excited. And I didn't have the heart to say to him at age twenty-seven, twenty-six, "You know, Dad, that's not my family." And he said, "Look I'm going to put your name in." And he didn't even write adopted on it. He just drew the lines without thinking about adoption, or maybe he put it in some other section, but I never saw it. Because this computer program—it's really amazing. It'll print out your whole family tree if you put the names in. It's wonderful. But I remember thinking, "Gosh, I would really like to know my family history." And that's been something that like these family trees drive me nuts! I'm sitting there talking to Terence last night, and he wants me to help him trace his family tree. Because Terence is like on this Africa kick, and so wants to see if he can trace himself all the way back. So when he was talking about it I started thinking again, you know, about family trees, and that maybe—My sister and I for the last four years have gone back and forth—well, I've gone back and forth—about doing a search. But it's hard. Those are really hard things—kind of assumptions we make about family.

As Lynn's discussion of her father's and her fiancé's genealogical quests shows, the question of roots resonates beyond the lives of adoptees. Indeed, since Alex Haley's *Roots* was published and televised in the 1970s, researching genealogies has become a fairly common endeavor in the United States (Watson 1996). Cultural studies scholar Julia Watson explains:

Genealogy is an abiding passion and a big industry in the United States. It establishes the family's collective biography as a *rooted* network that has *legitimately* and verifiably inhabited the past. Tracing one's ancestors is a hedge against mortality in an increasingly mobile, global world. . . . Books of genealogy refer to the "pedigree," the validated evidence documenting *ancestral identity*, transactions, and events. (emphasis added) (Watson 1996:297)

The assumption that identity is largely determined through our familial "bloodlines" is a prevailing sociopolitical allegory that underlies social understandings and political discourse about relationships between self, family, community, culture, race, nationality, ancestry, and social inequality. Lynn articulated one of the central points of contention for transracial adoptees who grapple with questions of family history. The history of her White adoptive family revealed that they owned land "up near Harper's Ferry, which was really *strange*." For her, this was strange because Harper's Ferry was the site of a violent slave rebellion in the nineteenth century. This information exemplified for her the divergent histories of her birth and adoptive families, and told her that her own familial histories reflected the institutional racism that characterized relations between Whites and Blacks in the United States. The racial differences and the lack of biological connections between Lynn and her adoptive family's ancestors prevented her from accepting their forebears as her own. As she said, such knowledge made her think, "Gosh, I would really like to know my family history."

The sense of being a person without a family history can be overwhelming. For adoptees this longing for a family history often sparks the desire to search for birth relatives. Gabrielle discussed her desire to know where she came from as follows:

Sandi: What is it that you're hoping to find?
Gabrielle: Um . . . I think . . . I think I really just wanted to know, you know, sort of where I came . . . come from. And I think that there's a little bit of wanting to find home, sort of feeling. Or family situation, or something like that . . . like fitting in and that

kind of thing. You know, those are the visibly kind of fringy de-
sires. I mean, they're important, but I'm also very logical and
like, "Oh, you can't have that." [both laugh] You know.
Sandi: So when you say, "To know where you come from." What
does that really mean in the context of adoption and your knowing your birth family . . . I mean your adoptive family?
Gabrielle: Hmm. I think it's sort of like a genetic . . . genetic kind of
. . . what's family stock? What do I come from? You know, what
race and past people? You know, what are their value sets and . . .
um . . . how do they perceive the world and . . . what do they do
on their weekends off? You know? What kind of food do they eat?
. . . and stuff. [laughs]

Not all adoptees feel compelled to resolve this yearning for familial,
and indeed racial roots/routes. The people I interviewed had resolved
this yearning in several different ways. For some, like Gabrielle, searching for their birth parents was a necessity; nothing less than biological
ties would fill this void. Others found resolution by claiming their adoptive family histories as their own, or by immersing themselves in the history and cultures of Blacks in Africa and the Diaspora, as Lynn had.
While adoptees have many perspectives on searching for their birth families and multiple motivations for wanting to search, this diversity is not
always represented in the rhetoric of the search movement.

While adoptees are often interested in finding their original parents
and being connected with their biological history, frequently the driving
force behind a search is a quest for identity. Ten of the twenty-two
adoptees I interviewed had either concluded a search or were engaged in
one at the time of the interviews. Interestingly, only two of the ten
adoptees on the East Coast had searched, whereas, of the twelve on the
West Coast, eight had either met their birth parents or were in the
process of searching. When they discussed their need to find their birth
parents they talked about something missing, a gap, an emptiness in their
sense of self that they needed to fill. This quest for identity is consistent
with the evidence from adoption search communities, in that the language is the same.

Significantly, this quest for "truth" involves interacting with the adoption agencies that largely determined who we, as adoptees, were to be-

come. For adoptees, searching involves interacting with—and often sub-verting—the policies and practices of the social institutions that guard our sealed adoption records—the discourses of our identities. Rarely is this quest embarked upon alone. In the last few decades of the twentieth century, a vital "search culture" developed that undertook, sometimes legally and sometimes not, the task of educating adoptees on search tech-niques, tapping valuable data banks, and supporting fellow searchers through the maze of government bureaucracy and the waves of emo-tional turmoil. Much of this work and community building now take place on the internet. This is truly a *discursive quest* for self, in which seekers follow routes of information they fervently hope will lead them to the "truth."

Christina Landon, who was twenty-eight years old when I interviewed her and lived in a predominantly White community in northern Califor-nia, was adopted when she was five. Prior to that she had lived with her birth mother, who was Mexican, and had some contact with her birth fa-ther, an African American. Then she was removed from that family and placed in foster care. She grew up with her White parents, two White sib-lings, and one Black brother in northern California. She discussed her search as follows:

Christina: I'm pursuing that [searching] myself.
Sandi: Are you?
Christina: Yeah, I'm having a friend help me do that. You know, if we can find them, then I'll decide if I want to go any further than that.
Sandi: What do you know?
Christina: What do I know? I know, I just know, one, that my dad was Black, and very tall, and didn't have a job. My mom was a call girl, and she loved me, but she couldn't afford to keep me. And that's the only reason why I'm going to—that's the only rea-son why I'm pursuing that. If I was just adopted, and I didn't know that, then I probably wouldn't. I would just live with it. There's something inside me that just needs that mother—My mom is great, but she's not my mom.
Sandi: Really?
Christina: I don't—I hate—

[turn tape over]

Christina: [inaudible] I think it's because of the skin color.

Sandi: Really?

Christina: Yeah. And, I just—She's not my mom. You know, I mean, there's nothing—it kills me to see you know, like, for instance, Gary's [her fiancé's]—It kills me to see the love and the friendship, the special little bond. My sister and my mom have this special little bond that me and my mom don't have. And maybe that's part my doing because I maybe didn't want to get that close with her like that.

Sandi: Well, you also didn't have the opportunity. When you come in at five, so much of that stuff has already happened.

Christina: You know, and I—There's just something about that relationship that's not there. Technically, on paper, and physically, she is my mom. But she's not—I call her mom. You know, and so that's why I want to pursue this. And if she's alive I'll make that decision if I want to go and see her. I guess I'd do something like writing her a letter, and if I never got a response back that will be my answer. You know, I'll still be hurt, but it'll be done with. That wall can come down.

Sandi: Some people even have someone call for them, stuff like that.

Christina: I might do that too. Because if, by all means, if she wants to be [pause] not found, that's her right and I will respect that. I hope that's not the case.

Sandi: What do you hope for?

Christina: I just hope I can see her once and talk to her, and let her know what I've done. I mean, I'll just tell her that I love her, even though I never even know her.

Sandi: Do you feel like you do love her?

Christina: Yeah, I feel she's my mother, and that's the one I love as a mother.

What was missing for Christina was the bond with her birth mother. Her search was driven by a sense of dislocation and longing for a particular kind of relationship with her mother. "There's something inside me that just needs that mother."

In her study of the adoption search movement in the contemporary

United States, Katarina Wegar found that the popular search rhetoric, academic studies drawn on by search activists, and media representations of reunions among birth families focused strongly on biological sources of identity formation. In fact, she found that psychological research on the issue often represented adoptees as "genealogically bewildered" and driven by nature to search for their biological origins. Psychology functions here as a normalizing discourse, asserting that adoptees who profess not to feel the need to search are repressing their true selves; searching is viewed as an expression of a universal human need (Wegar 1997:136).

One of the primary tenets of the culture of the search community that unites both adoptees and birth parents while on their quests is that a reunion is the only way that adoptees can heal their "primal wounds" and come to know their "real" selves (Verrier 1994; Lifton 1994). Indeed, much of the search literature and television discourse discusses searching as a sort of rite of passage for adoptees, a *rebirth* through the rewriting of the origin narrative. While the discourse is fueled by the tremendous loss that most adoptees feel, it is also infused with the power of biological and genetic ways of explaining the "nature" of identity.

While the desire to search for one's birth parents, and particularly for one's birth mother, is often keenly felt by adoptees, I also spoke with a number of people who did not feel that searching was the only way they could know who they were. Daniel Jacob, a transracial adoptee who was twenty-five-years old when I interviewed him and living in a primarily White area of northern California, was quite comfortable with his family and his sense of self.

> *Daniel:* I mean, and they—my mom and dad have come up to me and asked me . . . they've offered to help when I wanted to find my real parents. And I said no.
> *Sandi:* You don't think you'll ever do that?
> *Daniel:* No. 'Cause . . . I mean, they're my parents. The way I put it, they're my parents right now. My real parents . . . they raised me, they took me in, they took care of me. And plus, I wouldn't wanna go and disturb, you know, my mother . . . the other mother or father's family. You know, come back into their lives. Because I don't know how they feel.

For Daniel, his adoptive family was the primary source of his identity. I too have resisted the idea that my birth parents or birth mother are the only possible avenues through which I may discover my "true self." Indeed, I take issue with the notion that my "authentic self" exists somewhere deep down inside me or way out there in the world. I approach identity as a process rather than a fixed entity. As I discussed earlier, my birth mother and I came to know each other while I was researching this book. While her presence in my life is important, and has shaped my understandings of self and family, I can say with a fair amount of certitude that I had a strong sense of my own identity before she entered my life. A number of people have questioned me over the years about why I resisted the idea that I *needed* to search in order to know myself. I have given it a great deal of thought, and while I cannot claim to fully understand it, I have made some sense of my reaction. The concept of an "authentic self" linked to genealogical origins seems overly simplistic and to deny the influence and importance of my adoptive family in shaping who I am. It is dismissive of my parents, sisters, and extended kin, and it is very clear to me that I am very much a product of my life experiences as a member of that family.

Because Lynn also had ambivalent feelings about searching, we connected with one another from our first meeting. I interviewed her several times in 1994 but we rarely saw each other thereafter, although we touched base periodically either on the phone or through a common friend. The most recent interview I conducted with Lynn, in 1998, was structured as a dialogue between the two of us, focusing on changes in both our lives since we last talked.[3] In the following excerpt, we discussed an encounter I had at a birth parent/adoptee support group, in which I was directly confronted with the ideology of biology that infuses the search movement.

> *Sandi:* Let's see. What were we talking about? Searches. Karen [one of Lynn's sisters]. Um . . .
> *Lynn:* Well, what was really interesting I think was that we were talking about these support groups and trying them.
> *Sandi:* Oh, that's right. I went to one that was for...um...mostly birth mothers, but also adoptees were welcome. And it was one of the most horrible experiences of my life! [laughs]

Lynn: . . . of your life.

Sandi: They . . . jumped on me. They totally attacked me. . . . And
this woman was talking about how she wanted to find her birth
son and everything and she said, "Well, if he's like me he'd be
this way. If he's like his birth father he'd be this way." Going on
and on about this. And I said, "Well, you know, he might be like
his adopted parents, too." And just kind of added that perspective. And I said, "You know, I haven't found my birth parents,
but I do know that I'm an awful lot like my adoptive father. And
you know, there's some validity in that." And they just . . .
jumped on me like crazy. They were like . . . "You're deluded!
You're only saying that because you've never found your birth
parents and if you did you would see that you're really not like
your adoptive father, and . . ." I just could not believe it.

Lynn: They're the people who . . . it's interesting that they have
somehow bought into this that somehow you're gonna be un-
changed by this environment you're in. That's wild!

Sandi: It blew me away. Just blew me away.

Lynn and I shared a resistance to the idea that biology fully defines our
identities. While we both recognized that we are genetically embodied
people, we also saw the families, cultures, and communities in which we
were raised as important sources of socialization. However, it is understandable that the birth mothers at the meeting I attended would embrace a more biologically determinist view. Defining adoptees' lives
solely through biological ties supports their sense of self as the "real"
mothers, and validates their quest to reclaim their birth children through
reunions. I want to be clear that I support birth mothers' searches for
their children, and recognize their importance in adoptees' lives; it is the
biologically determinist discourse with which I take issue.

This focus on biology has been profoundly shaped by psychological
research on adoptees that is widely available within search communities.
The work of psychologist and adoptee Betty Jean Lifton has been extremely influential in search communities. It is often cited in bibliogra-
phies and book lists circulated by agencies and support groups. A number of my informants mentioned reading her work as well as that of psychologist Nancy Verrier. Both these authors draw on a view of kinship

and identity that is primarily grounded in biology to argue essentially that adoptees will never know their "true" identities until they "heal their primal wounds" through a reunion with their birth parents. This is a narrative steeped in the "ideology of authenticity." Indeed, Lifton speaks of adoptees themselves as *"not real."* In the preface to *Lost and Found: The Adoption Experience*, she explains:

> In this book I tell how the Adoptee, by being extruded from his or her own biological clan, forced out of the natural flow of generational continuity, feels forced out of nature itself. Lacking full knowledge of that clan, he or she feels an alien, an outsider, an orphan, a foundling, a changeling— outside the natural realm of being. (Lifton 1988:xii)

The biological clan is posited as the only locus of "the natural flow of generational continuity." The implication is that adoptive families and the relationships between their members are *unnatural.* There are certainly understandable reasons why some adoptees would respond to this view. Lifton's rhetoric draws on the feelings of emptiness and dislocation that adoptees often report. However, promoting reunions with birth parents—with the "natural" clan—as the *only* way adoptees can know who they are, is in my view a simplistic and irresponsible "solution." While many reunions bring joy and a sense of peace to the parties involved, others are painful and problematic, or simply unfulfilling. These are the stories that don't become TV movies-of-the-week.

The tension between "nature" and "nurture," or "biology" and "culture" is usually present in the discourse about adoptees. I employ the concept of social construction to encompass both culture and biology. To argue that identity is socially constructed is to see individual selves developing through complex interactions between biologically, genetically embodied people, cultural meaning systems, material circumstances, social institutions, public policies, and socioeconomic politics. With regard to the specific tension, generally present for adoptees, between heredity and environment, I accept recent scientific research that emphasizes the interdependence of these two categories, and points out that the separation of the two is conceptual rather than practical. Indeed, in my view, the existence and use of these categories as *separate* forces shaping individuals reflects Western dualistic frames of organizing the world. I am not arguing that these are not *real* forces, for in fact the widespread, unquestioning belief in and use of these two ways of explaining identity makes them real in their effects. Genetics is one system of meaning to explain who we are, but let us be clear that none of us—adoptees and non-adopted people alike—knows our actual DNA structure. Rather, we infer these genetic maps by comparing our phenotypic characteristics with those of our family members. Thus, it is the *cultural discourse of genetics*, as opposed to our DNA, that gives meaning to our identities.

The social weight of this discourse is apparent in the life stories of adoptees, many of whom have no familial genetic touchstones by which to guide our construction of family and self. Thus, the "truth" being sought in a search may range from the biological bond with the birth parents to knowledge of a genetic family history. The media often portrays reunions as joyous, unproblematic events, but few television versions go beyond the dramatic first meeting. In the lives of adoptees reunion experiences range from life-affirming to disturbing. The primary difference, however, is that in the lives of adoptees the reunion isn't the end of the story. It's just the beginning of what is often a profound redefinition of self.

Lynn's younger sister, Suzanne, a social worker herself, explained the importance to her of discovering her "story":

> *Suzanne:* You know, I think that there's . . . um . . . most days I feel like I'm very supported and very blessed to have this central . . . all these people around that I know care about me and that I consider my family. Um . . . but yeah, there's . . . there are days when I feel like I don't really belong anywhere. That it's all borrowed. You know. Um . . . I think I probably have more of a desire than Lynn to find my biological family. And we've talked a little bit about it. But that's always been a part of my desire to find out about our roots in that way. I think mostly because again most of my memories are from a little kid and I'd really like to know the true story of what really happened. . . .
>
> *Sandi:* What would you hope for with your birth mother? Or expect?
>
> *Suzanne:* Hmm . . . Just my story. I think because um . . . because the case notes that I've read really painted her as a little bit nutty, but I fully expect that she's not entirely together. Or at least at

that time she wasn't. And they said she was a little weird. That she showed up like for one of our visits on a day it was like 85 degrees out and she was wearing a wool jacket and wool turtle neck and a wool skirt and wool tights and boots up to here and things. . . . They said it was just odd. She just seemed a little off. And her mother was actually on drugs because of hallucinating.

Sandi: Oh wow.

Suzanne: And so there's kind of a sense that they might be a little left of center. [laughs] Um . . . so I have no illusions about who she is or what's going on. I'm also very clear that people don't just randomly give up their children, that situations had to have been pretty harsh in order for that to have happened. And so I'm not . . . if I were . . . I have no expectations that I would hear a pretty story. The story they commonly tell adopted kids, "She must have loved you very much to create this better life for you."

Although Suzanne talked about her "desire to find out about our roots in that way," her emphasis on discovering the "true story" indicated that she hoped to discover their *routes*. She knew the "story they commonly tell adopted kids," and was aware that that was not how she and Lynn entered the foster care system. She had childhood memories. She had the notes in their case file. Yet she was "also very clear that people don't just randomly give up their children," and she wanted to understand the circumstances in her birth mother's life that were so "harsh" that she finally relinquished her parental rights.

Searching for Birth Fathers

Most discussions of searches and reunions focus on birth mothers. As Judith Modell explains, comparison between adoptees' two sets of parents typically

focuses on the mother and virtually excludes fatherhood from the equation. This is true for several reasons: not only are adoptees more likely to think about the mother who gave away and the mother who took a child but also, as adoption illustrates, "mother" comes to represent "parent" more generally in American culture. (Modell 1994:228)

Birth mothers are also frequently unwed, and this often plays a role in the relinquishment of children. Mothers often bear the burden of decision or coercion.

Yet a number of the adoptees I interviewed also expressed a strong desire to meet their birth fathers. The determining factor was race. The people who longed to know their birth fathers were generally biracial adoptees with a White birth mother and a Black birth father. Thus, at heart their desire to know their birth fathers represented a need to connect with what they often described as the source of their racial identities. Indeed, Suzanne continued her discussion of her desire to search as follows:

> *Suzanne:* So I mean, if anything, I've got illusions about my biological father.
> *Sandi:* Yeah?
> *Suzanne:* Oh yeah. I mean, I was trying not to. But people have said to Lynn and I, they're like, "God you look like Sherry Belafonte" [Maybe it's] Harry. [both laugh]
> *Sandi:* That's exactly what Lynn said! [both laugh]
> *Suzanne:* There's a total fantasy there. And it . . . and I want it, I want to know.

Both Lynn and Suzanne felt a great deal of curiosity about their birth father. All they knew was that he was a leader in the Black community where they were born.

Brian, also the birth child of a White mother and Black father, keenly felt his birth father's absence in his life.

> *Brian:* I think I'd have been much, much, much better off if I would have had a positive Black male in my life. I needed one. I didn't have it. I didn't have any guidance. I'd sit there . . . and to me it's sad. Black man . . . what does it mean to be . . . ? I mean, I couldn't ask my father about being Black. It's sad. I grew up basically where I see it culturally White. You know, White family. You know . . . so a big part of me is like I am Black. But I could look at myself and say, "I'm a Black man." But a lot of me for a long time now is like, especially looking

back, there's a lot of me that was, "What does it mean to be
Black?" Who am I? You know?

Sandi: How did you answer that?

Brian: And I don't know how to deal with it. I didn't know how to
ask. I didn't know what to do. And it's not . . . I don't know. See,
I don't really have a . . . think anybody should say you can or cannot adopt a Black child because you're White. I know for me and
my family they should have put me into a Big Brothers Program.
Got me something, you know, and not been scared to talk about
it. But we didn't talk about it. Sure, I wouldn't have wanted to
go to Big Brothers. I'd have been like, "[Screw] that. I don't feel
like going there. I'm going off with my friends." And I think my
parents should have done it anyway. . . . All I saw of Black males
was violence and crime on the news and on TV.

While most of the people I interviewed expressed some curiosity about
their birth parents, very few of them were angry about being "abandoned." Brian continued:

Brian: I get really angry and I get really stupid feelings of, "You
just abandoned and left me!" You know? "You left me." . . . Um
. . . so yeah. I'd get really angry. I remember at that "Adoption's
the Right Thing" [a forum on adoption issues]. Everybody was
kinda being . . . it looked like something you'd see in the White
House. People dancing around the issues. And it was funny. It
was like, parents who gave their kids up here [gestures left]. And
kids who had been given up here [gestures right]. It was like . . .
separated. What up? You know? And I stood up and railed, man.
I was like, "[Screw] that! And then they left me. I get really
angry at 'em." And they're all, "But . . . but . . . but . . . but . . .
Now we wish you would . . ." "I don't give a . . ." Twenty-five
years later I wish. I wish . . . I wish. I grew up in a White family.
No Black role models. No nothing. You know. The more . . .
see, the more I think about it the more hyped I get about it.
Like, you might as well have f_____ threw me in a jungle and
left me. "Learn for yourself." You know? The more I think
about it the angrier I get at 'em. And the more I think like it's

incredibly important to have somebody of your race and sex to show you the right way.

Circumstances of Births and Adoptions

Cat: I remember drawing a picture of her when I was younger. And I remember drawing a picture of my dad, of my mom, and of my birth mother. Dad. Mom. Mom. You know. And I just remember doing that. . . . And I remember drawing this woman who looked just like me, except I pictured her as being a little bit darker skinned, with freckles, and a long pony tail.

One of the fundamental issues that adoption raises, particularly in the case of transracial adoption, is: How does the state define and regulate motherhood? *Who counts as a mother?* The closed adoption system in the United States both draws on and enforces social definitions of good and bad motherhood. In chapter 1 I discussed the ways in which young, poor, unwed mothers have been coerced into relinquishing their children for adoption. Rickie Solinger explains:

> Throughout American history, the particular populations of women whose motherhood status was vulnerable have shifted. But across time, the girls and women whose motherhood claims were ignored or denied shared a profound vulnerability, because they were defined as *possessing* attributes that counted as social demerits—qualities that marked them as not-mothers. Denial of their motherhood status was also fundamentally the result of what these females *lacked*: rights. (emphasis in original) (Solinger 1998: 382–83)

This history was evident in the stories of the adoptees I interviewed. Adoptees had been given a variety of reasons for their relinquishment, but one factor was constant: all their birth mothers had become pregnant outside the patriarchal boundaries of "legitimate" marriage. Two of them had had extramarital affairs. The rest were unmarried. The majority of the adoptees I spoke with were told that their birth mothers had been teenagers unable to care for and support a baby. Many of the mothers were young White women involved with African American men.

Three of the adoptees I spoke with were removed from their birth mothers by the social welfare system.

Lynn discussed her origins as follows:

Lynn: But it's hard, I mean, I think about it, you know, it's starting to stress me out more as I think about motherhood. And I never thought it would, but the more I think about having a kid I think, "Well, am I just going to give it up and make them do a family tree that begins with me?!" Is that what their family life will be? Do I do a search? Do I find like this mother—who couldn't cope? And I doubt—You know, she has a White kid. She chose to lead a certain type of life. You know, sometimes I think about, I remember this really came to me when I was like probably a sophomore in college and I was taking like a history—a Black history class. And we got to the sixties, and one of the things the teacher really wanted to talk about was kind of the interracial relationships that were going on. And I'm really a product of that. It was 1965; a lot of experimenting was going on. And so I'm a product of a very specific time too that sheds light on who I am. Whereas I look at like biracial kids now, and I think that their relationship to society is a little different. Oftentimes, there's not this kind of—I mean there is a little bit—but less of a stigma of having like a White parent and a Black parent. I mean, you see that a lot more on the West Coast.

Lynn quite consciously located herself historically as a product of the "experimenting" with interracial relationships that occurred in the 1960s. She mentioned the "choice" her birth mother made to relinquish her two biracial daughters for adoption. However, this matter of "choice" is more complex than it appears. How was this "choice" circumscribed by ideological and structural forces in society? This was a White woman married to a White man, who, as a result of an extended extramarital relationship, gave birth to two biracial daughters. We do not know what her options really were. We don't know what happened to their birth father. We do know that in the late 1960s the employment prospects for a single White woman raising two children were not auspicious and that finding housing in the Midwestern city in which they lived would have been difficult. We also know that a White woman who had "crossed the color line" was profoundly stigmatized in the White community in the 1960s. To what extent was her "decision" coerced?

For Lynn one of the most painful aspects of the story was that after her birth mother relinquished her and her sister she gave birth to and kept a White son. For Lynn this clearly demonstrated how profoundly her birth mother's "choice" was shaped by the prevailing race and gender norms of the time. The genealogy of Lynn's identity included the social circumstances that led to her birth parents' decision to relinquish their children, the policies and practices of the child welfare system that placed them first in a Black, working poor, foster home and then in an orphanage, and the social circumstances and public institutions that led to their adoption by White middle-class parents who raised them in a predominantly White community.

As a social worker, Lynn's younger sister Suzanne had gained access to their adoption records. She discussed the circumstances of their relinquishment as follows:

Suzanne: So I always joke with people and say, "I'm a love child." [both laugh] But it seems pretty likely that somehow they met on that level.

Sandi: Yeah. Mm hmm.

Suzanne: And that maybe the idea of having created these babies together was too much for them to deal with. Um . . . she . . . I mean, she clearly was having an affair and they just could be . . . and so . . . The records say that she was not completely emotionally stable. And that she really . . . she wanted to parent us but she didn't think she'd make a very good parent. And the reason why we were in . . . had visitation with her 'till we were about . . . 'till I was about five and a half was because she didn't wanna give up custody.

Sandi: Mm.

Suzanne: So it's hard to tell if she was actually talked into giving up custody. Um . . . it was definitely voluntary. But how voluntary I don't know.

Sandi: Yeah. What does voluntary mean in that context?

Suzanne: Yeah. She seems to have been really ambivalent about the whole thing. And yet they document sort of when she comes to visit us that she . . . she was very cold and she would sort of give us a hug and then that would be where she didn't really know how to relate to us. And that we called her Val from the beginning. Didn't call her mom, so . . .

The interlocking issues of gender, race, and class shaped the circumstances that led to Lynn and Suzanne being placed in foster care and eventually being adopted. What does "choice" mean in light of social stigma and limited economic and housing opportunities?

> Choice, like motherhood, has become a class privilege: for most women with economic resources, "choice" signifies the ability to make motherhood decisions. For women without, "choice" equals license and calls for restraints. "Choice" frames an updated set of class-based laws of procreation and provides a class-based guide to answering the question, Who is a mother? (Solinger 1998:396)

While feminists have actively debated the rights of women to choose abortion, much less attention has been paid to adoption. "Choice" has largely structured the feminist dialogue on reproductive rights. However, as critical race scholar Dorothy Roberts demonstrates, by framing these issues around choice feminists assume that all women have access to the same range of opportunities. This view neglects the interlocking forces of race and class. Her important analysis of race and reproductive rights demonstrates that Black and White women have historically been situated differently in relation to social institutions governing the range of "choices" available (Roberts 1997).

What does "choice" really mean for a pregnant teenage girl from a low-income family? What does it mean when the father of her child refuses to contribute support? What does "choice" mean when parents and social workers exert pressure on her to do "what is right" for the baby? What does it mean when she hasn't finished high school and has no job skills? When she has no support from family, no support from a boyfriend, and no options for child care?

The U.S. system of adoption turns on the issue of class. Families selected for adoption are predominantly middle class. In the 1990s, most of the children in the contemporary public child welfare system were there because they had been removed from low-income families that were already interacting with, and thus under the scrutiny of, the social welfare system. Clearly there are multiple issues involved in the selection of adoptive families, as in the removal of a child from his or her family of origin, often including abuse and/or neglect. However, from a macrosocial perspective, broad class patterns suggest that socioeconomic status significantly determines which families children will be removed from and into which families they will be adopted.

Brian discussed adoption and class in the course of his interview:

> *Brian:* When you're given up for adoption there's automatically a "I was left by my parents. And who am I? Who am I?" I have no blood. I have a family with no blood. I'm more [screwed] 'cause like my great grandpa hated me because I was Black. So, I have to deal with also the color line as well as, "I was left . . . for what? What did I do wrong? Why'd you leave me?" It's hard to rationally—I'll be talking to somebody. . . . I was talking to somebody today about it and what did they say? "Well maybe they financially couldn't afford it." Or, "Maybe, you know . . ." A lot of . . . I don't wanna hear that technical bull. I was left. You know. For whatever reason they left me. And I get angry at that. "Well, how can you be angry about that?" I'm like, "Well you grew up with your family. So you don't even know what you're talking about." . . . And there's plenty of families that look good on the outside and you'd be getting [screwed] up inside the house. So, who's to say they're going to someone better?
>
> *Sandi:* Yeah. True. Social workers can only see so much.
>
> *Brian:* You know, you might have . . . and that's a lot of the time it's a money thing. The secret . . . a lot of that to me, what I see is that's more a money thing. People who are broke, everybody knows they're getting whooped. You can hear it. The whole apartment building knows. That ain't no *secret*. Rich people, though . . . nobody know. The kids who get messed up in the house . . . you know, maybe they have a learning disability but

pop doesn't wanna hear it. "Where are the A's?" Smack! You know? So, who's to say they go to . . . I couldn't see myself giving my kid up for adoption. Like I said, I went to clinics a couple of times, you know, when we were getting abortions. And if the baby came, I'd deal with it. I'd bring my kid up. And I'm pissed that my parents didn't think like that. I'm pissed that they didn't do it.

Brian didn't have much sympathy for his birth parents' "choice" to relinquish him. However, as I noted, his birth mother may have been coerced into terminating her parental rights. He may have been removed from her care. He did not know what the circumstances were. He himself pointed out that class was at the heart of the issue. Poor people are under greater scrutiny by the social welfare system and are thus more vulnerable to the charges of abuse or neglect. We don't know Brian's birth mother's story, nor do we know the actual circumstances of most of the birth mothers of the people I interviewed. We do know that whatever their life circumstances—whether they were poor, teenagers, prostitutes, drug addicts, had engaged in an extramarital affair, or had participated in interracial relationships—they were socially "defined as *possessing* attributes that counted as social demerits—qualities that marked them as not-mothers" (Solinger 1998:382–83).

Christina was four years old when she was removed from her birth mother. She has been told that her birth mother was a Mexican "call girl." Her birth father was an unemployed African American man. In our interview she discussed how she imagined a life with her birth mother.

Christina: Because number one, if it wasn't for my adoptive mother and father where would I be now?
Sandi: Where do you think you would be?
Christina: Oh gosh. I've been around that one. Ooh.
Sandi: How do you imagine it?
Christina: Six feet under.
Sandi: Why do you say that?
Christina: Just 'cause of I . . . of the little bit out . . . you know, her little druggie . . . uh . . . that side of her.
Sandi: Hmm.

Christina: And I . . . either . . . and if I wasn't six feet under then I'd see myself on porn street.

Sandi: Say that again?

Christina: Porn street. [laughs]

Sandi: Oh, my god! That's really quite a dramatic picture.

Christina: But I . . . I don't have any good things to think about that side. I don't have any good thoughts about . . . I can't possibly see where anything would be good . . . 'cause I never was there.

Sandi: Wow.

Christina: I'm not . . . I could make up a whole bunch of stories. You know, what I . . . all the different ideas and thoughts that I'd thought. I definitely wouldn't be living up in this area. I would be totally . . . probably I wouldn't have been able to . . . I probably never would have went out of California [for college]. I don't . . . I don't think so. I probably would never have even left Salinas. I see myself being dirty and . . . I just . . . yeah. When I think of that I think of dirtiness.

Sandi: Because they were poor and the drug problem?

Christina: Yeah. And you know, who knows how many other people . . . kids are out there that they have that they've done the same thing with, you know?

Clearly Christina had internalized pervasive social views of poverty.

Found!

I began the previous chapter with a discussion of Elisa Jacob's sense of culture shock when she first found herself in a racially diverse college setting. In our first interview Elisa expressed anger at her parents over the way she was raised, and told me that she had been angry with them for a number of years. Having been raised in a predominantly White community with no awareness of racial issues, she responded to the culture shock she experienced at college by immersing herself in African American culture—essentially enculturating herself. At the time of our first interview she was searching for her birth parents. When we met again several months later she had been successful in her quest.

Elisa: It actually is interesting. I was gonna call you, and then you happened to call me. Because I have—It's just interesting. I've kind of had like this change of heart.

Sandi: Really?

Elisa: You know, and it's because I found my birth mother.

Sandi: Oh.

Elisa: And uh, it's like from the first conversation I had with her it was suddenly—I just became so grateful to my parents for—You know, just completely changed my perspective.

Sandi: Oh [surprised].

Elisa: You know, I still believe that I missed out on a lot and it could have been more, but it just completely changed my perspective on the thing that [long pause] what a huge deal it is for someone to adopt a child and take them in as their own. And it just really changed my perspective a lot.

Sandi: So tell me about your birth mother.

Elisa: I don't know that much about her yet. We've only had like two phone conversations. You know, she's in Atlanta. Um, she's married. She's got two kids, so you know, a half brother and sister.

Sandi: What are the ages?

Elisa: One's—the boy is twenty-five. The girl is nineteen.

Sandi: And you're twenty-eight?

Elisa: Twenty-six.

Sandi: Damn. That's really close.

Elisa: Yeah. It's interesting. And she said like—Well, I asked why she didn't abort, basically. That was one of the questions I asked, and you know, she said her parents had wanted her to. The only thing that saved me was you know, her best friend who was Catholic and said, "You can't do this." I thought that was interesting.

Sandi: Yeah.

Elisa: But um, you know, uh. [pause] It's hard to kind of describe. I actually have pictures and stuff. Um. But she seems like a really cool person. She said that [laughs] she's got back into therapy because of this, but it's a good thing, like me finding her. She was happy I found her, and you know, just brought all the—I guess during the time of my birth and stuff was a really bad time for her. But it brought it out into the open again and she could finally really deal with it. So she was happy I found her. That was good. You know, the worst thing is to think God, you're gonna contact her and she's gonna say, "No, I don't want to see you." So um. So in that respect it's been a good thing. And now I never have to sit and wonder about it. I thought it'd be a bigger deal.

Sandi: Huh.

Elisa: Like it'd fill this incredible hole or whatever. But I don't feel that, but maybe I'm just not realizing it yet.

Sandi: That's really interesting. Because I think a lot of adoptees talk about—when they're doing a search—that it is like that big hole that they're, you know, trying to find something to fill. Can you say more about how it doesn't resolve that for you?

Elisa: Um, see, you know, I don't think I can, because I've tried to figure it out myself—why it hasn't been a bigger deal. But then maybe I'm not realizing that it is a huge deal. You know, I can't—You know, it's pretty new, you know, the last two months this has happened so—You know I really haven't—just dealing with scripts and everything—that I don't think I've really had a chance to sit down and figure out what this whole thing means. So I can't really tell yet.

Sandi: Tell me about the first contact with her.

Elisa: It was funny. You know, it was really interesting. It's like once I got on the phone—you know, it's like we played phone tag for a minute and then we finally talked—it's like I only had like a couple questions, and it was good that she kind of kept the conversation going. It lasted about an hour and a half, I think. But, it's like after a while I didn't really know what to ask or what to say, so it was really good that she was asking questions or just talking, you know. You know, it's just really strange, you know, you're talking to someone where there's this incredible bond, yet you don't even know who it is.

Sandi: Yeah, it must be.

Elisa: So, you know, it was very strange. But like I said, she seems like a cool person.

Sandi: So what did she tell you about the circumstances of your birth?

Elisa: Just that you know, her parents didn't want her to keep it. And it was a really bad time in her life. And, um [long pause] I think that's pretty much what it was. You know, she wasn't married. You know this guy—they were dating but they weren't you know, really close, and it just wasn't a great situation.

Sandi: Do you have any desire to find him?

Elisa: Um yeah. And actually, it's interesting, you know, talking to my birth mother, you know, she asked what I consider myself. And I said Black and you know, it's like she says that she can't see that because she's White and she gave birth to me. But she says she can understand it, but can't—but for her I'm not Black I'm mixed. You know, so—

Sandi: Well, you get to define who you are for you. She can define you however she wants. [We both laugh.]

Elisa: Exactly.

Sandi: So in terms of racial identity you feel like it's important to touch base with him too?

Elisa: Oh yeah, yeah. He gave me the Blackness so, you know, it's important to see him.

Sandi: Well, and you found it yourself too. How has it given you empathy for your parents?

Elisa: Um, I think. I don't know, it's just like talking with her I was thinking God, what if—'cause you know, you always wonder well, what if I stayed with my birth parents or mother? How would I turn out? And just in talking to her—I don't know, maybe I realized that I wouldn't be where I am today and be everything I have if I had stayed with her. That it was a bad situation, you know, at that time. And also, you know, like I said just you know, for someone to take a child that isn't theirs but you know, raise it as your own, and consider your daughter. It just struck me while talking to her. And you know she was really upset for a minute—she started crying when she found that you know, it took three weeks for me to get adopted. But that's like *nothing!*

Sandi: I know, my God.

Elisa: But she was like saying you know three weeks—like at that age that's when you bond and that I was—You know, I just didn't have anyone for three weeks, but it's like some kids will languish for like six, seven, eight years or longer so, you know. I thought that was interesting.

For many adoptees the search and reunion are part of "the discursive practices by which the self establishes the 'truth' of itself in the relation it has with itself" (Poster 1993:66). Indeed, the search is often discussed as a quest for the "truth" of identity. Elisa's quest had led her to a "truth" of the self she had not expected to find—a newfound sympathy for and appreciation of her parents. Along with this had come a revaluation of the meanings of biological and adoptive kinship, and the relative forces of nature and nurture in shaping her life and sense of self. As she said with regard to her birth mother, "it's just really strange, you know, you're talking to someone where there's this incredible bond, yet you don't even know who it is." That was when she realized that if she had stayed with her rather than being adopted into her family, she would not have been the person she was then—both in terms of her success as a writer for television and film and in terms of *who she was.*

This was true in many ways. With regard to class, Elisa was probably correct that her adoptive parents were able to give her opportunities that her birth mother would not have had access to on a limited budget. But her comments resonated much deeper as well. Elisa had, since making the above comments, met her birth mother. After their meeting she felt even more strongly that she had been fundamentally shaped by her adoptive family. She was still searching for her birth father.

Cat's story of reunion with her birth family was very different from Elisa's. Her search process was easy and quick, and when she found them they were ecstatic. One of the first things her birth mother said was, "I married your father and you have three sisters." They had since divorced. At the time of our interview she had known them for three years. She had developed a close relationship with her birth sisters and mother, and had maintained her close relationship with her adoptive family. In the excerpt below, she discussed her two mothers.

Cat: It's real interesting 'cause I call Loretta mom now. One of 'em is my first mother, which is Loretta. And one of them is my mother. And they are both equally my mother. My adoptive mother, I've known her longer and has raised me, and I know

more about her. And I'm closer to her. But they are definitely
both my mothers. It's very strange. And I have two mothers,
none the less than the other. And I battled with that for a
long time.

When Cat first met her birth mother she went through what she called a
"honeymoon" phase. She was "clingy" with them, and for a while, she
pushed her adoptive family away. Following that, she became a little dis-
illusioned with her birth family and embraced her adoptive family as her
"real" family. Subsequently she had, after much struggle, come to a
happy medium. She said she wouldn't change anything about her life.
She felt very lucky to have "the best of both worlds."

> *Cat:* I was born. . . . Usually you say born into a family. Well I was
> born out of this family of abuse—never neglect, but abuse and a
> wrong kind of attention. And secrecy and pain and misery. And I
> was taken out of that family and put into this *wonderful* family
> that was all about no secrets, nurture, positive this, healthy this.
> And it was hard growing up, but I had this wonderful family.
> Then when I'm old enough to deal with it, I find my birth family.
> Am able to even meet and get to know my father. I don't know
> him very well, but I'm getting to know him. And so I know these
> people, and these other people who are potentially harmful to me
> when I'm growing up. But they can't harm me now. So I still
> have my adoptive family. And I have my birth family. And they
> know each other. And there's no secrecy. There's no lying.
> There's nothing. So I have the best of both.

The reason she was relinquished for adoption was that neither of her parents felt ready to be parents. They were in a relationship, but were not
ready to "settle down." Her birth father, a White man, wanted her birth
mother to have an abortion. Cat was with her birth mother for her first
two days of life; she assumed later that her birth mother was wrestling
with the idea of keeping her. Once again, we must consider the structural
reasons this would have been difficult. As a young, poor, Black woman
living in a predominantly White area, she would probably have had a difficult time finding a job that would have supported her and her baby.

These stories of birth and adoption reveal the complicated routes of adoptees' identities. They make clear the limitations of explaining lives solely through the tension between biology and culture. For when we explore the social circumstances of women's lives we see that the question of "choice" is problematic. When we consider the socioeconomic context within which such decisions are made, as well as the public policies shaping unwed mothers' reproductive behavior, it becomes clear that some women have more options than others. Some women—particularly those who are young, unmarried, poor, and of color—are defined primarily as breeders, as women who give birth, but do not mother. Conversely, the motherhood status of middle-class White women—the adoptive mothers of the people I interviewed—is supported and facilitated by public policies and social institutions concerned with the reproduction of particular kinds of families and citizens.

| FOUR |

Producing "IL/Legitimate" Citizens

Transracial Adoption and Welfare Reform

What follows are the opening scenes from the 1995 release of the feature film *Losing Isaiah.*

Credits appear on a black screen as a mellow saxophone-lead soundtrack eases in. As the title *Losing Isaiah* appears, some movement in the black screen becomes evident through increasingly visible streetlight beams and the muffled sounds of traffic. As the credits continue to appear the movement persists, and our aerial perspective reveals a full view of the city lights. As we fly above the Chicago skyscrapers, sirens and other city sounds intrude. Our perspective shifts from a view of light-sprinkled skyscrapers to a top-down gaze of the stark urban streets. A harder drum beat and synthesizer gradually replace the sax. As the streets within our view move further away from the crisply lit downtown we hear muffled yelling and distant sirens. The neighborhood becomes visibly impoverished as a distinctly urban contemporary sound claims the music and a soulful woman's voice rides the melody without words. Our view of the streets rolls into a succession of monotonous surfaces—cement, gray, pavement, darker gray. The movement of a shadow, then the tapping foot reveal that we've left the paved surfaces of the street for the inside view of cement walls. Our gaze follows the foot up a brown leg, across clothing and blanket to linger at a breast at which a Black infant is feeding. The camera pulls back to reveal the unkempt mother, rocking, eyes closed. She pulls her finger from the clutch of her infant, touches it to her temple, and grimaces with pain. Muffled conversation is evident in the background. She takes her child from her breast and he begins to cry. She buttons her shirt as she begins to leave the desolate room, but a woman stands up on the other side of the room and says, "You ain't leavin' that baby here, not hollerin' like that you

| 130 |

ain't." We cut to the woman walking down the tenement stairs carrying the child as he continues to cry. Outside looks like a war zone. In the distance a trashcan fire is blazing and we hear a man say, "Let's go girl. Okay baby, come on over here and be warm." Several men laugh. Another man says, "Come on now." The baby continues to cry. The woman's face is desperate. We continue to hear the muffled sounds of the men and then discern, "Come on babe, this some good shit. Come on you can have a little bit of this." The woman looks around for somewhere to leave her baby. She finds a box among piles of trash, places him inside, and says, "Okay Isaiah there you go. Okay? I'll be right back. Okay?" He cries loudly. She places the lid on the box and walks away. We continue to hear his cries as the camera lingers on the garbage pile. The camera cuts to the woman's hands lighting a crack pipe. We hear her inhale, her hands shake as she lights it again. As she exhales we hear her sounds of pleasure, "Um, umhmm, oh yeah, oh yes." The camera fades from a profile of her face into morning sky.

The camera pans across a freeway, a bridge, several streets, finally focusing on a garbage truck traveling down a road. The scene slowly fades into the moving blade of the garbage truck. Two men discuss basketball as they load bags and boxes into the compressor, lower the blade, and refill the bin. The blade pushes the lid off a box and the infant is revealed, inches from the compressor's force. Perspective shifts to a view from inside the truck's bin as the blade is lowered. One of the men hears the infant cry, sees him, and yells, "Holy shit. Stop the blade! Stop the blade! Stop it!" As the blade obscures the view of the baby the camera cuts to a blaring ambulance racing down the street. The scene shifts to a shot above the baby being wheeled into the hospital on a stretcher. Many sets of hands surround him. Perspective is shifted to the infant's viewpoint, as the faces of nurses, paramedics, and doctors jog beside the gurney shouting vital signs and instructions. He is put on a respirator.

The hospital social worker, an attractive White woman with blond hair, walks past the scene telling a White woman carrying a toddler, "It's a subdural hematoma, Mrs. Ianelli. He's five months old. You didn't think he might roll off that top bunk?" The woman responds, "He never did it before." The social worker continues, "Well now you know it's possible. He's not Peter Pan. He can't fly." A nurse approaches her, "We need you." She tells the woman, "You're going to have to wait here for x-rays," as she walks away. The nurse says, "At least she didn't dump him in a pot of boiling water, huh?" The social worker responds, "Yeah, she did that last month. Said his bath was too hot." As they near the infant the nurse explains: "This one was found in a dumpster." The social worker says, "Jesus" as she turns to look at him. The doctor queries, "Social services? He's not breathing on his own. Can you sign off?" She replies, "Sign off?" He clarifies, "Yeah, no extraordinary measures." She retorts, "Why don't we just dump him back in the garbage?" He says, "Alright lady, play God." She turns to the baby and looks at him, smiling. Soft music begins to play as she watches him breathe, she looks at his hands and feet. She is momentarily entranced. His body begins to shake. A woman's voice says, "Looks like a brain bleed." The social worker yells, "This infant is having a seizure." The doctor returns, orders, "Phenobarbital, stat. NICU." Just before racing off with the baby, he turns to her and says, "What'd I tell you?"

This series of scenes dramatizes the question: " *Who decides what makes a mother?*" This was the question used as the tag line in advertisements for the 1995 film, released at the height of political and public policy discussions about "fit" versus "unfit" mothers in the context of welfare reform and transracial adoption legislation.

Losing Isaiah raises a wide range of issues regarding race, gender, class, and family in its dramatization of the circumstances leading to transracial adoption. The representation of the Black mother embodies society's most horrific view of Black women as mothers. *She abandons her baby in a trash heap so she can get a fix.* This aspect of the story provides viewers a palpable explanation of how and why the number of Black children in foster care increased dramatically in the 1980s and 1990s. It dramatizes one of the central tenets of the mainstream narrative of transracial adoption, namely, that Black folks can't take care of their own children. The racial narrative continues with the salvation of the infant by the White social worker, who eventually adopts him.

As public discourse about transracial adoption emerged in 1993 and 1994 following the introduction of the first of several legislative proposals, a wave of television talk shows, made-for-television movies, and cinematic films began appearing in the spring of 1994 about adoption, foster care, and the relative "fitness" or otherwise of poor and middle-class mothers. However, *Losing Isaiah* was the only feature film of which I am aware specifically concerned with transracial adoption. Legislative agendas do not exist in isolation from popular culture and public opinion. As Graeme Turner explains, "What is clear is that the world 'comes to us' in the shape of stories" (Turner 1988:68). Public policy agendas draw on broader social stories about race and identity, gender and family, class and work, that are widely available in popular culture. It is through stories that political issues such as transracial adoption are given meaning for a broad segment of the public.

In popular contemporary narratives surrounding the issues of transracial adoption and welfare reform, Black women are represented as drug addicted and poor, and thus "fit" as breeders but "unfit" as mothers. Black children are shown as fragile, frail, drug addicted, unwanted, and indeed disposable. In stories like *Losing Isaiah*, Black children are un-cared-for and unwanted by their Black families, and thus must be saved by those fit to save, and redeem these lost children—White women. The broader sociopolitical message is that Black families have been destroyed by the "culture of poverty" and their innocent children must be saved from the same fate. Salvation and redemption come in the form of White nuclear families, possessors of "family values."

When the film was released, the Personal Responsibility Act, part of the new Republican congressional majority's *Contract with America*, had only recently been introduced in January 1995. This original version of the bill was particularly concerned with reducing "illegitimacy," and as a means to that end, legislated the removal of all restrictions on transracial placements, prohibiting the consideration of race in placing a child for adoption. *Losing Isaiah* was certainly topical. Indeed, it went into production in 1993, during the public debate over the Multiethnic Placement Act. The film was previewed for selected groups of transracial adoptees and parents, various opinion makers, social workers, and civil rights groups across the country along with the usual screenings to more general audiences. The *Los Angeles Times* reported, "In Washington, where a bill has been introduced in Congress that would make it illegal to consider race when placing children with prospective families, politicians also were invited to see *Losing Isaiah*." (Welkos 1995:F1). A number of social workers and agency directors I interviewed reported being invited to openings in their locales.

"Illegitimacy" is consistently cited, by conservatives and centrists alike, as the primary cause for social chaos and decline, evidenced by crime, poverty, gang violence, and drug abuse, and usually represented as a primarily Black problem that has begun to spread to White families.

The fact that politicians presented *transracial* adoption as a means of reducing "illegitimacy" reveals their concern with the regulation of Black women's reproductive behavior. Public discourse has been saturated with rhetoric about "family breakdown" as the cause for contemporary social ills. At the heart of this political debate is the fiercely held belief that this supposed "breakdown of the family" fails American society through a failure of *socialization*. In the most conservative version of this story, the inability of unwed mothers to properly "civilize" their "illegitimate" children threatens the demise of a free society not only by creating of a permanent "underclass," but also by failing to socialize "productive citizens" capable of ensuring U.S. competitiveness in the global market economy. Indeed, the argument posits a crisis in American democracy and locates its source in the bodies of young, poor, and primarily Black women and their children—the future citizens of this capitalist democracy.

These concerns are played out in public policy dialogues at the intersection of transracial adoption and welfare reform. Social policies regulating adoption have been discussed as a concrete means of engineering and enforcing the literal social construction of "legitimate" families and identities. The issues raised in this public discourse show how profoundly social policy shapes the identities and everyday lives of people living in the United States. Public policy is at the matrix of culture, knowledge, and power. It shapes who we become and how we live our lives.

I begin by mapping out the public narrative about transracial adoption, drawing on federal legislation passed in the 1990s, discussions of this legislation in the Congressional Record, editorials, and news coverage. I then offer the counternarrative that emerged from my ethnographic interviews with sixteen social workers and directors of public and private adoption agencies on the East and West Coasts. Next, I explore transracial adoption discourse in the context of policy dialogues about welfare legislation. Following that, I consider the ways in which public policy on adoption and the social welfare system furthers the social construction and maintenance of particular kinds of families and identities. Finally, I explore this legislative discourse as an institutionalization of conservative social visions that serve to map out "legitimate" and "illegitimate" social identities and their place in the national socioeconomic order.

Bad Mothers, Good Mothers

The congruence of the messages in *Losing Isaiah* with the conservative politics of the moment was not lost on several reviewers. In a scathing critique of the film, Duchess Harris discussed the character of the crack-addicted mother, played by actress Halle Berry, in light of historic "controlling images" of Black women:

> Berry's character reinscribes the controlling image of the black woman as negligent breeder—semi-literate and crack addict—in a way that is dangerous. Her Jezebel/Mammy/Sapphire depiction of this character subverts the activist rhetoric of "strong black womanhood" that Berry espouses in celebrity interviews. Her character is an exaggerated welfare queen that will support the arguments of House Speaker Newt Gingrich as easily as *Forrest Gump* became an icon for the GOP. (Harris 1995:48)

In a similar vein, James Verniere observed:

> In step with the new conservatism, the film also suggests that attempts to help the less fortunate are doomed to failure and probably create only resentment. *Losing Isaiah* may even appeal to the angry white men who will be perfectly happy to see Khaila as a typical urban, black woman. Notably, the only other African-American family in the film is headed by an abusive, drug-addicted, single mother (Spike Lee's sister Joie Lee). (Vernier 1995:sec. SCE.S03)

If we broaden the frame further we may consider this story of race and family as a narrative of race and nation. What ideological work does this story accomplish? Cultural critic Hazel Carby suggests that such narratives of salvation preserve the interests of the White middle class in times of perceived national crisis (Carby 1993). She discusses Hollywood filmmakers' symbolic uses of Los Angeles's Black neighborhoods; her remarks shed light on the darkness of Chicago's inner city in the opening scene of *Losing Isaiah*. She argues that such landscapes "are important sites not just for the representation of death and destruction but for the enactment of social and political confrontations that constitute a threat to national stability" (Carby 1993:239). An air of death and destruction pervades the site of Isaiah's abandonment; indeed, it powerfully likens the inner city to a war zone. It is Khaila's abandonment of Isaiah that constitutes a threat to national stability, for it signifies the "breakdown of the family." In this war zone the battle has already been lost: "immorality" has annihilated "family values"; drug abuse has imperiled a healthy future; poverty has destroyed hope. An abandoned Black infant threatens the future of the nation, for he symbolizes another "lost generation" of "super-predators"—gang members, criminals, and drug addicts.

In this context, the White social worker and her family who save Isaiah from a desolate future as a dislocated member of the "underclass" "save" the White middle class as well by socializing him *as one of their own*, and symbolically diminish the violent, inner-city Black threat to class security. In Hazel Carby's words (in her discussion of the film *Grand Canyon*): "The resolution we are offered uses black bodies as a means to white salvation" (Carby 1993:245).

The ideological punch of *Losing Isaiah* is further revealed through an exploration of the changes made in the film from the 1993 novel by Seth J. Margolis. The most fundamental and striking transformation involves Isaiah's origin narrative. As discussed, in the film he is abandoned by his birth mother before being saved and ultimately adopted by a White woman who is a social worker in the hospital to which he is admitted. However, in Margolis's novel the birth mother does not abandon the child, and the adoptive mother is not a social worker but a photographer's representative. Somehow—it is never revealed how—the White couple locates Isaiah and his birth mother at home. They offer to adopt him, and pay expenses. The birth mother, a crack addict in the novel as well as the film, does not want to be a mother, and thus accepts $25,000 for the child. The narratives of abandonment and salvation for these two mothers that emerged in the film version are consonant with the political climate of 1995.

Narratives of Politics

The sources of the social narratives I explore are varied, and thus different "truth" claims emerge. Some texts, such as news reports or statements of "fact" made by Senate or House members on the floor of Congress, are commonly regarded with certitude in the public sphere. Conversely, we are typically taught as children that "fictional" stories are not "true," but belong to the realm of the imaginary.

In the 1990s, as the right wing social agenda was forcefully asserted and centrists and liberals edged closer to the right, adoption was paired with welfare reform in ways that disturbed those of us concerned with the lives of poor women and their children. It is certainly useful—indeed, necessary—for progressive academics to address the fundamental inaccuracies in the conservative and centrist political narratives that make causal connections between "illegitimate" births and such social problems as poverty, crime, drugs, and gang violence. It is accurate to point out, as numerous scholars have, that poor women and children, as well as immigrants—many of them elderly and/or disabled—and families of children with disabilities, were scapegoated in the political debate about welfare reform. But I believe there was much more going on. What was the *social function* of such causal narratives in an era of economic downsizing, disinvestment in inner cities, increasingly dramatic disparities between the poor and the wealthy, and the juridical and legislative dismantling of affirmative action? How were such widespread, individualistic narratives used to highlight particular perspectives and obscure others? Conservatives successfully fashioned appealing and accessible social fables that provided an easily identifiable enemy, simple explanations for complex social problems, and a sense of stability and security for those floundering in the swiftly changing society of the late-twentieth-century United States. This is, perhaps, one of the keys to the successful resurgence of the right in recent U.S. politics.

Political narratives that offer explanations for social issues do not exist in isolation from other forms of public discourse. Scholars in a number of fields—perhaps most notably cultural studies and critical race theory—have applied a narrative analysis to legal and/or legislative texts as well as "fictional" stories in popular film and television.[1] Legal scholar and literary critic Laura Hanft Korobkin explains the interplay of "truth"—claiming texts and "fabricated" stories in considering legal discourse: "Coherent and effective narratives of past events will always resonate intertextually with other narratives, factual and fictional, about similar events. The circulation of influence from literature to life and back again simply brings out the narrative logic that underlies the litigative process; it does not violate it" (Korobkin 1996:232).

This understanding allows for an approach to the politics of narratives and the narratives of politics that focuses on questions of ideology, power, and representation. A common analytical tool in much of this work is the concept of *genealogical* analysis. In essence we must ask: What is the social function of a particular racial representation? What does this representation of race signify beyond the particular meanings conveyed within the given text? And, of course, we must ask: Why has this narrative appeared here and now? Cultural studies scholar Hazel Carby suggests that: "These narrative genealogies, in their production of this symbolic power, have significant political resonance when they are produced in response to a perceived crisis in the formation of a society. The process of inscribing national issues on black bodies accomplishes the ideological work that is necessary for the everyday maintenance of systems of racial injustice and inequality" (Carby 1993:236). Thus, Carby argues that popular narratives, in their allegorical power to explain sociopolitical "truths," are ideological justifications for oppression and inequality. This framework is useful in considering social narratives of adoption and welfare reform.

Narratives of Salvation: Adoption, Race, and Disability

During the week of August 19, 1996 President Clinton signed into law two pieces of legislation that quickly began to reshape the lives of millions of poor women and their children. After more than three years of intense public dialogue regarding the philosophies and pragmatics of families, poverty, work, and government aid, the Personal Responsibility and Work Opportunity Reconciliation Act of 1996 (welfare reform) became law, as did the Small Business Job Protection Act of 1996 (most commonly known as the minimum wage bill). The primary significance of the minimum wage bill in this discussion is a section devoted to the promotion of adoption. The law provides a $5,000 to $6,000 tax credit to families that adopt. More controversially, the legislation removes all restrictions on transracial placements and prohibits the use of race in considering the placement of a child for adoption.

Transracial adoption has been a provocative topic since it first came to public notice in the 1960s and 1970s. When the practice first began gaining popularity in the 1960s many White parents and social workers regarded it as a solution to the steady decline in White infants available for adoption and to the need for adoptive families by Black and mixed race children in foster care. Additionally, integrationist politics often led White adoptive parents to consider the biracial families they constructed as a step toward a more humane "color-blind" world (Ladner 1977). This climate changed after the public debate that followed the 1972 NABSW statement against transracial adoption. This statement placed the highest value on the development of Black cultural identity and survival skills for African American children living in a racist society, and led to a shift in policy in favor of "racial matching" between children and parents. Subsequently, individual agencies and county and state governments throughout the United States developed both formal and informal policies and practices regarding adoption and the placement of children of color, in keeping with local needs, concerns, and populations. While most researchers and practitioners agree that the number of Black children placed transracially significantly declined after the early 1970s, the practice did not cease altogether. Conversely, the political debate in the 1990s placed the highest value on an ostensible desire to end discrimination against Black children in foster care through the promotion of "color-blind" adoptions.

The contemporary public narrative emerged through news coverage, editorials, television talk shows and newsmagazines, fictional television dramas, cinematic films, and political rhetoric. While individual accounts varied, a generally coherent story emerged as the dominant or preferred view of transracial adoption as a social issue.[2] A range of both complementary and conflicting "facts" were presented. Some versions included critical perspectives as well as supportive views, while others insisted on the simplicity of the solution to the perceived crisis in child welfare. As the work of cultural studies scholars has demonstrated, the meanings of media texts are not inherent. Rather, they emerge through viewers' individual and collective readings. Fictional and nonfictional representations of the issue of transracial adoption are sites of struggle over the social and political meanings of race and identity, gender and family, individuals and the role of the state.

Media texts offer both the dominant readings of these issues as well as oppositional readings. Cultural studies scholar Herman Gray argues: "Because of this constantly shifting terrain of meaning and struggle, the representations of race and racial interaction in fictional and nonfictional television reveal both the elements of the dominant racial ideology as well as the limits to that ideology" (Gray 1995:431). Thus, I consider the representations of transracial adoption in public discourse—in both nonfictional and fictional texts—as a field of available readings. There are openings for resistant interpretations within any ideological narrative, but the possibilities for such opposition are circumscribed by the boundaries and logic of the story as well as the tenor and history of the power relations involved.

The dominant narrative that emerged in public discourse in roughly the first half of the 1990s begins with the assertion that the number of Black children in foster care increased dramatically in the past decade, and that race is *the* factor keeping Black children in foster care. The narrator typically bemoans the inadequate numbers of Black families able to adopt, but cites an increasing demand for "adoptable" children among Whites. The narrative continues with the information that there are plenty of White families willing to adopt Black children. People in favor of transracial adoption say the solution is simple: let White families adopt African American children. They argue that the only barriers to the implementation of this simple solution are (what they call) "racist" racial matching policies.

In a letter to the *New York Times* Elizabeth Bartholet, a law professor who has been particularly vocal in arguments against racial matching, explicated this aspect of the narrative:

> It is true that this legislation (the Multiethnic Placement Act) was originally developed in recognition of the fact that child welfare workers throughout the country are holding children of color in foster and institutional care for years at a time rather than placing them in permanent adoptive homes, solely because of their reluctance to place children transracially. (Bartholet 1993c:A24)

The contemporary public dialogue has been dominated by arguments against racial matching policies and characterizations of the National Association of Black Social Workers as the "new racists." In a *Washington Post* editorial, Ellen Goodman explained: "What keeps many children and parents apart is not the old-fangled segregation created by whites who oppose racial mixing. It's the new-fangled segregation now supported by a small but powerful group of black Americans who support 'racial matching'" (Goodman 1993:Editorial page).

The story continues with the argument that racial matching policies and practices keep African American children waiting in long-term "foster limbo" while social workers search for Black parents. This is followed by an argument in favor of transracial adoption, supported by reference to the "empirical evidence" demonstrating how well-adjusted transracial adoptees are. In a September 5, 1995 U.S. Senate discussion of the adoption legislation originally part of the welfare reform bill, Senator McCain cited the "sound research" conducted by Simon and Altstein, which concluded that "interracial adoptions do not hurt the children or deprive them of their culture." Senator McCain argued that: "By incorporating strong and reasonable antidiscrimination provisions in the Conference Report, we will help to remedy the national problem of children being held in foster care because the color of their skin does not match that of the individuals who wish to adopt them" (U.S. Senate 1995).

This narrative, while not immune to public corrections and critiques, won out as "truth" in the policy battle. This view of transracial adoption drew momentum from a number of sensationalized court battles in which White foster parents fought to adopt their Black foster children against the wishes of social service agencies; several such cases were cited in political dialogues. One of the major forces behind the crafting of this social narrative was Harvard lawyer and adoptive parent Elizabeth Bartholet. She has published widely and has been actively engaged in these legislative battles. Her 1991 and 1992 articles, "Where Do Black Children Belong?" appeared early on in the renaissance of this issue, and were successful in shaping the dominant narrative; all the basic elements of the argument were present in Bartholet's published work.[3] Along with a group of influential lawyers, she forcefully lobbied for legislation prohibiting any attention to race in the placement of a child for adoption.

The critiques and cautions about the cultural identities of Black children adopted into White families are dismissed by assertions that the "empirical evidence" of academic research demonstrates that transracial adoptees grow up well-adjusted. The "empirical evidence" directly cited by most proponents of this view is one longitudinal study conducted by Simon and Altstein. There are a number of problems with this study, chief among them the fact that the authors dismiss the concerns of the National Association of Black Social Workers as "political" in relation to their own "scientific"—and by implication apolitical—research. This dismissal correlates with a research agenda that "measures adjustment" but does not consider how transracial adoptees construct and define a sense of racial identity.[4] It is interesting that this particular study is used in the public discourse to *legitimate* the dominant public narrative advocating the promotion of "color-blind adoptions." The research was positioned and discussed as "apolitical" because it was "scientific." Yet as cultural studies scholarship of the past few decades has demonstrated, the results of science and social science research are not unproblematically "objective" and removed from power dynamics. As Mark Poster explains, "Far from neutral statements of truth, the discourses of science emerge fully implicated in practices of domination" (Poster 1993:64). This is evident in the social debate over transracial adoption.

The "scientific" research conducted by Simon and Altstein entered the political discourse through a number of channels. The final book in their study, released in 1994, stated its position in its title, *The Case for Transracial Adoption*. The authors' public comments and political actions were used in public policy dialogues as *evidence* in favor of transracial adoptions. During the early stages of congressional consideration of the Multiethnic Placement Act, which was designed to make transracial placements easier, Howard Altstein submitted a statement to sponsoring Senator Howard Metzenbaum's office in support of the bill (Altstein 1993). While Altstein sought to influence Congress, Rita Simon promoted the bill along with their new book in both scholarly and popular publications.[5] Their research was credited in the *Chronicle of Higher Education* with helping to influence the Texas legislature pass a law designed to promote transracial adoptions (Wheeler 1993).

Elizabeth Bartholet, who became one of the most vociferous opponents of racial matching after adopting two children from Peru, has relied on Simon and Altstein's work to argue for the removal of all restrictions to transracial placements. She has submitted letters to Congress, published op-ed pieces, written articles in law reviews, interdisciplinary journals, and scholarly anthologies, and published *Family Bonds: Adoption and the Politics of Parenting*, a book targeted at a general audience (Bartholet 1993a). In all her publications she draws on Simon and Altstein's longitudinal study to bolster her argument that racial matching discriminates against Black children in foster care and White parents seeking to adopt. This argument promotes "color-blind"—transracial—

adoptions as the solution to largescale problems in the U.S. child welfare system. Bartholet and others suggest that White families who adopt Black and mixed-race children will solve the problems of overpopulation in the foster care system and the disproportionate representation of racial-ethnic minorities in that population. However, this argument obscures the question of why so many African American and multiracial children are channeled into the foster care system in the first place. It promotes a narrative of Black family pathology and White "family values." It obscures a systemic analysis of poverty, and of racial and gender inequality in the labor market. It promotes an *individual* solution to a *systemic* social problem.

Several racial messages emerge from this argument. Read in a social context that conflates race and class, it tells us that the "culture of poverty" has so devastated "the Black family" that African Americans cannot take care of their own children. This is ultimately a *salvation narrative*, in which White families, bearing the torch of "family values" in popular representations, are the only families—or mothers—who can *save* Black children. Yet we are told time and again that these altruistic efforts are hindered by "racist" Black social workers who value a political cause over the "best interests" of children.

If we unquestionably accept this view of transracial adoption, the logical policy initiative would be one that encourages the adoption of Black children into White families. Yet this perspective must be examined more closely in light of the political stakes driving much of the discussion, and the racial context in which these views are expressed. Legislative pressure to disregard racial matching in adoptive placements is exerted most fiercely by two primary constituencies: Whites arguing for the "right" to adopt any child they desire, and conservative policy pundits whose primary interest is, I argue, a sort of *cultural eugenics* geared toward both the regulation of poor women's reproductive capacities and the socialization of their children into "productive citizens." This by no means describes all White families hoping to adopt Black children or all the political actors involved in these debates. There are certainly participants in this dialogue who are sincere in their concern for children in foster care.

Yet this view of the crisis has taken shape within an already existing movement primarily set in motion by legislators and prospective White adoptive and foster parents concerned with "reverse discrimination" in the adoption system. The parallels in the language of the 1996 adoption legislation with subsequent moves against supposed "racial preferences" in affirmative action are striking. The concern with "reverse discrimination" impinging on the "rights" of White families to adopt a child of color is evident in the range of sanctions the policy imposes and allows for. The federal policy

> provides that neither the State nor any other entity in the State that receives funds from the Federal Government and is involved in adoption or foster care placements may—deny to any person the opportunity to become an adoptive or a foster parent, on the basis of the race, color, or national origin of the person, or of the child, involved; or delay or deny the placement of a child for adoption or into foster care, on the basis of the race, color, or national origin of the adoptive or foster parent, or the child, involved. (United States Congress 1996: Public Law 104-188, sec. 1808)

The law empowers individuals aggrieved by such violations to bring legal action against the state or other violating entity in any U.S. district court. States who violate this law once will receive a 2 percent deduction in state aid for that quarter, 3 percent for the second violation, and 5 percent for subsequent violations; deductions will be made each quarter until the violation is corrected. Private agencies found in violation will remit all funds received from the state.

We must read this institutionalization of a "color-blind" child welfare system in the context of contemporary racial politics. This controversial issue has emerged at a time when affirmative action is under attack as "reverse racism," the Supreme Court has issued a number of landmark rulings supporting this popular view as well as a "color-blind" legislative system in the United States, the passage of the California Civil Rights Initiative in 1996 has legislated the dismantling of affirmative action in that state, and racist hate groups and armed militias are on the rise.

The ideological narrative of race and class in the United States posits that racial inequality existed in the past but was eradicated by the civil rights movement. This argument supports one of the central ideologies of this capitalist society, namely, that everyone has an equal chance in the economic marketplace, and that, lack of success is therefore due to individual failure rather than systemic inequality. In discussing the social and legislative gains of the civil rights movement, Howard Winant argues that:

despite these tremendous accomplishments, patterns of institutional dis-crimination proved to be quite obstinate, and the precise meaning of race, in politics and law as well as in everyday life, remained undefined. The am-biguity of race in the post–civil rights period has now reached the point where any hint of *race consciousness* is viewed suspiciously as an expression of *racism.* (emphasis in original) (Winant 1994:67)

Those for whom "color blindness" is a goal may perceive attention to racial survival skills and the African American cultural identities of tran-sracial adoptees as racist separatism. Their assumption—or at least de-sire—is that race does not matter and should not be highlighted; their primary explanatory category for attention to race is racism. Questions of racial identity and survival skills do not fit neatly into their racial worldview. Additionally, calls for the creation of a Black cultural identity by transracial adoptees are further devalued by the "culture of poverty" thesis that has been widely accepted by both centrists and conservatives. In a context in which U.S. poverty is largely represented as Black, "Black culture" merges with a "culture of poverty" in the popular imagination.

The "culture of poverty" explanation has had a profound influence on public policy discussions in the second half of the twentieth century and has been one of the central explanatory systems drawn on in the con-temporary discourse about adoption and the social welfare system. An-thropologist Oscar Lewis coined the term in his 1959 study of Mexican families, in which he argued that people living in conditions of poverty develop a culture or way of life in response to their exclusion from main-stream society. Social commentators have extrapolated Lewis's concept to explain the causes and perpetuation of poverty in general. This generic "culture" is generally said to be characterized by female-headed house-holds, laziness, lack of motivation, lack of a work ethic, and an orienta-tion toward the present. Sociologist Stephen Steinberg discusses Lewis's explanation for intergenerational poverty as follows:

Once a culture of poverty is formed, he argues, it assumes a "life of its own" and is passed on from parents to children through ordinary channels of culture transmission. As Lewis writes: "By the time slum children are age six or seven, they have usually absorbed the basic values and attitudes of their subculture. Thereafter they are psychologically unready to take full advantage of changing conditions or improved opportunities that may develop in their lifetime" (Lewis 1966:5). The adaptations of one generation thus become the inherited culture of the next, creating a self-perpetuating cycle of poverty. (Steinberg 1989:107)

There are three particularly salient issues here. First, this formulation, as co-opted from Lewis's study, obscures the systemic causes of poverty and inequality by essentially blaming poor families for causing their own poverty through a lack of morals or good values. In the contemporary public discourse regarding family and poverty, middle-class families are cast as the indisputable possessors of good "family values," and their location in the middle class is assumed to be a result of these values. Second, this explanation suggests that public policies designed to eradicate poverty and inequality in the labor market are futile; if such a culture takes on "a life of its own" it is unlikely to be displaced by social policies. Finally, and perhaps most significant in relation to questions of adoption and race, this culture is sustained and reproduced through familial channels of socialization, leading to a "self-perpetuating cycle of poverty."

The politics of family, race, and poverty are complex issues. The dominant policy argument regarding transracial adoption asserts that the "reverse racism" of Black social workers who support and enforce racial matching policies is the only significant barrier keeping Black children from permanently leaving the "limbo" of foster care through adoption. Thus, proponents of this position argue that the solution to the problems of the U.S. foster care system is national legislation abolishing the use of race in the adoptive placement of children. This is a convenient and appealing social narrative. However, despite its attractiveness, the social workers I interviewed believed it will probably do virtually nothing to change the lives of children of color in foster care.

The View from Here: Social Workers' Counternarrative

Sharon Williams was director of a private adoption agency specializing in the placement of African American children in the San Francisco Bay area, and member of the NABSW, when I interviewed her in 1995. She discussed the gap between her view of the issues in transracial adoption and the way such issues are represented in the media as follows:

Sharon: I don't know if you saw [pause] um [pause] um, uh, oh, the child's name is Isaiah.
Sandi: Losing Isaiah?
Sharon: Yeah, *Losing Isaiah.*
Sandi: Oh yeah. Did you see it?
Sharon: I saw it. Of course I was invited to the premiere. And I thought, well, it had all the sensational stuff happening in there but it was clear to me that families sometimes—I can see them saying, "Oh this is fine. This is our child that we adopted." And they don't mind other people looking at them. Because in fact they get a lot of attention from people looking at them. But when it becomes more of an issue, I think, for families—and the movie couldn't go into that—is when the child gets older. So the scene where the little boy is putting his hand inside of his sister's hand and she asks him the question, "What's the difference?" And he says, "Your hand is bigger than mine." And I think in the audience where I was you know everyone went "ahhhh." You know, but I said ask that same little child that when he's older, and it won't just be that "Your hand is bigger than mine." And it's the innocence that we try to capture. Because when you look at transracial placements they are not happening with kids that are over two years of age. But the number of kids that are languishing in the foster care system are kids that are older. So have we really impacted adoptions when we say well, any home is okay, and the reason that there's a problem is that there are not enough homes?

Several issues emerge here. The scene from the film that Sharon cited involved Isaiah, a three-year-old African American boy who was adopted into a White family. What made the scene powerful for some viewers, including a number of film critics, was the child's "color-blind" response when his White older sister placed his hand in hers and asked, "What's the difference?" Isaiah had not yet learned about racial difference. He only saw that his hand was smaller. But as Sharon Williams pointed out, he would learn to see race as he grew older. The transracial adoptees that Isaiah represents may grow up learning that they live in a "color-blind" world, but they will inevitably learn at some point that the rest of society is not like their "color-blind" family. And these lessons may be learned in quite a painful way. While the issue of racial difference in transracially adoptive families may be minor in the early years, it often becomes more pressing as children reach adolescence.

Sharon Williams raised another issue central to the public policy dialogue. As she pointed out, most transracial placements involve infants and young toddlers, yet these are generally not the children languishing in foster care. The children in foster care who are most in need of adoptive families and the most difficult to place are over three years old, are members of sibling groups, and/or have emotional, physical, or developmental disabilities. While the public discourse has been dominated by assertions that it is race that keeps children in foster care, my interviewees contended that it is race as it interacts with these other issues that makes adoptive placements more difficult.

The perspective of social workers and agency directors who are involved in the daily practices of adoption and foster care is quite different from what we encounter in public discourse. During 1995 and 1996, I conducted in-depth interviews with sixteen directors and social workers in public and private adoption agencies that were part of an interactive network in the placement of "special needs" children in California and the Mid-Atlantic region. Four of those I interviewed were African American women, three of them members of the NABSW, and one was a Black man, also an active member of the NABSW. I interviewed ten White women and one White man, none of whom, to my knowledge, were members of the NABSW. I have changed all my interviewees' names and the names of their agencies to protect their privacy.

My identity as an adoptee not only shapes my political concerns in this analysis; it also affected my interviews with the social workers. I usually disclosed that I am an adoptee at an early stage of an interview. This information never failed to evoke a warm response. To many of the social workers I was like one of "their kids." This connection served as a bridge of alliance. Seeing me as a part of their world strengthened their sense that we could work together as allies against the legislators they saw as being out of touch with the needs of children.

Social workers, while subject to the same public rhetoric about transracial adoption and welfare reform as the rest of us, are also in the unique position of enacting and enforcing many of the social policies crafted in the halls of Congress and the Executive Office. Working in the social welfare system gives them a different perspective on the possible effectiveness of legislative measures and the impact such policies may have on the families and children that they interact with on a daily basis. While I want to be clear that I do not see their perspectives as "truth" in relation to the political allegories in the public realm, I believe their social location gives them a useful vantage point accessible to few people outside these social institutions. My interviews with these social workers made palpable to me the possible ramifications of the new policies in the lives of families and children. In view of the connection between identity, family, and public policy, it is evident that the public debate regarding state support to poor women and those most "fit" to parent their children will have major social consequences.

There was unanimous agreement among those I interviewed that lifting the restrictions on transracial placements would do little or nothing to help the growing population of children waiting in foster care. The primary reason they gave for their view that this legislation would not accomplish what it set out to do was that *race is not the sole factor that keeps a child in foster care.* While the mainstream narrative equates a child's "special needs" status with race, in fact this is only one factor among several that make adoptive placements more difficult. The consensus among my informants was that in most areas of the country what classifies a child as "special needs" was a combination of factors, one of which was race. Race interacts with three other variables: age, being a member of a sibling group, and disability.

Agency workers verified that the number of children entering foster care had increased dramatically in the 1980s and 1990s. They attributed this largely to rising levels of poverty, the dismantling of social supports for poor women and their children, and what they identified as a growth in addiction to drugs and alcohol. They argued that these factors had not only increased the number of children being removed from their families of origin, but had also changed the population of children entering care. A number of social workers argued that an increase of drug exposure *in utero* had led to the proliferation of a broad range of physical, developmental, and emotional disabilities. Linda Stevens, director of an East Coast agency for Black children, explained:

Linda: I started working in child welfare in 1969. I was there briefly, and then came back in '74, and I've seen a huge increase in the severity of the problems the children have in the foster care system. A decrease in the number of healthy infants being placed voluntarily, and a great increase in the number of children coming into foster care because of abuse and neglect. And I think the most dramatic shift was occurring probably in the mid-'80s as the crack epidemic began to hit. At the same time that there was a huge effort to prevent children from coming into service in the first place, so there were a lot of prevention services that were put into place in the 1980s. There was a great emphasis on keeping children in foster care for only a very short period of time, putting dramatically intensive services into the birth family. And when children did come into foster care getting the children back either with the birth families or with relatives. So that those children who actually came into foster care and those children who stayed in foster care and had their plan changed to adoption were the most damaged children. Damaged by drug exposure prior to birth. Damaged by living in a crack household. And damaged because the birth parents did not have the potential and many times the extended family didn't either, because there was just epidemic drug involvement.

The "crack epidemic" was cited by a number of social workers as the cause of an increase in drug exposure *in utero,* and a corresponding growth in a new range of "disabilities." They reported that these issues had created a population of children in foster care who were very hard to place in adoptive homes because they were profoundly difficult to parent. Many of these kids had health problems and/or disabilities that would need ongoing medical and/or psychological care.

It is important to read the narratives of social workers through the lens of public discourse as well. They were not immune to media narratives about the "pathology" of the "underclass." As Dorothy Roberts documents, the surge in the use of crack cocaine in the 1980s ushered in a wave of media panic involving drug exposure *in utero,* primarily among African Americans. As she explains, "The press often gave medically inaccurate descriptions of crack's impact on children. The *New York Times,* for example, stated that pregnant women were 'producing a new generation of innocent addicts,' erroneously implying that babies exposed prenatally to crack are all born automatically hooked on the drug" (Roberts 1997:156).

This frenzy over newborn crack addicts led to "predictions of the tremendous burdens that crack babies were destined to impose on law-abiding taxpayers" through hospital care, foster care, and public education for "permanently damaged" children that would "ultimately prey on the rest of society as criminals and welfare dependents" (Roberts 1997:157). Such predictions increased the vigilance of health care workers and social workers in testing and monitoring the drug exposure of infants primarily born to low-income women of color (Roberts 1997). This led to an increase in the removal of infants from mothers at birth.

In an interview in 1996 Elizabeth Fisher, a child welfare supervisor in the Social Services Department of a major Bay area county agency, discussed the way that children entered foster care:

Sandi: So, the kids that come into the county system, how do they get into the system generally? I mean, we have this idea about you know, infant relinquishment—the *old* mythology of what it used to be like. Is it like that at all?

Elizabeth: It's not like that, at least in public agencies. Um . . . we get children because we have filed a petition in juvenile court alleging that the biological parents either aren't available or aren't able to care for these kids. Most of them are filed in infancy. Some, you know, are filed on parents who get to take babies home, but can't care for them.

Sandi: So they're all really taken away from their families?

Elizabeth: Yes.

Sandi: Do you get infants?

Elizabeth: No. We don't get any child in this project [adoption] until long-term placement is adjudicated as the permanent plan.

In other words, even children removed at birth waited for a period of time in foster care while mothers underwent drug treatment or completed other aspects of reunification plans. Thus, most children did not become available for adoption until they were at least a few years old (depending upon their age when they entered foster care), and many were part of sibling groups. The goal was generally to keep siblings together, and it was often difficult to find families willing or able to adopt more than one child at a time. Children who were over three years old were more difficult to place as well.

"Disability" is no longer defined in terms of recognizable physical and/or developmental limitations. A majority of the children in foster care have some kind of physical, developmental, emotional, or behavioral disability, many of which are attributed to drug exposure *in utero*. A healthy Black infant who is not a member of a sibling group and has not been exposed to drugs does not qualify as a "special needs" child in the San Francisco or Washington, D.C., areas and will be easy to place.

Theresa Sanchez, Special Needs Adoption Program Coordinator in another Bay area County Social Services Department explained her view of recent adoption legislation in an interview in 1995:

Theresa: First of all, I don't buy the premise behind the Metzenbaum bill [the Multiethnic Placement Act of 1994]. Time will tell, but . . . You know, the so-called premise is that it will keep—it will stop the delay of placements. I don't believe that because I don't see that the Caucasian families who come to us—I don't think will be any more open to older children who are very involved with "special needs" than the families of color who have come to us. My fear is that the Caucasian families who don't have access to Caucasian children will be choosing the children of color who the families of color also want. . . . I think there is going to be competition over the wrong kids. And you know, perhaps there will be a few children who will be matched, but I don't think overall it's a solution. I think there are children that no families right now are very open to. . . . People who know anything—who really know who's out there, who's looking for kids, who the kids are don't buy it.

The dominant narrative depends on a particular version of the history of Black children in the adoption and foster care system. This view ignores the history of systematic disregard for children of color demonstrated by the child welfare system until social protest led to reforms in the 1960s and 1970s, and the decline in availability of White infants led many Whites to consider adopting Black infants. Also largely ignored in the mainstream discourse is the history of discrimination, both overt and covert, experienced by African American families in the U.S. social welfare system.

The public narrative asserts that the 1972 statement by the National Association of Black Social Workers opposing transracial adoption stopped the practice altogether, and that the association's power continues to enforce racial matching policies. The power of Black social workers is greatly exaggerated. As discussed above, all my informants—most of whom were not members of the NABSW—stated that transracial adoptions had continued to take place, though at a slower pace than they did in the late 1960s and early 1970s, when the largest number of such placements were made. All recognized the tensions surrounding the position statement, and several White social workers cited it as a critical moment in raising their own consciousness about racial issues.

Dr. Harriet Morrison, founding director of one of the Bay area's private agencies focusing on special needs adoptions, and a member of the NABSW, emphasized the importance of considering the 1972 position statement in historical context. She explained that the position against transracial placements was an attempt to draw attention to the fact that in the United States Black families have not been valued or protected. It was an attempt to convey that:

> *Harriet:* We are somebody. We have a responsibility to take care of our families, and to demand respect inside the communities and *especially* outside the community. And to do less than that is a kind of death for us. . . . I think it really was a message saying: *We are somebody.* We *can* take care of our families. We can be other than domestics and kind of be always the least accomplished in society. And I think it was a call to protect, expand . . . I'm searching for words here, Sandi.

| 153 |

Sandi: Respect?

Harriet: Respect, but take charge and elevate the family, offset the increasingly demeaning press that was being put out about our families.

As was true at the end of the twentieth century, Black families were the target of a great deal of negative public attention in the late 1960s and early 1970s. In *Black Families in White America,* Andrew Billingsley commented on the treatment of Black families in family studies scholarship in 1968: "Two tendencies, then, are current in studies of American families. The first, and most general, is to ignore Negro families altogether. The second is to consider them only insofar as they may be conceived as a social problem" (Billingsley 1968:198).

Indeed, a great deal of negative press constructing Black families as a social problem had grown out of the 1965 Moynihan Report which characterized African American families as a "tangle of pathology." Billingsley explained that "coming just at the time the nation was trying to find a single cause of the Watts riots, Moynihan's thesis struck a responsive chord in the collective American breast" (1968:199–200). The NABSW's position paper denied that African American families were "pathologically" deviant from White middle-class values. It read:

Ethnicity is a way of life in these United States, and the world at large; a viable, sensitive, meaningful and legitimate societal construct. This is no less true, nor legitimate for Black people than for other ethnic groups. . . . Overt ethnic identification, especially for Blacks, was long suppressed by the social and political pressures speaking to total assimilation of all peoples in that great melting pot. . . . Black people are now developing an honest perception of this society; the myths of assimilation and of our inferiority stand bare under glaring light. We now proclaim our truth, substance, beauty and value as ourselves without apology or compromise. The affirmation of our ethnicity promotes our opposition to the trans-racial placements of Black children.

The family is the basic unit of society; one's first, most pervasive and only consistent culturing life experience. Humans develop their sense of values, identity, self concept, attitudes and basic perspective within the family group. Black children in white homes are cut off from the healthy

development of themselves as Black people, which development is the normal expectation and only true humanistic goal. (NABSW 1972:1)

The position paper's alleged assertion that transracial adoption was "cultural genocide" has haunted the organization ever since; the association
is continually castigated for this view and cast as villains in the popular
narrative. In fact, that phrase did not appear in the actual position statement. While the NABSW is repeatedly cited as continuing to hold such
a position, its stance regarding such placements has in fact changed since
1972. In the late 1990s its position emphasized the preservation and
support of Black families. It stressed that more emphasis on family
preservation could stem the tide of children in need of out-of-home care.
When adoptions were necessary it stressed that every effort should be
made to place children in homes of similar racial and ethnic backgrounds
whenever possible, but that transracial placements were appropriate in
certain circumstances. Its 1990s position stated quite explicitly that children should not languish in foster care unnecessarily.

While some agencies are more successful than others at placing children in same-race families, all the social workers I interviewed affirmed
their belief in the importance of racial matching in adoption. One of the
most common statements I heard was that adoption is hard enough for
kids—there are almost always abandonment, attachment, and identity issues to be dealt with—that placing a child in a family of another race
added further complication in their lives. A child who looks starkly different from other members of his or her family is *always* visible as an
adoptee; transracial adoptees can never "pass" as "regular" people when
with their families. The social workers and adoptees I interviewed
stressed the importance of awareness and education for families that did
decide to adopt transracially. A number of agencies had a list of questions
they asked White families to consider, including the racial makeup of the
community they lived in, the diversity of their social circle, and the feelings of their extended families. One agency asked whether or not the parents had African American friends who were close enough to them to feel
comfortable about pointing out a racist or problematic comment or act
by the parents if there was one. They stressed that one of the most important things that White families should be aware of was that they

would not be able to do everything for their child that he or she would need. Margaret Danielson, an adoption worker for many years on the East Coast and the White adoptive parent of twelve Black and multiracial grown children, emphasized the limitations of White parents who raised Black kids:

> *Margaret:* The bottom line is, just because—We did everything right. You know, we moved to the city. They were in integrated schools, integrated everything. What we do is raise White kids in Black bodies. No matter what we do, because we can't do anything else. And so when they go out into the world it's like a gigantic shock. They're much more comfortable with Whites than Blacks. But Whites are always much more comfortable with them [than with other Blacks].

While she recognized her own limitations as a White parent, she also stressed the importance of parents making every possible effort to become a multiracial family in a multiracial community, not just in color but also in culture.

Most of the social workers I interviewed strongly advocated the recruitment of African American families as one of the normal activities of adoption agencies. The NABSW, along with other social workers and groups like the Children's Defense Fund and the Child Welfare League, lobbied against the 1996 legislation. This lobbying effort included a strong push to include funds earmarked for recruitment in the allocation of federal block grants for child welfare. The logic behind the legislation was the premise that there were not enough Black families willing or able to adopt Black children. While it is true that in most areas of the country fewer African American than White families approach adoption agencies, this must be understood in the context of a history of institutional discrimination in the U.S. social welfare system. Dawn Day's research has shown that African Americans have encountered institutional racism at every stage of the adoption screening process (Day 1979). The 1980 National Urban League Black Pulse Survey of a nationally representative sample of African American families found that three million heads of household expressed interest in expanding their families through the formal adoption of a Black child (Hill et al. 1993:33).

Recruitment efforts in the greater San Francisco Bay area and other parts of the country have shown that Black families are not reluctant to adopt but reluctant to subject themselves to the intense scrutiny of the child welfare system. This is what keeps many Black families from approaching agencies. Three of the agencies I visited in the San Francisco area—one public, two private—were involved in a successful collaborative recruitment campaign. They met with tremendous success when they approached African Americans in community settings and simply explained how many children they had that needed families.

The counternarrative that emerged in my interviews with social workers and agency directors regarding the adoptive placement of children with "special needs" problematizes the ways in which transracial adoption is represented in political rhetoric and the popular media. The public narrative sees race as the determinant of "special needs" status; this argument co-opts the language of racial equality and in the process denies the saliency of disability, age, and membership in a sibling group. A primary point of contention concerns the definition of "special needs," which make adoptive placements more difficult and less likely. When race alone is seen as the determinant of a child's fate in the child welfare system, the simple and logical policy solution is to remove the supposedly "racist" barriers to transracial placements. The understanding of the social workers I spoke with was that those publicly arguing for the increase of transracial adoptions were primarily interested in Whites gaining "access" to Black *infants*, without stating that explicitly. Margaret Danielson discussed the new legislation:

Margaret: The government has passed a law that you must place, you know [without regard to race]. Of course, that doesn't mean that everyone is going to, nor did it mean that anybody wouldn't have before. Where the problem is that that law came as a response to parents who wanted babies. I mean nobody was going to— If somebody came in and wanted a twelve-year-old Black girl with c.p. [cerebral palsy], you know, anybody would have done— They would have told the people you best move your butt—you know, they're not going to lose a placement for that kid. It's the people out there baby-grabbing. And so, it's not going to really change anybody's policies.

The public narrative relied on the life experiences of "special needs" foster children to argue for the "right" of Whites to adopt the prized "commodities" of the adoption market, namely, healthy, nondisabled infants. The fulcrum of this argument was race.

The social workers I interviewed did not deny that children of color were affected differently than White children in the adoption/foster care system, but they identified the sources of and solutions to the inequality of the system in other ways. Most importantly, they made it painfully clear that the popular narrative regarding adoption and race did not respond to the needs of most African American children. In fact, it obscured the needs of children of all racial-ethnic groups with a broad range of physical, developmental, emotional, and behavioral disabilities, as well as older children and members of sibling groups. Race does affect the chances a child has for permanent adoptive placement, but typically it is race as it intersects with disability, age, and/or status as a member of a sibling group that makes adoptive placement more difficult and prolongs a child's stay in foster care.

Socializing "Productive Citizens"

There is a growing consciousness that children are *at risk*. But the point I want to make here is

> that there is also a growing sense of children themselves as *the risk*—and thus of some children themselves as people out of place and excess populations to be eliminated, while others must be controlled, reshaped, and harnessed to changing social ends. Hence, the centrality of children, both as symbolic figures and as objects of contested forms of socialization, in the contemporary politics of culture. (Stephens 1995:13).

Questions of race, gender, class, and family have become intimately intertwined with the politics of culture, nation, and citizenship in the public policy and media discourse regarding adoption and welfare reform. When this cultural dialogue is placed in the context of conservative policy discussions about poverty, family, and governmental support a new aspect of the narrative is made apparent—that *children are the risk*. The central concern in this public discourse is the use of social policy to engineer the socialization of "legitimate"—that is "productive" middle-class—citizens. Because adoption policy literally regulates the social construction of identity, it offers us a rich site for exploring the ubiquitous power of social policy in shaping the lives of Americans. It also discloses a conservative social vision that maps out the "appropriate" locations for "legitimate" and "illegitimate" identities in the socioeconomic landscape. Drawing on public policies, the Congressional Record, news, editorials, and other published work, in this section I discuss the conservative social narrative surrounding adoption and welfare reform.

When it comes to transracial adoption, questions of socialization and race are inseparable. When the myth that race alone relegates children to foster care is debunked, conservative policymakers and advocates claiming to abolish racial discrimination in the child welfare system lose the central point of their argument. Additionally, the ostensibly altruistic salvation narrative of transracial adoption in which White families alone are deemed capable of "saving" Black children from the fate of urban poverty, crime, drug addiction, and chaos reads distinctly like a 1990s urbanized version of the "White man's (or family's) burden" of "civilizing the natives." In fact, the insidious nature of this argument is apparent in the conservative political discourse advocating adoption as a "solution" to the "social ill" of "illegitimacy." Alongside the language regarding the "best interests" of children through the promotion of "color-blind" adoptions, is the discourse of children as a risk, threat, and unsocialized menace to civil society. In this perspective children and teens in the inner city threaten to become a generation of criminal "super-predators."

The representational context for this discourse is rife with dangerous images of inner-city Blacks. Herman Gray explains:

> The black underclass appears as menace and a source of social disorganization in news accounts of black urban crime, gang violence, drug use, teenage pregnancy, riots, homelessness, and general aimlessness. In news accounts (and in Hollywood films such as *Colors*), poor blacks (and Hispanics) signify a social menace that must be contained. Poor urban blacks help to mark the boundaries of appropriate middle class behavior as well as the acceptable routes to success. (Gray 1995:431)

Urban "gangsta" films work intertextually with nightly newscasts of inner-city crime to provide a readily available array of images and narratives that vigorously punctuate the political rhetoric warning of ominous social threats emerging from the "breakdown of the family." Policy discussions both on the floor of Congress and in published works have cited "family breakdown" as the root cause for the major social problems in the late-twentieth-century United States. In congressional testimony on welfare and "illegitimacy," William J. Bennett explicitly linked family, race, citizenship, and the maintenance of civil society:

> Every civilized society has understood the importance of keeping families together. They have known, too, that you cannot raise young boys to become responsible citizens unless there are other good men in their lives— men who will spend time with them, discipline them and love them. (Bennett 1995)

Charles Murray, a conservative policy analyst and one of two primary Republican advisors on welfare reform in the 104th Congress, testified to the House Subcommittee on Human Resources as follows:

> My proposition is that illegitimacy is the single most important social problem of our time—more important than crime, drugs, poverty, illiteracy, welfare or homelessness because it drives everything else. Doing something about it is not just one more item on the American policy agenda, but should be at the top. (Murray 1994)

Bennett's and Murray's social vision is codified in the language of the welfare legislation of 1996. A long list of "the negative consequences of raising children in single-parent homes" is cited, including the greater likelihood of children's poor academic performance, the higher rates of arrest for teens, higher incidence of teenage pregnancy, and higher rates of violent crime in neighborhoods with large populations of single-parent families. The bill then states:

> Therefore, in light of this demonstration of the crisis in our Nation, it is the sense of the Congress that prevention of out-of-wedlock pregnancy and reduction in out-of-wedlock birth are very important Government interests and the policy contained in part A of title IV of the Social Security Act (as amended by section 103(a) of this Act) is intended to address the crisis. (United States Congress 1996: Public Law 104-193, sec. 101)

Though Republicans were not successful in pushing through the most draconian version of the Personal Responsibility Act, the law dismantled the U.S. social welfare system. Federal entitlement to benefits ceased, giving way to the allocation of block grants to facilitate state-run assistance programs. The version of the bill President Clinton eventually signed into law placed a five-year lifetime limit on benefits, required able-bodied adults to work after two years, required minors to be enrolled in school and living at home or with a responsible adult, required unwed mothers to cooperate in identifying paternity, disallowed support to anyone convicted of a felony drug charge, and denied benefits to *legal* immigrants.

As I have discussed, the same week this bill was signed into law, legislation was also signed providing a substantial tax deduction to couples who adopt and barring federally funded adoption agencies from considering race in the adoptive placement of a child. It is no accident that these bills were paired. In fact, up until the final version of the welfare reform bill, the legislation removing all restrictions on transracial adoption was part of the Personal Responsibility Act and was located in the section designed to combat the so-called epidemic of "illegitimacy." As is evident in the language of the legislation itself, this social narrative posits "illegitimacy" and single-parent families as the cause of poverty and social ills, and declares that the prevention of out-of-wedlock pregnancy and the promotion of two-parent families are in the best interests of the Nation.

Though these social problems are unproblematically cited as the outcome of family forms that deviate from two-parent nuclear families, feminists and other progressive scholars explain them as the consequence of poverty. Contrary to the seemingly irrefutable perspective of conservatives and centrists sounding the alarm about social decay and "family breakdown," there is a respected body of literature disputing the causal connections made here between single-parent families and poverty, crime, and immorality. In her book *In the Name of the Family* (1996), sociologist Judith Stacey provides a detailed analysis of the "new familism" widespread among right-wing and centrist politicians, as well as non-feminist sociologists, whose work has been used to justify public policies designed to promote middle-class, two-parent, heterosexual families. The new orthodoxy regarding the relative merits of two-parent and single-parent families draws on the work of such sociologists as Judith Wallerstein and Sandra Blakeslee (1989), Sara McLanahan and Gary

Sandefur (1994), William Galston (1993), and David Popenoe (1988) to establish as "truth" the belief that a stable marriage provides the best situation for children, and that single-parent and stepfamilies are detrimental to the healthy development of children:

> through interlocking networks of think tanks, organizations, periodicals, and policy institutes, these social scientists have been constructing a virtual scholarly and popular consensus in the media in support of the very narrative about universal family values that succumbed to feminist and other forms of scrutiny in academia. Saturating the media-beltway world they have come to inhabit with the ideology of new familism, they misleadingly maintain that social science has confirmed Moynihan's warning about the socially destructive effects of single motherhood, illegitimacy, and fatherless families. (Stacey 1996:97)

Stacey effectively critiques this system of explanation through a close examination of the ways in which this particular construction of academic knowledge developed and became accepted as social scientific "fact." She exposes the common sources of the funding of many of these centrist scholars and the "incestuous . . . reciprocal citation practices of these cultural crusaders" (Stacey 1996:59). She reveals that research countering the view of single-parent families as pathological was marginalized and downplayed by centrist scholars, as they exaggerated the benefits to children of having two married parents. She emphasizes that: "Most research indicates that a stable, intimate relationship with one responsible, nurturant adult is a child's surest route to becoming the same kind of adult. In short, the research scale tips handily toward those who stress the quality of family relationships over their form" (1996:60).[6]

The writings of both Daniel Patrick Moynihan and Charles Murray were influential in changing the public perception that single-parent families are harmful to children to the belief that out-of-wedlock births are at the root of most contemporary social problems. The new orthodoxy among conservatives and centrists alike was that "illegitimacy" was responsible for most of the social ills of the late twentieth century: poverty, sexual "immorality," crime, drug abuse, drug trafficking, gang violence, and the general "social decay" of inner cities in the United States. In his discussion of the rising percentage of "illegitimate" births to Black women (he cited 68 percent in 1991), Murray drew on one of the central theses of the 1965 Moynihan Report on Black families, namely, that single mothers were incapable of properly socializing and disciplining their sons, to explain what he saw as the social chaos of inner cities: "But if the proportion of fatherless boys in a given community were to reach such levels, surely the culture must be 'Lord of the Flies' writ large, the values of unsocialized male adolescents made norms— physical violence, immediate gratification and predatory sex. That is the culture now taking over the black inner city" (Murray 1993).

Central to this narrative of socialization was an unabashed belief in the relative "unfitness" of poor mothers versus "fitness" of middle-class ones. The danger cited was Moynihan's ominous threat of a Black "matriarchal" culture that flaunted its disregard for the strictures of patriarchy. As political writer Richard Cohen explained, "We fear our children, not because there are too many of them, but because too many of them lack fathers" (Cohen 1993).

In his 1994 essay, "Poor Suffering Bastards: An Anthropologist Looks at Illegitimacy," published in the conservative Heritage Foundation's journal *Policy Review*, Foundation Fellow David W. Murray articulated the connections between marriage, socialization, and the threat of social chaos as follows:

> Here is the pertinent meaning of the "legitimacy" of children: Legitimacy is nothing more nor less than the orderly transfer of social meaning across the generations. Remember that children are the ultimate illegal aliens. They are undocumented immigrants to our world, who must be socialized and invested with identity, a culture, and an estate. By conferring legitimacy marriage keeps this process from becoming chaos. (D. Murray 1994:10)

This social narrative was a foundational myth in the 1996 dismantling of the U.S. social welfare system. In this view, Aid to Families with Dependent Children was seen as the cause of out-of-wedlock births, the assumption being that poor women got pregnant in order to secure government subsistence. Thus, the "solution" to this social crisis lay in social welfare reform. Charles Krauthammer advised, "Stop the welfare checks. The check, generated by the first illegitimate birth, says that government will play the role of father and provider. It sustains a deranged social structure of children having children and raising them alone and abandoned by their men" (Krauthammer 1993). Social commentators gave Charles Murray credit for first introducing the argument that the simple remedy was to abolish AFDC as this would force unwed mothers to find jobs or rely on their families for support, removing the incentive for, and increasing the stigma of, out-of-wedlock births.

It is at this juncture that this social narrative takes on gothic tones. Murray explicated the next piece of his social vision as follows: "What about women who can find no support but keep the baby anyway? There are laws already on the books about the right of the state to take a child from a neglectful parent" (Murray 1993). Murray argued that the only social policy initiative radical enough to alter the inevitable fate of children born into a "culture of poverty" was to remove all restrictions on transracial adoption, and to make all adoptions irrevocable and as easy as possible for two-parent families (Murray 1993; 1994).

I read this social dialogue as a sort of *cultural eugenics* geared toward both the regulation of poor women's reproductive behavior and the social construction and socialization of economically "productive citizens." When compared to the eugenic movement of the early twentieth century that sought to prevent White "race suicide" through the control of fertility among poor women and women of color, the insidious racial agenda of the 1996 legislation seems clear. Sociologist Kristin Luker discusses women's sexuality and "illegitimacy" in the context of the eugenic movement:

> Whether passive victim or willing participant, the young woman who was sexually active, particularly outside marriage, and particularly when intercourse led to an out-of-wedlock birth, was perceived as deviant, unfit. And the problem did not end with her: her child represented the antithesis of reformers' hopes for societal improvement, by becoming yet another link in a chain of unfitness. Born to an immature and presumably unfit woman, the illegitimate child evoked reformers' worst fears for future generations. (Luker 1996:36–37)

In the early years of the twentieth century these social fears led to movements for eugenic sterilization and birth control among poor women and immigrants. In the post-Holocaust and post–civil rights movement era such racist and classist inclinations must adopt a more "race-neutral" veneer. While essentialist racism—the pseudoscientific explanation of the supposed inferiority of "non-White" people—was the "legitimating" knowledge driving the eugenics of the early twentieth century, at the end of that century "cultural determinism" joined biology as the engine of racial oppression. The focus on biological heritability led to efforts to curtail the "excess" fertility of undesirables; in a framework dominated by the "culture of poverty" social engineering was envisioned through adoption. Considered in this light, policies concerning adoption—that is, which men and women the state sanctions as "fit" parents—serve both to "legitimate" children born out of wedlock and to regulate their "proper" socialization into "virtuous" citizens through the construction of "legitimate" two-parent, middle-class, heterosexual families.

The construction of "legitimate" nuclear families is discussed as necessary for the good of the nation. Indeed, out-of-wedlock births are represented as a threat to Western civilization. As George Will explains: "Democracy depends on virtues that depend on socialization of children in the matrix of care and resources fostered by marriage" (Will 1993). However, underlying this concern over democratic virtue lurks the more base consideration of the future of U.S. competitiveness in the global market economy. Richard Cohen's editorial makes the connections clear: "About 1.2 million children are being born annually in single-parent homes. Without mature males as role models (not to mention disciplinarians), they are growing up unsocialized—prone to violence, unsuitable for employment and thus without prospects or hope" (Cohen 1993).

The key phrases here are "growing up unsocialized" and "unsuitable for employment." Once again, the work of Charles Murray, along with Richard Herrnstein, makes the connections clear. The central thesis of Herrnstein and Murray's *The Bell Curve: Intelligence and Class Structure in American Life* (1994) is that IQ determines economic and social success, and that the global economy is based on the manipulation of information. Thus, the future economic viability of the United States is dependent on its citizens with high IQs—what the authors of *The Bell Curve* call the "cognitive elite." From their perspective, "productive" citizens are not defined by hard work, but by superior intelligence. Unproblematically accepting the belief that IQ tests accurately and objectively measure intelligence, they argue that African Americans are less intelligent than other racial groups; they state that on average Blacks score fifteen points less than Whites on IQ tests. They use this skewed data to account for racial stratification, arguing that poverty among Blacks is due to genetic inferiority rather than discrimination and oppression.[7] In their circular logic one's socioeconomic location is also evidence of one's intelligence. Not surprisingly, they argue that women with low IQs typically have "illegitimate" children, and of course, given their hereditarian logic those children inherit their mothers' incapacity for mental achievement. "Naturally," they are destined to live on the margins of society, never achieving for themselves, forever draining government resources.

However, Herrnstein and Murray do see one glimmer of hope for these lost children. Because for them intelligence is overwhelmingly shaped by genetics (they concede a small measure of influence to the environment), they believe social programs such as Head Start are doomed to failure. Yet they see one exception, and it is here that we come back to the intersection of socialization, public policy, and adoption. They argue that adoption is the only social intervention radical enough to raise the IQs, and thus the chances for economic success, of poor "illegitimate" children. The slippery quality of their arguments is undeniable here: when the biologically determinist explanation does not suit their argument they shift their emphasis to the cultural. The added bonus, they explain, is that "In terms of government budgets, adoption is cheap; the new parents bear all the costs of twenty-four-hour-a-day care for eighteen years or so" (Herrnstein and Murray 1994:416). They continue:

> If adoption is one of the only affordable and successful ways known to improve the life chances of disadvantaged children appreciably, why has it been so ignored in congressional debate and presidential proposals? Why do current adoption practices make it so difficult for would-be parents and needy infants to match up? Why are cross-racial adoptions so often restricted or even banned? . . . Anyone seeking an inexpensive way to do some good for an expandable number of the most disadvantaged infants should look at adoption (1994:416).

In Murray's editorial on welfare reform and adoption he also provided an option for "unadoptable" children: orphanages (Murray 1993).

Thus, in this social vision, children whose proper socialization cannot be ensured should be warehoused in public institutions. For those children not placed in adoptive homes Murray argued the government should "spend lavishly on orphanages." *The Bell Curve*, a racist, vitriolic book, was released shortly after Murray had laid out the basic elements of his reactionary social vision for welfare reform in the *Wall Street Journal* and in congressional testimony, and in many ways it can be read as the "scientific evidence" for his theories regarding work, poverty, and family. *The Bell Curve* is, in a sense, the "legitimating" text for Murray's draconian "solutions" to poverty, "illegitimacy," crime, and "family breakdown." As Judith Stacey astutely observes, social science has supplanted religion as the ultimate source of "truth" in centrist and conservative political discourse on families. However, as countless scholars from the sciences, social sciences, and humanities have demonstrated, this is by no means a "legitimate" scholarly work. As geneticists Joseph L. Graves and Amanda Johnson make clear:

> If a measurable depression in mean African American performance on specific cognitive tests exists, it is undoubtedly the result of the destructive physical and social environments in which the majority of African Americans have been forced to live in the United States over time. Without the elimination of the toxic conditions to which African Americans have been and are exposed, the debate concerning genetic differentials in generalized intelligence is scientifically meaningless. (Graves and Johnson 1995:290)

In my reading this narrative linking national economic strength, citizenship, intelligence, socialization, race, and adoption is fundamentally about what should be done with the people this information-based capitalist economy has no use for—the supposedly unintelligent masses who have become surplus labor. We continually return to the question of *socialization.* The options presented by Murray and others for the children the state removes from "unfit" unwed mothers—those unable to survive in this economy without AFDC—involve socialization and warehousing. Surplus children will be housed in orphanages or group homes, while residual adult labor will be channeled into prisons. The children placed for adoption will be raised by predominantly White, middle-class, heterosexual married couples in accordance with the "family values" of "legitimate," "productive" citizenship.

| CONCLUSION |

Narratives of Identity, Race, and Nation

I am interested in under what circumstances, for whom, and to do what in the world the political subject is constructed. In other words, *the state thinks the subject too*. Thus, to some extent, what we think of ourselves in relation to the world, what we imagine ourselves to be in relation to the world, is also, under most circumstances, at least partially a state project. (emphasis added)

—Lubiano 1996:65–66

Gabrielle: Well, I think identity is an issue, and then also bringing in sexuality and everything. I think that I'm always trying to search, and trying to find out, and trying to uncover, and trying to understand what Creole is, and where they live and what they eat, and what kind of music they listened to. I think that if I had stayed with my original family a lot of that would have just been given to me, and I would look and see faces similar to mine, at least in certain lights. Um, and you know that, in actuality hasn't been part of my experience. And so, I kind of have to seek it out. It's not handed to me. And so I don't know. It's hard for me to speculate on what might have been.

How was Gabrielle's identity a "state project"? The county adoption agency placed her in a White family, and told them she was Mexican and Creole. She was raised in a community and culture dominated by White-ness. In her mid-twenties she requested and received her "non-identifying information." This government document provided two significant classifications: "Negro/white" and "illegitimate." How did the state shape and direct the *routes* of Gabrielle's identity?

This genealogy of transracial adoptees' identities considers the social construction of adoptive selves through the patterns of language, narrative, and knowledge, the social mappings of power and policy that commingle to compose the multiple meanings of their lives. This interdisciplinary ethnographic study has brought together two areas of inquiry that are typically addressed separately—the study of identity and the study of public policy. I have demonstrated through a holistic, multifaceted analysis of the adoption issue that the identities of transracial adoptees are constructed and shaped by a broad range of factors, including the politics of family, race, and poverty; social policies regulating governmental aid; public policies governing child welfare and adoption; the practices of adoption agencies; existing cultural meaning systems, particularly those relating to race; media narratives; the social relations which bind adoptees to their communities; and the enculturation they receive from their families. While the dominant public voices in these social debates claim that their sole concern is the well-being of children in foster care, an exploration of the political and racial context in which the issue of transracial adoption has reemerged makes it clear that this debate has broader ramifications.

The social and political meanings of transracial adoption have differed in the two periods in which it became controversial—the 1970s and the 1990s—in ways consistent with the racial tenor of the times. As the public debate took shape between 1993 and 1996 the issue of White families adopting Black children became particularly charged, as it was paired with conservative proposals for welfare reform. Indeed, as I discussed in chapter 4, transracial adoption was presented as a "profamily," "antiracist," and "color-blind" *solution* to the so-called epidemic of "illegitimacy" in the United States. "Illegitimate" families—female-headed households—are typically represented as an inherently Black social problem that has spread to White families, thus endangering the whole of society by failing to socialize "productive" citizens. The social narratives drawn on to promote the adoption of Black children by White families represent Black families as incapable of taking care of their own children, and White families as the only hope for the "salvation" of African American children from inner-city poverty.

Yet in a political context in which "illegitimacy" is viewed as the *cause* of poverty, crime, violence, and teen pregnancy, the object of this "salvation" story goes beyond the individual child to the deliverance of society as a whole from the social chaos that a future generation of inner-city gang members, criminals, and teenage mothers threatens. Consequently we must question the state's representation of transracial adoptees' identities as unproblematic. In the service of the political and racial agenda noted above, the state has represented existing research on transracial adoption as "empirical proof" that adoption into White families is in the "best interests" of Black children, while delegitimating criticism of this social practice as ideological and racist. However, as I have discussed, the existing research does not adequately address the processes of identity formation among transracial adoptees.

I have demonstrated, based on my ethnographic interviews with twenty-two transracial adoptees, that while individual experiences vary greatly on account of specific familial and community relations, one thing is undeniably clear: the development of a meaningful sense of racial identity is profoundly complex and problematic for African American and multiracial adoptees raised in White families. While all these adults have managed to work out the racial implications of their lives for themselves, their acquisition of cultural maps to enable such negotiation has typically been a struggle. It is evident that transracial adoptees' identities and families are constructed and maintained through the complex interplay of the role of the state, racism, structural inequality, cultural meaning systems, and personal agency. Simplistic readings of transracial adoption as being categorically and unproblematically in both Black children's and society's "best interests" are thus unconvincing.

In the multifaceted, interdisciplinary analysis in this book I have been particularly concerned with the *social functions* of political allegories about transracial adoption and welfare reform. I would like to consider these questions of power and knowledge by mapping out the principal streams of discourse surrounding this social issue. I hope in this way to recontextualize the issue of transracial adoption to show that it is part of a broader and deeper landscape of meaning in the contemporary United States. The three central tensions interwoven throughout the social narratives about adoption involve culture and biology, "legitimacy" and "illegitimacy," and competing and contested definitions of race. In this chapter I address these three tensions as they relate to the key issues that emerged in this study. I then consider the implications of this book for the study of identity, family, race, and policy, and the directions it suggests for public policy about transracial adoption.

Culture, Biology, and Social Structure

Discussions of adoption in the Western world almost inevitably raise questions about biology and culture. In fact, the conceptualization of "nature" and "nurture" as the two factors responsible for human variability and individuality originated in the late nineteenth century with the infamous British eugenicist Francis Galton, and studies of adoptees as a means of exploring the relative influences of culture and biology on intelligence were first conducted in the early decades of the twentieth century (Cadoret 1990:25–27). In Galton's dualistic schema, nature was viewed as permanent and immutable and was thus cast as the stronger force in shaping human identity. With the rise of scientific racism, biological forces were seen as the source of the supposed inferiority of Blacks and other non-White peoples. Such pseudoscientific disciplines as phrenology and craniometry produced "scientific truths" supporting claims of inferiority that were used to justify oppression and rationalize inequality. Understandings of nature versus nurture in the shaping of identity have, from the inception been intertwined with questions of what defines race.[1]

In the contemporary moment these understandings are still routinely invoked in discussions about what shapes individual identities, whether adopted or not. In a society that idealizes "ideologies of authenticity," including biological kinship, adoptees often feel these issues deeply. The lack of information about our birth families often translates into frustration that we have no family medical history, no (known) biological ancestors, no (biologically based) physical resemblance with our families, and no sense of physical connection to our parents or knowledge of our birth. We know we have "alien" origins that guide our bodily development with biological, genetic maps sketched in indecipherable code.

The adoptees I interviewed discussed their identities through the categories of biology and culture, often mourning their lack of knowledge of a biological heritage. However, transracial adoption adds another element to the picture, for most of my informants felt the absence of their original *cultures* as well. While a few who were raised in predominantly White communities with little interaction with other African Americans or knowledge of Black culture did not feel compelled or comfortable enough to explore such issues in adulthood, most of the people I interviewed had (re)constructed their own sense of racial identity as Black people living in a racially stratified society. Indeed, they often experienced a sense of *culture shock* when they first encountered Black folks. Frequently, their quest for cultural knowledge and survival skills had been motivated by blatant racist treatment and the confusion and pain arising therefrom.

However, while tensions between biology and culture in the construction of self were evident in my interviewees' identity narratives, there was another overriding factor present in every origin story I heard: the power of public policies and social institutions in the construction of their lives as members of the families they were placed in. It was striking how aware most of them were of the public policy issues involved in the regulation of transracial adoptions; indeed, several mentioned having researched the topic for school projects. Adoptees cannot help but be aware of the role of the state in constructing who we are when the story of our beginnings typically involves elements like "the home study" and being picked up at the agency rather than coming home from the hospital. Among transracial adoptees, the apparent differences in commonly identified "racial characteristics" between their families and themselves are the subject of discussion and serve to regularly remind them of the "constructedness" of their families and identities. They are always visible as adoptees; they cannot "pass." Though people who were not adopted rarely feel the presence of the state in the formation of their identities as keenly as do adoptees, everyone living in the United States is affected by public institutions such as the educational system, the labor market, the health care industry, and the legal system, among others.

The lives of adoptees demonstrate the complexities involved in the concept of the social construction of identity. Often this phrase is taken to mean the "cultural" side of the nature-nurture tension, but that assumption disregards the role of social structure in the shaping and constructing of individual identities. This is particularly important

when considering the social construction of race. As the work of multiracial feminists has emphasized, considering the sources of diversity
and difference solely in *cultural* terms obscures the oppression and inequality that various racial-ethnic groups have endured (Baca Zinn and
Dill 1994). For example, systemic racism and exclusionary public policies have led different forms of family to thrive and survive among
African Americans, Latinos, and Asian Americans. Because different
racial-ethnic groups have been assaulted and oppressed by the state in
various ways, their cultural responses to social inequality, their survival
skills, have varied as well. Too often, cultural explanations for diversity
end up blaming the oppressed for their failure to thrive in the capitalist
marketplace.

A focus on cultural differences alone often translates into arguments
by "social constructionists" and cultural studies scholars that deny the
power of biology; focusing on culture to the exclusion of politics and
policy often forces progressives, through the logic of the dualistic contrast, into an untenable opposition to biology that cannot hold its own
in public debate. In my view, identity formation is shaped by the biological, embodied aspects of being, the cultural meaning systems available
to individuals, and the public policies, social institutions, and political
economy of the society in which a person lives.

Public dialogue about transracial adoption and welfare reform represents culture and biology as the two primary explanations for racial difference and social inequality, and usually explains such differences as
rooted in families. Historically, Black families have been represented as
pathologically deviant from the White middle-class nuclear family norm,
and over time biology and culture have been invoked in various ways to
explain such supposed difference. The spurious assertion that "matriarchal" single-parent families embody a "tangle of pathology" is grounded
in Daniel Patrick Moynihan's report of 1965, which draws on E.
Franklin Frazier's work on Black families published in the 1930s and
1940s. Cultural studies scholar Gitanjali Maharaja argues:

> As one of its dubious achievements, the Moynihan Report continued a tra-
> dition in U.S. society that has historically constructed the black body as
> the exemplary site through which anxieties about the (re)production of

labor, the nuclear family, and gender have been played out, all in the national interest. (Maharaj 1997:97)

As I discussed in chapter 4, contemporary conservatives have drawn on Moynihan's thesis regarding the supposed inability of unwed mothers to properly socialize their sons into "productive" citizens. In the current moment this supposed pathology is attributed—most notably by Murray and Herrnstein—to biological inferiority, but the more widespread explanation attributes such deviance to the "culture of poverty."

Culture has often been offered by progressive scholars as a counter to essentialist and biologically determined racism. Yet the widespread, indiscriminate use of culture as the *cause* of unemployment, crime, violence, and "illegitimacy" forces us to rethink the explanatory uses of this key concept. Cultural explanations for social inequality—particularly the "culture of poverty" theory—have gradually come to indicate an inflexible and determinant set of group characteristics that locate *values* as the source of poverty and social decay. This explanation focuses its blame on individuals and groups, and is commonly used as a means of obscuring the structural and economic causes of oppression. As Carla Peterson and Rhonda M. Williams explain:

> Today, it seems that both culture and nature conspire to damn poor women in general, and poor Black women in particular. The horror of today's welfare reform lies in the truths masked by narratives of culture, nature, race, and gender. (Peterson and Williams 1997:10)

In short, in public discourse, what culture masks is power. The "culture of poverty" explanation, so widely accepted by conservatives and centrists alike, obscures the role of the state in perpetuating and enforcing inequality, placing the blame on individuals and families. As Sanford F. Schram puts it:

> Insisting that family breakdown is a cause rather than a symptom of growing poverty allows social policy to continue to legitimate itself in spite of the failure of social policy to address the collapse of the family wage system. To be sure, blaming female-headed families for growing poverty provides a convenient and culturally ascendant way to deflect attention from the deleterious effects of the changing economy on the poorer segments of society. (Schram 1995:157)

This narrative deflects attention from economic dislocation, discrimination in the labor market, disinvestment in inner cities, and decreasing social support for low-income families by ascribing welfare dependency and poverty to a lack of hard work and "family values."

"Legitimate" Knowledge/"Illegitimate" People

Considerations of *legitimacy* obviously underlie the labeling of children born into single-parent families as "*illegitimate*." What does this "commonsense" category mean? What does it say about a society that only children born into particular kinds of families—nuclear families headed by two married heterosexual parents—are considered *legitimate* people, *legitimate* citizens? What does it mean for a society when the federal government declares it a national priority to "combat illegitimacy"? At the very least it indicates that the state assumes a powerful role in producing and supporting families it believes will raise citizens who will contribute to society in "productive" ways—that is, patriarchal nuclear families. Simultaneously, the state will punish and even sunder apart the kinds of families that supposedly (re)produce "undesirables"—that is, single-mother families. *Legitimacy* is only conferred through patriarchally sanctioned marriages.

Questions of *legitimacy* enter this public discourse in other ways as well. Indeed, in Gramsci's view, questions of legitimacy lie at the heart of the concept of hegemony (Gramsci 1971). Such bodies of social knowledge as science, social science, religion, and legislative proclamations defining "the good of the nation" delineate what counts as "legitimate" families, mothers, children, and social behavior. Power relations are largely enforced by consent; particular constructions of "legitimate" social identities are chosen because they come to be seen as "common sense" (Gramsci 1971:182).[2] In the case of adoption we see social definitions of "legitimacy" codified in public policy, as it is through their interaction with state-sanctioned social institutions that "illegitimate" children are transformed into "legitimate" citizens.

The public debate about welfare, "illegitimacy," and "family values" provides a language for discussing racial anxieties and social inequalities that appears deceptively "race neutral." Critical legal scholar Kimberle Crenshaw explains:

In part to offset potential contradictions between the formal discourse of racial equality on the one hand and the social and political realities of black marginalization and disempowerment on the other, race has gradually reemerged from both the center and the right as a *discourse of legitimation.* The continuing marginal condition of African Americans within the post-apartheid society has been a stubborn fact that can not be dismissed. Either the claims of equality's promise have been false and much more radical remedial strategies are warranted, or there is something wrong with blacks that formal equality simply cannot "fix." (emphasis added) (Crenshaw 1997:108)

Race has become a discourse of legitimation in the sense that both cultural and biological definitions of racial "difference" have reemerged as *legitimate* ways of accounting for the continued economic and social marginalization of African Americans in the United States. This construction of "legitimate" social knowledge functions as an agent of power by deflecting attention from the failure of the United States to achieve racial equality in the labor market, in housing, in education, and in the social welfare system. As Peterson and Williams argue, "narratives of family breakdown obliterate seismic shifts in the macroeconomy within which Black and non-Black families struggle to survive" (Peterson and Williams 1997:9). Such narratives also serve as a justification for such punitive legislative agendas as the termination of entitlement to AFDC payments.

Shifting and Competing Definitions of Race

As the new millennium dawns, scholars have noted the relevance of Du Bois's pronouncement a century ago that the problem of the twentieth century would be the "problem of the color line." While movements for social justice brought dramatic changes to the U.S. racial order in the twentieth century, the "problem of the color line" is still very much a defining factor of social and political life. Competing theories of race and inequality battle for hegemony, for justice, for peace in families, neighborhoods, schools, media, the penal system, the social welfare system, and the legislature. In this section I consider racist essentialism, "color-blindness," and a racial formation analysis in addressing the most salient aspects of racial meaning to emerge in this work.

Conclusion

Though race is a central issue in the public dialogues about welfare reform, the language employed often appears to be race "neutral." The tacit racial agenda of the 1996 welfare reform legislation was evident in several ways. Representations linking race, gender, poverty, and welfare are so prevalent in American society that the images that spring to most people's minds when they hear the term "welfare mother" are Black; the political rhetoric does not need to be explicit. As Michael Katz explains: "In popular impressions (although not in fact), the color of the underclass is black" (Katz 1993). In the post–civil rights era conservatives and centrists have fashioned a public language devoid of explicit racial references that nevertheless promotes a racist social program. Howard Winant explains:

> First . . . neoracism has effectively rid itself of any overt adherence to racial prejudice or advocacy of discrimination. Second, and by far more important, neoracism has moved beyond biologism to an understanding of race rooted in supposed cultural differences, a position that permits a far more flexible range of racist political practices. (Winant 1994:100–101)

In fact, the seemingly antiracist discourse regarding transracial adoption exemplifies this analysis. As I discussed in chapter 4, the dominant narrative that emerged in the 1990s touting transracial adoption as necessary for the "salvation" of Black children in foster care made its case against racial matching policies by labeling them racist and discriminatory. Race was cited as the sole factor that kept children in foster care, and racial matching policies were portrayed as the only barriers to permanent families for "special needs" children; transracial adoption was cast as a "color-blind" and antiracist practice that could "save" such children from the limbo of foster care.

While this is an appealing and convenient narrative, a different story emerged in my interviews with social workers and adoption agency directors who were responsible for the adoptive placement of "special needs" children. They stressed that legislation removing restrictions on transracial placements would do very little to change the lives of children in foster care. The primary reason they cited was that the factors defining a "special needs" child and thus accounting for the length of time a child spends in out-of-home care are complex. They made it very clear that race alone rarely relegates a child to long-term foster care. Rather, it

| 177 |

was the interaction of race with disability, age, and being part of a sibling group that made some children more difficult to place in adoptive families. The pairing of legislation on welfare and transracial adoption, and the belief that this pairing was a "solution" to "illegitimacy" indicates the importance of race and gender in the welfare reform debate. Indeed, it reveals the insidious agenda driving this culturally eugenic vision. If race were not a central issue in welfare reform, transracial adoption would not be seen as a solution to the problem of out-of-wedlock births. When considered side by side this legislative agenda promotes a traffic in Black children from poor single women who, it is assumed, cannot properly socialize them, to middle-class White families who, it is assumed, will instill in them the "family values" of the work ethic and responsible, "productive" citizenship.

The racial agenda of conservatives is also evident when we consider the roots of these arguments. This view of socialization, single-parent families, and social crises is directly drawn from social narratives of Black families as pathological. As I have discussed, conservatives and centrists believe there is a crisis in American democracy rooted in a "breakdown of the family." The supposed demise of "the family" is signaled by the proliferation of single-parent families, typically represented as Black. The control of Black women's reproductive behavior is presented as a solution to a national "crisis." Thus, in the words of Toni Morrison (in her analysis of the Hill-Thomas controversy): "as is almost always the case, the site of the exorcism of critical national issues was situated in the miasma of black life and inscribed on the bodies of black people" (Morrison 1992:x).

The public dialogues regarding transracial adoption and welfare reform provided a language and a narrative frame that enabled White anxiety about racial "others" to be articulated in race-"neutral" terms. Kimberle Crenshaw makes clear:

> Thus while the triumph of the ideology of colorblindness has effectively rendered explicit racist discourse entirely unsuitable within mainstream political debate, a residual degree of racist sentiment among a substantial part of the white population remains amenable to appropriately coded racial appeals. (Crenshaw 1997:105)

In fact, "color-blindness" both allows for and necessitates "coded racial appeals," for the goal of this ideology is race neutrality, which demands the denial of race and racial difference. As Kimberle Crenshaw and Gary Peller explain, "From this vantage point racism consists of the failure to treat people on an individual basis according to terms that are neutral to race" (Crenshaw and Peller 1993:60). Any attention to race, then, deviates from the goal of neutrality and is considered racist.

Narrative analyses of policy argue for the importance of recognizing that public policy dialogues are *public* discussions situated in complex discursive, legislative, and sociopolitical histories. Omi and Winant's theoretical framework for the study of race—"racial formation"—"has all kinds of ramifications for state deployments of narratives that ensure a particular global economy" (Lubiano 1996:65). Omi and Winant's conceptualization of "racial projects" is helpful in making connections between race, power, nation, narration, and individual identity:

> Projects are the building blocks not just of racial formation, but of hegemony in general. Hegemony operates by simultaneously structuring and signifying. As in the case of racial oppression, gender- or class-based conflict today links structural inequality and injustice on the one hand, and identifies and represents its subjects on the other. (Omi and Winant 1993:68)

Lubiano explores the connections between racist representations and individuals as follows:

> "Like being mugged by a metaphor" is a way to describe what it means to be at the mercy of racist, sexist, heterosexist, and global capitalist constructions of the meaning of skin color on a daily basis. Whether or not I am a card-carrying believer in distinctions of racial biology, I am nonetheless attacked by the hegemonic social formation's notions of racial being and the way those notions position me in the world. Like a mugging, this attack involves an exchange of assets: some aspect of the social order is enriched domestically and internationally by virtue of material inequities stabilized and narrativized by race oppression and I lose symbolically and monetarily. Further, I am physically traumatized and psychologically assaulted by an operation that is mystified. It goes on in the dark, so to

speak—in the dark of a power that never admits to its own existence. (Lubiano 1996:64)

Lubiano's vivid description of the "assault" on her person by such oppressive narratives points to the political investments and the power issues involved in the reproduction of such social meanings—"some aspect of the social order is enriched." What, then, is the social function of the pathologizing discourse describing welfare mothers as incapable of properly caring for and socializing their children? Of "illegitimate" births as the cause of poverty, crime, and social decline? In her analysis of Foucault's treatment of racism,[3] anthropologist Ann Laura Stoler argues that "the discursive production of unsuitable participants in the body politic" is used as a means of maintaining and justifying inequality and social exclusions that are "codified as necessary and noble pursuits to ensure the well-being and very survival of the social body by a protective state" (Stoler 1995:62). In this view welfare reforms are represented as "necessary and noble" attempts to secure the safety and well-being of the broader society by "breaking the cycle" of "illegitimacy," intergenerational poverty, and crime. Peterson and Williams explain that:

> Unmarried mothers live outside the naturalized cultural norm, unable to rear proper national subjects. Enslaved by their passions, lacking self-control, poor women cannot be left to their own devices. They are the antithesis of the self-regulating citizen. It is the racialization of gender deviancy that marks "welfare mothers" as threatening cultural aberrations that compel draconian shifts in social policy. The "welfare queens" that haunt popular landscapes are African Americans. (Peterson and Williams 1997:8)

The "racialization of gender deviancy" colors poor women Black, and thus, in conservative political fables, the threat to society that their potentially dangerous progeny pose necessitates radical intervention to disrupt the racial socialization imparted by their "pathological" families. For, as Murray and Herrnstein argue, the only social intervention radical enough to measurably improve the prospects for poor Black children becoming "productive" citizens is *adoption*. The next step in the narrative, then, involves the transformation of "unsuitable" citizens through transracial adoption.

This state narrative regarding race, nation, and citizenship "thinks the subject(s)" in this political allegory in particular ways (Lubiano 1996:65). I will outline the various subjects represented in the hegemonic narrative concerning welfare reform and transracial adoption to highlight the investment of the state in perpetuating these representations. Black families are portrayed as dysfunctional and pathological, and therefore incapable of properly caring for and socializing their own children. They are typically figured as single-mother families. This view of Black families emerges in both the narrative of welfare mothers and the assertion that there are not enough Black families willing to adopt African American children, thus necessitating transracial adoptions. Black children are portrayed as disposable, unwanted, and endangered, as well as a potential menace to civil society in the form of gang members, drug dealers, criminals and teenage mothers. In popular narratives White families are seen as middle-class, heterosexual, married, two-parent families who possess "family values." In transracial adoption narratives they are cast as the "color-blind" saviors of poor Black, often crack-addicted children, who believe that "love is more important that race." In these same allegories Black social workers are represented as "politically correct racists" who are willing to disregard the needs of Black children to further their own separatist political goals. In discourse concerning welfare reform and transracial adoption the U.S. Congress constructs itself as a benevolent paternalist practicing "tough love" for the "good of the nation," and combating the racism of the child welfare system. Finally, transracial adoptees are portrayed as well-adjusted "color-blind" people whose identity development has been relatively problem-free and who, it is often implied, possess none of the anger or "reverse racism" that many Blacks raised in African American families supposedly have. The findings of the ethnographic interviews I conducted with social workers and transracial adoptees, as well as my analyses of popular and political texts, have demonstrated that these representations are largely political fictions.

What I would like to consider now is the logic of the allegory these characters populate. The point I want to stress is that the story doesn't work without race. I am inspired here by Toni Morrison's brilliant narrative analysis of the O. J. Simpson trial, in which she attempted to construct "a believable narrative" of "an un-raced figure executing the murders" (Morrison and Lacour 1997:xii). She found that all her "efforts collapsed into nonsense. Without the support of black irrationality . . . the fictional case not only could not be made, it was silly" (1997:xiii). Similarly, the narrative of welfare reform, transracial adoption, and the salvation of middle-class White America hinges on a long history of racial narratives that have permeated social texts and cultural understandings. As noted, the structure of this story follows the logic of the "White man's burden" of "civilizing the natives." In the Western world Whites have been depicted as capable of "saving" and "civilizing," while Blacks have historically been constructed as "savages" in need of civilization.

If we cast all the characters as White and distinguish them along class lines, the narrative changes significantly. There would basically be no story because there would be no conflict in need of resolution, nor an "internal other" in need of containment. First, the logic of the story depends on the threat of what Stoler describes as "unsuitable participants in the body politic"; racism is central to the "discursive production" of such internal enemies (Stoler 1995:62). Second, White children relinquished by or removed from low-income women would seamlessly and invisibly be incorporated into White middle-class society; they would "pass" as "normal" (nonadopted) members of their families and communities. In fact, that was the story largely played out from the 1940s through the mid-1960s in the U.S. adoption system.

This alternate scenario clarifies one of the necessary components of the state narrative, which is that its seemingly antiracist stance with regard to transracial adoption obscures the racist agenda driving welfare reform that I have called cultural eugenics. The constructed threat of a racialized "other" is used to legitimate the dismantling of the federal economic safety net, the channeling of federal money into the building of prisons, the maintenance of a large percentage of governmental resources committed to military defense, and the cutting of capital gains taxes. Transracial adoption provides the quality of *salvation* and *redemption* to this story. Not only does it representationally provide for the "salvation" of inner-city Black children, but it also allows for the "redemption" of Whites from the "burdens" of racism and guilt by affirming as "color-blind" and antiracist those politicians and advocates who favor transracial placements and Whites who adopt Black children. Thus, this narrative enacts what Foucault (1990), in his discussion of "racisms of the state," calls the "constant purification" of society: "It is a racism that a society will practice against itself, against its own elements, against its own products; it is an internal racism—that of constant purification— which will be one of the fundamental dimensions of social normaliza- tion" (Foucault 1990 as quoted in Stoler 1995:55).

American society attempts to "purify" itself of racial "others" through policies which promote the removal of Black children from single- mother families and their placement in White two-parent middle-class families. The language of racial purification reminds us of the parallels between the eugenic movement of the early twentieth century and the cultural eugenics of the current political moment. In its contemporary form, adoption and socialization, have replaced birth control and steril- ization in the service of what Foucault refers to as "normalization." The shift from an emphasis on biological determinism as the source of sup- posed racial-ethnic inferiority to the contemporary focus on "cultural de- terminism," especially evident in the "culture of poverty" thesis, has al- lowed the insidious eugenic agenda to adopt a "color-blind" veneer of benevolence. Thus, this narrative of salvation "purifies" Whites of the guilt of, or at least the appearance of, racism.

Ironically, transracial adoptees struggle with the very allegories used to justify transracial adoption in trying to construct a positive sense of self as African Americans. Pervasive representations of Blacks as poor, uned- ucated, criminal, drug addicted, welfare dependent, pregnant teenagers, and generally pathological—in contrast to "normal" White middle-class people—permeate the lives of transracial adoptees, necessitating self-de- finition in opposition. However, as I discussed in chapter 3, adoptees must *learn* that these images are not truly representative of African Americans. This task can be monumental for adoptees who grow up iso- lated from other Blacks, raised by parents with no understanding of the need to teach their children skills to delegitimate such narratives of iden- tity and race. A few of my informants who were raised in homogeneous White communities accepted such stereotypical representations as true, and distanced themselves from African Americans by defining themselves as "exceptions" who were more like Whites than Blacks.

However, most of the adoptees I interviewed responded in more re- sistant ways. The identities of the transracial adoptees I spoke with can be read as counternarratives in two specific respects. First, their struggle to construct a coherent, positive sense of racial identity and acquire survival skills to deal with racism contrasted directly with the one-dimensional, unproblematic ways in which their identities are represented in the dominant social allegory promoting transracial adoption. Second, the complex, fluid, multiply defined sense of racial being that many of them articulated challenged received notions of race as fixed and immutable, and redefined the way we understand the social construction of a sense of racial-ethnic identity—not only for transracial adoptees, but for all of us living in the contemporary, racially and ethnically diverse, power-differential United States.

As I have noted, the dominant public narrative in favor of transracial adoption portrays Black children raised in White families as well-adjusted children and adults for whom the construction of a sense of racial identity has been basically unproblematic. However, as I demonstrated in chapter 3, all my informants identified racial identity as an "issue" that had demanded their particular attention. To be sure, the specific struggle for self-definition was different for each adoptee. Yet even adoptees who were raised in multiracial contexts by parents who were sensitive and aware of race experienced difficulty and often pain over their racial identity. Andrea Bailey, who was raised by racially conscious parents in a racially diverse community, discussed her "identity issues" as follows:

> *Andrea:* I feel like to some extent I'm very strong. Interesting, I don't why. I mean, I'm strong when it comes to work and when it comes to school and being disciplined and being a good stable friend kind of stuff. You know, that kind of stuff. And I think that has to do with just having a good family and feeling like I'm capable of doing anything I want to do. And I know I am capable, but then the issues that I do have—not knowing where I fit in, not knowing really what my purpose is in life, that kind of stuff— I think has to do with [pause] with uh, the adoption.
> *Sandi:* How is it connected to the adoption?
> *Andrea:* I feel like I'm in like several different worlds, and I don't know exactly where I fit in.
> *Sandi:* What worlds are they?

Andrea: A White world, a Black world, a middle-class world. Um. And I don't feel like I'm living out the life that I was necessarily born to live out.

Sandi: So when you say the life you were born to live out, how do you envision that?

Andrea: You see, that's also contradicting, because I don't necessarily believe in destiny. I don't believe in destiny at all, and I think my life has proved that. You know? But I feel like I was born in one condition, and now I'm totally living out a different one. And I wonder, is that wrong?

The portrayal of transracial adoptees by people promoting "color-blind" adoptions is simply too neat and unproblematic. Adoptees' counternarratives of identity, family, and race challenge naturalized notions of race as a discreetly defined immutable biological category, and of "normal"—read two-parent, biological—families. I have referred to Gabrielle's story in some depth throughout this study. The ambiguity of her (physical) racial identity, her discovery in her midtwenties that she was classified at birth as "Negro/white," and the continual redefinition of where she "belonged" racially all indicate the "constructedness" of her fluid, multiply defined self. In the excerpt that follows, she discussed receiving her "papers," that is, her "non-identifying information":

Gabrielle: I got that and um finally looked at it. And from that I got a lot of descriptions about people, and the story. And you know, a lot of bad typing, you know, and whatever. Um, I—It gave me a lot more sense of like, I actually have relatives. You know, I was actually *born* and things like that aren't—like we don't know that for sure.

Sandi: Other people take for granted "I was born. And there's someone in my life who knows I was born and was there." Like we should be so lucky.

Gabrielle: Yeah. It's so big.

Sandi: So what does that mean? Because that strikes me as being really powerful, that sense of—especially how you put it "I found out that I was born." What do you mean when you say that?

Gabrielle: Um, just that it acknowledges that I come from somewhere, that I have a past, that I'm actually related to people.
Sandi: Were you a county adoption?
Gabrielle: Yeah. Um. So, uh, you know, just looking at all these
aunts and uncles, and brother and sister, albeit half, but still. Just
you know, there's a lot of people. So I was just— It was a lot to
look at. You know, I tend to look at Black people around and
Mexican people, and try to see myself in them a lot more. And
try to acknowledge how I maybe do look like that a little bit, in
some parts—body type or whatever. It was good. Because my hair
has always—I mean, hair is such a big thing. . . . And just looking
at body types in general. I mean, like, I look like those Black girls
over there. And you know, I don't have to like kill myself at the
gym trying to look like these White girls over here! It's like that's
how I am. I need to like own that and not fight it. And so much
growing up was like not knowing really why I am this genetic
stock, and not knowing why I have a big butt or have kinky hair
or whatever. . . . I feel like I have a foot in the door many places,
and I don't feel a hundred percent any one of the things that I
am. But you know, I feel interested in all of them. You know,
Mexico and Spain, that whole connection. Um, the French, the
American Indian, the African American, all of that.

"I actually have relatives. You know, I was actually *born*." This knowledge is often experienced as a revelation by adoptees. We know, logically,
that we were born like everyone else was, but often we don't *know it*
until it's confirmed on a government document like Gabrielle's "papers," or narrated by a birth parent. I had a similar reaction when I first
met my birth mother: *I was actually born. I actually look like someone. I
came from someone's body, not only from a government agency.* While nonadopted people typically take for granted the "naturalness" of their identities and familial relationships, adoptees often take for granted the "constructedness" of ours. However, from a cultural studies perspective, *all*
identities and families are socially constructed and "fictive." Whether or
not a biological tie exists between a parent and child, the *familial relationship* is constructed and codified through cultural meaning systems,
social interaction, the media, social institutions, and public policies.

Adoptees' identities both point to the cultural and structural forces shaping racial-ethnic identity, and raise fundamental questions about the meanings of such social categories. Gabrielle's knowledge that she "was" both Mexican and Creole provided her with a new set of cultural references through which to see herself. At the same time, the disjuncture between that information—her official government racial-ethnic designation—and her lack of insider cultural knowledge about those groups raises questions about what racial-ethnic identity means. Such disjunctures denaturalize racial and ethnic identity and point toward the importance of considering both cultural meaning and social structure when exploring the meanings of biological inheritance.

Cultural Studies/Policy Studies

The genealogy of transracial adoptees' identities that I have mapped out in this study suggests that the provocative juncture of policy and cultural studies can provide new perspectives on identity, family, and race as socially constructed through cultural meaning and social structure. Much good work has been done in the area of policy studies, but often missed are the ways in which public policies shape the way people live. An ethnographic approach to policy can remedy such absences by focusing on the micro level of experience. Ethnographic and cultural studies perspectives can also contribute to policy studies through their emphasis on exploring legislative agendas in cultural, social, political, historical, and representational contexts. The use of narrative as an analytical tool can flesh out the ways in which policy decisions are shaped by the media and public opinion. Additionally, ethnographic methods can be used to explore how members of a particular profession or cultural group perceive the current or future effectiveness of social policies.

The issues raised in both welfare reform and transracial adoption demonstrate how profoundly social policy shapes the everyday lives of people living in the United States. American studies must explore public policy at the matrix of culture, knowledge, and power, which together shape who we are and how we live our lives. Indeed, in recent years cultural studies has moved toward more direct engagement with public political issues. Paul Lauter argues that the field is and should be moving toward an engagement with public political issues:

I think American studies can most usefully be understood not as a discipline that, from a remote and academic standpoint, surveys a particular historical and cultural territory but as a framework within which people engage in those most significant of intellectual ventures, changing or policing the society in which we live. (Lauter 1995:186)

Public policy is a particularly rich area of exploration for American cultural studies, and one that has too long been neglected. Inquiry at the intersection of policy studies and cultural studies can broaden and deepen our understandings of how social policies function in society and shape the identities, families, and lives of people living in the United States. Attention to public policy challenges us to carefully consider the ways in which we employ culture as an analytical category in our research, our teaching, and our forays into the public political realm. Exploration of the current social and political uses of the "culture of poverty" thesis should caution us as we engage in "cultural" analysis. Consideration of how adoptees' lives have been constructed through social institutions and the policies that govern them should prompt us to recognize that race, gender, family, and identity are socially constructed.

Attending to the forces of social structure in the shaping of people's lives broadens and enhances approaches that only consider culture and biology, and displaces frameworks that obscure the role of power in the development and maintenance of families and identities of various races and ethnicities. It is important for American studies scholars to consider public policy issues in our work because it will enrich our understanding of the people living in the United States and the social forces shaping their lives. Yet, we should engage ourselves in policy debates for another reason as well. An interdisciplinary approach to the workings of government can contribute to necessary and worthy political struggles for equality and social justice. In my view, scholars have a responsibility to engage in battle when we find ourselves in a critical political moment, such as the present.

Adoption, Race, and Policy

The social practice of adoption, viewed here as a system of legitimation and social construction, creates particular kinds of families, and thus particular "subjects"—adoptees—through the regulation of women's reproductive behavior, according to racialized, gendered, and class-specific definitions of legitimate social identities. As the unequal history of transracial adoption illustrates, public policies regulating the use of race in the child welfare system have profound implications for Black and multiracial children in the adoption and foster care system. This practice raises fundamental questions about the inscription of ideology in social policy, and the differential impact such policies have on children and families in a diverse range of racial-ethnic groups.

I am not arguing "for" or "against" the practice of transracial adoption. This issue is too complex for that. Rather, I would like to see this debate reframed. Adoption policies must be considered as part of the broader political context. Narratives of White middle-class families "saving" children of color should be replaced by discussions of the power inequalities built into the child welfare system. My critique of transracial adoption is *not* aimed at individual families. My criticism concerns the role of the state in regulating the reproductive and parenting behavior of primarily young, poor, single women of color and White women with children of color. We must consider who the children are, how they came into the system, and what social circumstances led them there. It seems highly unlikely, considering the tenor of the times, that the 1996 legislative changes to transracial adoption policy will be reversed any time soon. However, this should not deter us from discussing these issues. Indeed, if transracial placements are to increase, open discussions should continue to explore how we can make such placements as beneficial to children and their families as possible. The experiences of my informants suggest that awareness of and education about questions of racial identity, racism, survival skills, and social inequality are profoundly important for transracially adoptive families. If Black and biracial children are to be adopted into White families, agencies should provide pre- and postadoption educational workshops and counseling services when necessary.

Although the issues that arise in transracial adoption cannot be easily resolved, the following four points may facilitate greater sensitivity to the needs of the children and families involved. First, a structural critique of the adoption and foster care system is a necessary component of any analysis of transracial adoption. Attempts to solve a crisis in the foster care system that focus almost exclusively on the individual and familial levels by encouraging Whites to adopt Black foster children without addressing the systemic inequalities built into the structure of the U.S. child welfare system are simply cosmetic. They do nothing to alleviate the circumstances that lead more Black children than White children into the social welfare system, nor do they address the issues that keep them from getting out. They fail to address the social circumstances that make it difficult for low income, single women of color to keep and raise their children.

Second, an understanding of this issue depends on the recognition that each constituent in the practice of transracial adoption—children, birth parents, and adoptive parents—has had a different history and a different relationship to the social institution of adoption, and these differences should be made apparent and respected. As I have indicated, the public adoption system in the United States as we know it today developed following World War II primarily to serve the "needs" of infertile White, middle-class, heterosexual married couples. The privilege of being White and middle class was inscribed in the system through screening policies which identified White middle-class nuclear families as the social norm to be reproduced and emulated, as well as more tacit assumptions and practices that privileged this group over others. Indeed, the 1996 federal legislation prohibiting the consideration of race in adoptive placements further empowered Whites to adopt any available child, regardless of race, and was, in fact, explicitly crafted in conjunction with welfare reform legislation to reproduce White middle-class heterosexual nuclear families. The majority of children in foster care are there because they have been removed from their families of origin. Whatever the stated reason for their removal, poverty is frequently a significant factor. Many birth mothers are poor people whose personal agency is circumscribed both by a discriminatory labor market and an intrusive social welfare system. In fact, the governmental regulation of the reproductive behavior of poor women of color has a long history in the United States (Roberts 1997). As the history of this issue makes apparent, children of color were virtually ignored by the adoption system for many years, until the rising number of children of color in foster care and the decline in available White infants led to an increase of transracial placements throughout the 1960s and early 1970s. In my view, all children in the U.S. adoption market have been commodified. However, this is particularly disturbing in the context of welfare reform legislation that makes it more difficult for poor women to support themselves and their families, and thus increases the likelihood of children being removed from poor single-mother families, and subsequently adopted into middle-class nuclear families—the kind the system is designed to reproduce.

Third, in light of the ways in which the use of racial categories has created varied histories of interaction with the child welfare system, it is crucial to recognize that race is not a static, immutable concept, and has had vastly different meanings for people in a range of racial-ethnic groups. The dominant meanings of race drawn on by the state in determining the life courses of Black and White children must be considered critically in order to reveal how such definitions maintain and legitimate inequalities in the dissemination of social services for children and their caretakers.

Finally, if those involved in this debate are truly interested in serving "the best interests of the child," they must listen to the voices of the children who have been through this system. At a fundamental level, this involves moving beyond essentialist racial categories and "color-blind" denials of race, and learning to hear the multiply defined identity narratives of people whose life experiences have placed them on the boundaries between the too often polarized cultures and communities we call Black and White.

NOTES

Notes to the Introduction

1. The categories "Black" and "White" are particularly problematic in the context of transracial adoption. Many of the children of color placed in White families are considered to be of "mixed race," but they are defined as Black in U.S. society. "In the United States, the black/white color line has historically been rigidly defined and enforced. White is seen as a 'pure' category. Any racial intermixture makes one 'nonwhite'" (Omi and Winant 1986:60). I use the terms Black and African American interchangeably, and I capitalize all the racial classifications—including White—both to show respect for the cultural groups these terms represent and to highlight the constructed and falsely unified character of these racial designations.

2. Sociologist Joyce Ladner's qualitative study, *Mixed Families: Adopting across Racial Boundaries* (1977) is an important and insightful exception notable for its attention to the sociocultural context—particularly in terms of race—in which transracial adoption has been practiced. Also of note is Dawn Day's *The Adoption of Black Children: Counteracting Institutional Discrimination* (1979). While the focus of Day's work was not solely transracial adoption, her analysis placed the practice in the context of a history of institutional discrimination based on race. In significant contrast to other studies, Ladner and Day attend to the fundamentally different relationship of Black and White children to the child welfare system in the United States through history, and the way these unequal relationships have been shaped by sociopolitical definitions of race.

3. See Roberts 1997 for a discussion of the ways in which Black women's reproductive behavior has historically been targeted as a means of reducing poverty.

4. For a detailed discussion of this policy debate, see Patton 1996.

5. The term "super-predators" is attributed to Representative Bill McCollum (R-Fla.) (Editorial 1996). In the 1990s adoption was one of several strategies promoted by conservatives to "handle" the "underclass" through either transformation or elimination. Other political strategies of the 1990s involved welfare reform and policies regulating the criminal justice system.

6. I draw on the use of racial meaning systems outlined by Frankenberg (1993).

7. Racial-ethnic is a term used by multiracial feminists to denote groups that are culturally distinct and legally and socially subordinated in U.S. society. It suggests the complex interplay of culture, ethnicity, and race both at the level of group identity and societal inequality (Baca Zinn and Dill 1994).

Notes to Chapter 1

1. The number of children in the U.S. foster care system increased dramatically from 276,000 in 1986 to between 450,000 and 500,000 in 1993. In that year, children of color were said to comprise approximately 40 percent of U.S. children in foster care. (Background Information, Multiethnic Placement Act of 1993(4), S. 1224). However, these figures can be misleading, in that they do not reflect the number of children in foster care whose parental rights have been terminated, making them available for adoption. "In 1991 adoption is the goal for approximately 75,000 of the (then) 400,000 children in foster care. Half of the children (approximately 37,500) are legally free for adoptive placement; the other half remain in legal limbo." (Information adapted by the National Adoption Information Clearinghouse from a report from the U.S. House Select Committee on Children, Youth, and Families (December 1989), and from a survey of selected states by the North American Council on Adoptable Children.)

2. Some of the earliest efforts began with American farmer Harry Holt (founder of the Holt organization) in the early 1950s, and involved the placement of Korean children displaced during the Korean War. Native American children were targeted by the Indian Adoption Project, administered jointly by the Bureau of Indian Affairs and the Child Welfare League of America in the late 1950s. Approximately seven hundred children were placed in transracial and conventional homes before Native American opposition led to the demise of the program. See Silverman and Feigelman (1990).

3. In 1955 the Minority Adoption Recruitment of Children's Homes (MARCH) was organized to find homes for Black, Native American, and Chicana/o children in the San Francisco Bay area. Minnesota's Parents to Adopt Minority Youngsters (PAMY) was founded in 1957 and Canada's Open Door Society in 1959. The Council on Adoptable Children (COAC) and chapters of the Open Door Society were formed throughout the 1960s in Canada and the U.S. Ladner (1977).

4. See, for example, Chestang (1972); Jones (1972); Chimezie (1975).

5. McRoy and Zurcher (1983:138). McRoy and Zurcher's study stands out

among the social work research for its comparative approach between transracial adoptees and Black children adopted into Black families.

6. For an in-depth discussion of these issues, see Harding (1993).

Notes to Chapter 2

1. I found my informants through various sources. Many were referred to me by friends and acquaintances who were aware of my research. Often one informant led me to others. Several people were referred to me by social workers that I interviewed. This word of mouth process provided me with a number of informal social groupings of adoptees and adoptive families, as well as several individuals who were not socially connected to other transracial adoptees.

2. See Gooding-Williams 1993; Wong 1994.

3. Psychological stage theories track the development of individual identity through a series of four or five stages from a point at which people accept a negative stereotypical understanding of Blackness to one at which they define a positive sense of racial identity.

4. Root (1992); Zack (1993, 1995); Reddy (1994); Haizlip (1994); Funderburg (1994); Williams (1995); Obama (1995); Scales-Trent (1995); McBride (1996); Minerbrook (1996); Root (1996); and Thompson and Tyagi (1996).

5. The term "good hair" derives from a perspective that values light skin and hair that is closer to that of European Americans.

6. Gooding-Williams (1993:164). I am indebted to Gooding-Williams's brilliant use of Fanon in his analysis of the Rodney King verdict.

Notes to Chapter 3

1. See Wegar (1997) for an analysis of search narratives in popular culture.

2. See Robert Gooding-Williams (1993) for a discussion of sociopolitical allegories.

3. The interview was structured this way because I was asked to write an essay focusing on my relationship with one of the people I had interviewed. The essay, "Routes of Identity: Dialogues on Race, Gender, and Adoption," will appear in an anthology focusing on life history research (Patton 2001).

Notes to Chapter 4

1. See, for example, Williams (1991); Morrison (1992); Carby (1993); Gooding-Williams (1993); Delgado (1995); Morrison and Lacour (1997); Wing (1997).

2. In this section I draw on a wide range of public texts to present the dominant narrative that emerged, including Tisdale (1991); Bartholet (1991, 1992a, 1992b, 1993a, 1993b, 1993c); Kennedy (1993, 1994); Simon, Altstein, and Melli (1994); Weiss (1994); Hunt (1995); Fagan and Fitzgerald (1995).

3. See Bartholet (1991) for the version of this article that contains citations.

4. The major studies of transracially adopted individuals and their families do not address how race is defined; rather, the disciplinary and methodological boundaries of the studies rely on positivistic assumptions that translate into research practices that approach race as a "natural" fact of identity. Adoptees are unproblematically considered to "be" Black or White. Thus, rather than being seen as an "objective" framework for gathering "facts," the assumptions of positivism mystify the power relations through which hegemonic definitions of race are constructed and maintained. The "scientific" methodology employed by Simon and Altstein encodes racial categories in static and immutable ways. Linguistically, race is "assigned 'object' nature" (Van Dijk 1987:33), bearing out Omi and Winant's assertion: "Although abstractly acknowledged to be a socio-historical construct, race in practice is often treated as an objective fact: one simply is one's race; in the contemporary U.S., if we discard euphemisms, we have five color-based racial categories: black, white, brown, yellow, or red" (Omi and Winant 1993:10).

5. See Jeffrey (1994); Simon (1993).

6. For a detailed discussion of these issues see Dill, Baca Zinn, and Patton (1999).

7. For critiques of this work, see Fraser (1995); Graves and Johnson (1995); Jacoby and Glauberman (1995); Kincheloe, Steinberg, and Gresson (1996).

Notes to the Conclusion

1. See Harding (1993) for discussions of scientific racism.

2. For discussions of Gramsci's view of hegemony and legitimacy, see Omi and Winant (1994:67); Ross (1989:55).

3. Stoler examines a text by Foucault that is only available in Italian.

BIBLIOGRAPHY

Abramovitz, Mimi. 1989. *Regulating the Lives of Women: Social Welfare Policy from Colonial Times to the Present.* Boston: South End Press.

Adler, Patricia A., and Peter Adler. 1987. *Membership Roles in Field Research.* Newbury Park, Calif: Sage Publications.

Agar, Michael H. 1986. *Speaking of Ethnography.* Newbury Park, Calif.: Sage Publications. The Publishers of Professional Social Science. 2.

———. 1992. "Stretching Linguistic Ethnography over Part of a State." *Journal of Linguistic Anthropology* 1(2):131–42.

Altstein, Howard. 1993. "Transracial Adoption: A Demonstrated Successful Alternative to Non-Permanent Options." Statement submitted to Senator Howard Metzenbaum in support of the Multiethnic Placement Act, 26 July.

Amott, Teresa L., and Julie A. Matthaei. 1991. *Race, Gender, and Work: A Multicultural Economic History of Women in the United States.* Boston: South End Press.

Anderson, Benedict. 1991. *Imagined Communities.* 2d ed. London: Verso.

Andujo, Estela. 1988. "Ethnic Identity of Transethnically Adopted Hispanic Adolescents." *Social Work* 33(6) (November–December): 531–36.

Anzaldua, Gloria. 1987. *Borderlands/La Frontera: The New Mestiza.* San Francisco: Spinsters/Aunt Lute.

Appell, Annette R. 1998. "On Fixing 'Bad' Mothers and Saving Their Children." In *"Bad Mothers": The Politics of Blame in Twentieth-Century America,* edited by Molly Ladd-Taylor and Lauri Umansky. New York: New York University Press.

Armstrong, Louise. 1995. *Of "Sluts" and "Bastards": A Feminist Decodes the Child Welfare Debate.* Monroe, Minn.: Common Courage Press.

Augustin, Natalie A. 1997. "Learnfare and Black Motherhood: The Social Construction of Deviance." In *Critical Race Feminism: A Reader,* edited by Adrien Katherine Wing. New York: New York University Press.

Baca Zinn, Maxine. 1990. "Family, Feminism, and Race in America." *Gender and Society* 4(1): 68–82.

———, 1994. "Feminist Rethinking from Racial-Ethnic Families." In *Women of*

Color In U.S. Society, edited by Maxine Baca Zinn and Bonnie Thornton Dill. Philadelphia: Temple University Press.

Baca Zinn, Maxine, and Bonnie Thornton Dill, ed. 1994. *Women of Color in U.S. Society.* Philadelphia: Temple University Press.

Background Information, Multiethnic Placement Act of 1993(4), S. 1224.

Bagley, Christopher. 1993. "Transracial Adoption in Britain: A Follow-Up Study, with Policy Considerations." *Child Welfare* (May–June): 285–99.

Barnes, Annie S. 1987. *Single Parents in Black America: A Study in Culture and Legitimacy.* Bristol: Wyndham Hall Press.

Barrett, Susan E., and Carol M. Aubin. 1990. "Feminist Considerations of Intercountry Adoptions." *Woman and Therapy* 10: 127–38.

Barth, Richard, Jill Duerr Berrick, and Neil Gilbert, ed. 1994. *Child Welfare Research Review, Vol. 1.* New York: Columbia University Press.

———. 1994. "Adoption Research: Building Blocks for the Next Decade." *Child Welfare* 73(5) (September–October): 625–38.

Bartholet, Elizabeth. 1991. "Where Do Black Children Belong?" *University of Pennsylvania Law Review* 139: 1163–256.

———. 1992a. "Against Racial Matching." *Reconstruction* 1(4): 44–55.

———. 1992b. "Where Do Black Children Belong? The Politics of Race Matching in Adoption." *Reconstruction* 1(4): 22–43.

———. 1993a. *Family Bonds: Adoption and the Politics of Parenting.* Boston: Houghton Mifflin.

———. 1993b. "Legislating Race Separatism," *Chicago Tribune* (November 5): Editorial section.

———. 1993c. Letter to the editor, *New York Times* (December 8): A24.

Bates, J. Douglas. 1993. *Gift Children: A Story of Race, Family, and Adoption in a Divided America.* New York: Ticknor and Fields.

Battaglia, Debbora. 1995. "Problematizing the Self: A Thematic Introduction." In *Rhetorics of Self-Making,* edited by Debbora Battaglia. Berkeley: University of California Press.

Beck, Melinda. 1988. "Willing Families, Waiting Kids." *Newsweek* (September 12): 64.

Behar, Ruth, and Deborah A. Gordon, ed. 1995. *Women Writing Culture.* Berkeley: University of California Press.

Benet, Mary Kathleen. 1976. *The Politics of Adoption.* New York: Free Press.

Bennett, William J. 1995. "Prepared Testimony by William J. Bennett before the Ways and Means Subcommittee on Human Resources, U.S. House of Representatives, Re: Increase in Illegitimacy." *Federal News Service,* sec: In the News (January 20).

Berman, Claire. 1974. *We Take This Child: A Candid Look at Modern Adoption.* Garden City: Doubleday.

Billingsley, Andrew. 1968. *Black Families in White America.* New York: Simon and Schuster.

Blankenhorn, David. 1995. *Fatherless America: Confronting Our Most Urgent Social Problem.* New York: Basic Books.

Boris, Eileen, and Peter Bardaglio. 1987. "Gender, Race, and Class: The Impact of the State on the Family and the Economy, 1790–1945." In *Families and Work,* edited by Naomi Gerstel and Harriet Engel Gross. Philadelphia: Temple University Press.

Brantlinger, Patrick. 1990. *Crusoe's Footprints: Cultural Studies in Britain and America.* New York: Routledge.

Brodzinsky, David M., and Robin Marantz Henig. 1992. *Being Adopted: The Lifelong Search for Self.* New York: Doubleday.

Brodzinsky, David M., and Marshall D. Schechter, eds. 1990. *The Psychology of Adoption.* New York: Oxford University Press.

Burlew, A. Kathleen, and Lori R. Smith. 1991. "Measures of Racial Identity: An Overview and a Proposed Framework." *Journal of Black Psychology* 17(2) (spring): 53–71.

Cadoret, Remi J. 1990. "Biologic Perspectives of Adoptee Adjustment." In *The Psychology of Adoption,* edited by David M. Brodzinsky and Marshall D. Schechter. New York: Oxford University Press.

Caputo, John, and Mark Yount, eds. 1993. *Foucault and the Critique of Institutions.* University Park, Pa.: Pennsylvania State University Press.

Carby, Hazel. 1993. "Encoding White Resentment: Grand Canyon—A Narrative for Our Times." In *Race, Identity, and Representation in Education,* edited by Cameron McCarthy and Warren Critchlow. New York: Routledge.

Carp, Wayne E. 1998. *Family Matters: Secrecy and Disclosure in the History of Adoption.* Cambridge: Harvard University Press.

Caughey, John L. 1982. "Ethnography, Introspection, and Reflexive Culture Studies." *Prospects* 7: 115–39.

———. 1984. *Imaginary Social Worlds.* Lincoln: University of Nebraska Press.

———. 1986. "Epilogue: On the Anthropology of America." In *Symbolizing America,* edited by Herve Varenne. Lincoln: University of Nebraska Press.

———. 1994. "Gina as Steven: The Social and Cultural Dimensions of a Media Relationship." *Visual Anthropology Review,* 10(1) (spring): 126–35.

Chestang, Leon. 1972. "The Dilemma of Biracial Adoption." *Social Work* 17(3) (May): 100–105.

Chimezie, Amuzie. 1975. "Transracial Adoption of Black Children." *Social Work* 20(4) (July): 296–301.

Clark, Clifford E., Jr. 1989. "Ranch-House Suburbia: Ideals and Realities." In *Recasting America: Culture and Politics in the Age of Cold War*, edited by Lary May. Chicago: University of Chicago Press.

Clifford, James, 1986. "Introduction: Partial Truths." In *Writing Culture: The Poetics and Politics of Ethnography*, edited by James Clifford and George E. Marcus. Berkeley: University of California Press.

————. 1988. *The Predicament of Culture: Twentieth-Century Ethnography, Literature, and Art*. Cambridge: Harvard University Press.

————.1997. *Routes: Travel and Translation in the Late Twentieth Century*. Cambridge: Harvard University Press.

Clifford, James, and George E. Marcus, eds. 1986. *Writing Culture: The Poetics and Politics of Ethnography*. Berkeley: University of California Press.

Cohen, Richard. 1993. "Dealing with Illegitimacy." *Washington Post* (November 23): Editorial page.

Coker, Ruth. 1996. *Hybrid: Bisexuals, Multiracials, and Other Misfits under American Law*. New York: New York University Press.

Cole, Elizabeth S., and Kathryn S. Donley. 1990. "History, Values, and Placement Policy Issues in Adoption." In *The Psychology of Adoption*, edited by David M. Brodzinsky and Marshall D. Schechter. New York: Oxford University Press.

Collier, Jane Fisburne, and Sylvia Junko Yanagisako. 1987. *Gender and Kinship: Essays toward a Unified Analysis*. Stanford: Stanford University Press.

Collins, Patricia Hill. 1990. *Black Feminist Thought: Knowledge, Consciousness, and the Politics of Empowerment*. Boston: Unwin Hyman.

Coontz, Stephanie. 1992. *The Way We Never Were: American Families and the Nostalgia Trap*. New York: Basic Books.

Crapanzano, Vincent, Ergas Yasmine, and Judith Modell. 1986. "Personal Testimony: Narratives of the Self in the Social Sciences and the Humanities." *Items* 40:2.

Crenshaw, Kimberle Williams. 1997. "Color-Blind Dreams and Racial Nightmares: Reconfiguring Racism in the Post–Civil Rights Era." In *Birth of a Nation 'hood: Gaze, Script, and Spectacle in the O. J. Simpson Case*, edited by Toni Morrison and Claudia Brodsky Lacour. New York: Pantheon Books.

Crenshaw, Kimberle Williams, and Gary Peller. 1993. "Reel Time/Real Justice." In *Reading Rodney King/Reading Urban Uprising*, edited by Robert Gooding-Williams. New York: Routledge.

Cross, William E., Jr. 1991. *Shades of Black: Diversity in African-American Identity*. Philadelphia: Temple University Press.

Daniel, G. Reginald. 1996. "Black and White Identity in the New Millennium: Unsevering the Ties That Bind." In *The Multiracial Experience: Racial Borders as the New Frontier*, edited by Maria P. P. Root. Thousand Oaks, Calif.: Sage Publications.

Davis, Angela Y. 1981. *Women, Race, and Class*. New York: Vintage Books.

Day, Dawn. 1979. *The Adoption of Black Children: Counteracting Institutional Discrimination*. Lexington, Mass.: Lexington Books, D. C. Heath.

Dean, Amy E. 1991. *Letters to My Birthmother: An Adoptee's Diary of Her Search for Her Identity*. New York: Pharos Books.

Dean, Mitchell. 1996. "Foucault, Government and the Enforcing of Authority." In *Foucault and Political Reason: Liberalism, Neo-liberalism, and Rationalities of Government*, edited by Andrew Barry, Thomas Osborne, and Nikolas Rose. Chicago: University of Chicago Press.

de Lauretis, Teresa. 1988. "Displacing Hegemonic Discourses: Reflections on Feminist Theory in the 1980s." *Inscriptions: Feminism and the Critique of Colonial Discourse* 3(4): 127–44.

Delgado, Richard. 1995. *Critical Race Theory: The Cutting Edge*. Philadelphia: Temple University Press.

Dill, Bonnie Thornton. 1988. "Our Mothers' Grief: Racial Ethnic Women and the Maintenance of Families." *Journal of Family History* 13(4): 415–31.

———. 1994. "Fictive Kin, Paper Sons, and Compadrazgo: Women of Color and the Struggle for Family Survival." In *Women of Color in U.S. Society*, edited by Maxine Baca Zinn and Bonnie Thornton Dill. Philadelphia: Temple University Press.

Dill, Bonnie Thornton, Maxine Baca Zinn, and Sandra Patton. 1993. "Feminism, Race, and the Politics of Family Values." *Report from the Institute for Philosophy and Public Policy* 13(3) (summer): 13–18.

———. 1999. "Race, Family Values, and Welfare Reform." In *A New Introduction to Poverty: The Role of Race, Power, and Politics*, edited by Louis Kushnick and James Jennings. New York: New York University Press.

Du Bois, W. E. B. 1903. *The Souls of Black Folk*. New York: Penguin Books.

Duke, Lynne. 1992. "Couples Challenging Same-Race Adoption Policies." *Washington Post*. (April 5): A1.

Dunn, Robert G. 1998. *Identity Crises: A Social Critique of Postmodernity*. Minneapolis: University of Minnesota Press.

Duster, Troy. 1996. "The Prism of Heritability and the Sociology of Knowledge." In *Naked Science: Anthropological Inquiry into Boundaries, Power, and Knowledge*, edited by Laura Nader. New York: Routledge.

Editorial. 1996. "Super-Predators." *Washington Post* (August 17): A24.

Edelman, Marian Wright. 1986. *Families in Peril: An Agenda for Social Change.* Cambridge: Harvard University Press.

Egan, Timothy. 1993. "A Cultural Gap May Swallow a Child." *New York Times* (October 12): 8, 16.

Emerson, Robert. 1983. *Contemporary Field Research.* Boston: Little Brown.

Evans, Maureen McCauley. 1993. "Transracial Adoption: Questions and Challenges for Children and Parents Alike." *Washington Post* (November 8): Style section, B5.

Fagan, Patrick F., and William H. G. Fitzgerald. 1995. "Why Serious Welfare Reform Must Include Serious Adoption Reform." *Heritage Foundation Reports* no. 1045 (July 27): 1–28.

Falk, Laurence L. 1970. "A Comparative Study of Transracial and Intracial Adoptions." *Child Welfare* 49(2) (February): 82–88.

Fanon, Frantz. 1967. *Black Skin, White Masks,* translated by Charles Lam Markmann. New York: Grove Press.

Faraday, Annabel, and Kenneth Plummer. 1979. "Doing Life Histories." *Sociological Review* 27(4): 773–98.

Fausto-Sterling, Anne. 1985. *Myths of Gender: Biological Theories about Women and Men.* New York: Basic Books.

Feigelman, William, and Arnold R. Silverman. 1984. "The Long-Term Effects of Transracial Adoption." *Social Service Review* 58: 589–602.

Fiske, John. 1987. "Culture and Television." In *Channels of Discourse: Television and Contemporary Criticism,* edited by Robert C. Allen. Chapel Hill: University of North Carolina Press.

Foucault, Michel. 1978. *The History of Sexuality. Vol. 1: An Introduction,* translated by Robert Hurley. New York: Vintage Books.

———. 1990. *Difendere la societa.* Florence: Ponte alle Grazie.

Frankenberg, Ruth. 1993. *White Women, Race Matters: The Social Construction of Whiteness.* Minneapolis: University of Minnesota Press.

Franklin, Donna L. 1997. *Ensuring Inequality: The Structural Transformation of the African-American Family.* New York: Oxford University Press.

Franklin, Sarah. 1990. "Deconstructing 'Desperateness': The Social Construction of Infertility in Popular Representations of New Reproductive Technologies." In *The New Reproduction Technologies,* edited by Maureen McNeil, Ian Varcoe, and Steven Yearley. New York: St. Martin's Press.

Fraser, Steven, ed. 1995. *The Bell Curve Wars: Race, Intelligence, and the Future of America.* New York: Basic Books.

Frazier, E. Franklin. 1939. *The Negro Family in the United States.* Chicago: University of Chicago Press.

Fricke, Harriet. 1965. "Interracial Adoption: The Little Revolution." *Social Work* 10(3) (July): 92–97.

Friedman, Susan Stanford. 1998. *Mappings: Feminism and the Cultural Geographies of Encounter.* Princeton: Princeton University Press.

Funderburg, Lise. 1994. *Black, White, Other: Biracial Americans Talk about Race and Identity.* New York: William Morrow.

Fuss, Diana. 1995. *Identification Papers.* New York: Routledge.

Gabriel, John. 1998. *Whitewash: Racialized Politics and the Media.* London: Routledge.

Galston, William A. 1993. "Causes of Declining Well-Being Among U.S. Children." *Aspen Institute Quarterly.* 5(1): 68.

Garber Marjorie, Rebecca L. Walkowitz, and Paul Franklin, ed. 1996. *Fieldwork: Sites in Literary and Cultural Studies.* New York: Routledge.

Gediman, Judith S., and Linda P. Brown. 1989. *BirthBond: Reunions between Birthparents and Adoptees—What Happens After . . .* Far Hills, N.J.: New Horizon Press.

Gerstel, Naomi, and Harriet Engel Gross. 1987. *Families and Work.* Philadelphia: Temple University Press.

Gill, Owen, and Barbara Jackson. 1983. *Adoption and Race: Black, Asian, and Mixed Race Children in White Families.* New York: St. Martin's Press.

Gilroy, Paul. 1993. *The Black Atlantic: Modernity and Double Consciousness.* Cambridge: Harvard University Press.

Ginsburg, Faye D., and Rayna Rapp, eds. 1995. *Conceiving the New World Order: The Global Politics of Reproduction.* Berkeley: University of California Press.

Goodenough, Ward H. 1981. *Culture, Language, and Society.* 2nd ed. Menlo Park, Calif: Benjamin/Cummings.

Gooding-Williams, Robert. 1993. "Look a Negro!" In *Reading Rodney King/Reading Urban Uprising,* edited by Robert Gooding-Williams. New York: Routledge.

Goodman, Ellen. 1993. "Adoption—The New Racism." *Washington Post* (December 11): Editorial page.

Gordon, Deborah A. 1995. "Border Work: Feminist Ethnography and the Dissemination of Literacy." In *Women Writing Culture,* edited by Ruth Behar and Deborah A. Gordon. Berkeley: University of California Press.

Gordon, Linda, ed. 1990. *Women, the State, and Welfare.* Madison: University of Wisconsin Press.

Gramsci, Antonio. 1971. *Selections from the Prison Notebooks,* edited and translated by Quentin Hoare and Geoffrey Nowell Smith. New York: International Publishers.

Graves, Joseph L., Jr., and Amanda Johnson. 1995. "The Pseudoscience of Psychometry and *The Bell Curve.*" *Journal of Negro Education* 64(3) (summer): 277–94.

Gray, Herman. 1995. "Television, Black Americans, and the American Dream." In *Gender, Race, and Class in Media: A Text Reader,* edited by Gail Dines and Jean M. Humez. Thousand Oaks, Calif.: Sage Publications.

Gresham, Jewel Handy. 1989. "The Politics of Family in America." *The Nation. Special Issue: Scapegoating the Black Family* (July) 24/31.

Grow, Lucille J., and Deborah Shapiro. 1974. *Black Children/White Parents: A Study of Transracial Adoption.* New York: Research Center Child Welfare League of America.

Haizlip, Shirlee Taylor. 1994. *The Sweeter the Juice: A Family Memoir in Black and White.* New York: Simon and Schuster.

Hall, Stuart, 1996. "New Ethnicities." In *Stuart Hall: Critical Dialogues in Cultural Studies,* edited by David Morley and Kuan-Hsing Chen. London: Routledge.

Haraway, Donna J. 1991. *Simians, Cyborgs, and Women: The Reinvention of Nature.* New York: Routledge.

Harding, Sandra. 1987. *Feminism and Methodology.* Bloomington: Indiana University Press.

Harding, Sandra, ed. 1993. *The "Racial" Economy of Science: Toward a Democratic Future.* Bloomington: Indiana University Press.

Harris, Duchess. 1995. "More than Memorabilia? Khaila as Jezebel, Mammy and Sapphire in Losing Isaiah." *Colors.* 4(4) (July–August): 46–49.

Harrison, Faye V., ed. 1991. *Decolonizing Anthropology: Moving Further toward an Anthropology for Liberation.* Washington, D.C.: Association of Black Anthropologists, American Anthropological Association.

Hasian, Marouf A., Jr. 1996. *The Rhetoric of Eugenics in Anglo-American Thought.* Athens: University of Georgia Press.

Helms Janet E. 1990. *Black and White Racial Identity: Theory, Research, and Practice.* New York: Greenwood Press.

Herrnstein, Richard J., and Charles Murray. 1994. *The Bell Curve: Intelligence and Class Structure in American Life.* New York: Free Press.

Herskovits, Melville J. 1941. *The Myth of the Negro Past.* Boston: Beacon Press.

Higginbotham, Evelyn Brooks. 1992. "African American Women's History and the Metalanguage of Race." *Signs: Journal of Women in Culture and Society* 17(2) (winter): 251–75.

Hill, Robert B., Andrew Billingsley, Eleanor Engram, Michelene R. Malson, Roger H. Rubin, Carol B. Stack, James B. Stewart, and James E. Teele. 1993.

Research on the African-American Family: A Holistic Perspective. Westport, Conn.: Auburn House.

Hodes, Martha, ed. 1999. *Sex, Love, Race: Crossing Boundaries in North American History.* New York: New York University Press.

Hoksbergen, R. A. C., ed. 1986. *Adoption in Worldwide Perspective: A Review of Programs, Policies, and Legislation in Fourteen Countries.* Berwyn: Swets North America.

Hollinger, Joan Heifetz. 1992. "Responses to Bartholet." *Reconstruction* 1(4): 49–51.

Hollingsworth, Leslie Doty. 1997. "Effect of Transracial/Transethnic Adoption on Children's Racial and Ethnic Identity and Self-Esteem: A Meta-Analytic Review." In *Families and Adoption,* edited by Harriet E. Gross and Marvin B. Sussman. New York: Haworth Press.

hooks, bell. 1995. *Killing Rage: Ending Racism.* New York: Henry Holt.

Hoopes, Janet L. 1990. "Adoption and Identity Formation." In *The Psychology of Adoption,* edited by David M. Brodzinsky and Marshall D. Schechter. New York: Oxford University Press.

Hopson, Darlene Powell, and Derek S. Hopson. 1992. *Different and Wonderful: Raising Black Children in a Race-Conscious Society.* New York: Simon and Schuster.

Hunt, Albert R. 1995. "The Republicans Seize the High Ground on Transracial Adoption." *Wall Street Journal* (March 9): Section A, 19.

Isaacs, Asher D. 1996. "Interracial Adoption: Permanent Placement and Racial Identity—An Adoptee's Perspective." *National Black Law Journal* 14(1): 126–56.

Jackson, Fatimah Linda Collier. 1992. "Race and Ethnicity as Biological Constructs." Working Paper from the Bioanthropology Research Laboratory, University of Maryland, College Park (March 10).

Jackson, James S., Wayne R. McCullough, and Gerald Gurin. 1988. "Family, Socialization Environment, and Identity Development in Black Americans." In *Black Families,* edited by Harriette Pipes McAdoo. 2d ed. Newbury Park, Calif.: Sage Publications.

Jacoby, Russell, and Naomi Glauberman, eds. 1995. *The Bell Curve Debate: History, Documents, Opinions.* New York: Random House.

Jeffery, Clara. 1994. "A Question of Color." *Washington City Paper* (28 January–3 February): 21.

Johnson, P. , J. Shireman, and K. Watson. 1987. "Transracial Adoption and the Development of Black Identity at Age Eight." *Child Welfare* 66: 45–56.

Jones, Edmund D. 1972. "On Transracial Adoption of Black Children." *Child Welfare* 51(3): 156–64.

Katz, Michael B. 1989. *The Undeserving Poor: From the War on Poverty to the War on Welfare.* New York: Pantheon Books.

———. 1993. "The Urban 'Underclass' as a Metaphor of Social Transformation." In *The "Underclass" Debate: Views from History*, edited by Michael B. Katz. Princeton: Princeton University Press.

Kennedy, Randall. 1993. "Kids Need Parents—of Any Race." *Wall Street Journal* (November 9): Editorial page.

———. 1994. "Orphans of Separatism: The Painful Politics of Transracial Adoption." *American Prospect* 17 (spring): 38–45.

Kincheloe, Joe L., Shirley R. Steinberg, and Aaron D. Gresson III, eds. 1996. *Measured Lies: The Bell Curve Examined.* New York: St. Martin's Press.

Kirk, Jerome, and Marc L. Miller. 1986. *Reliability and Validity in Qualitative Research.* Beverly Hills, Calif.: Sage Publications.

Korobkin, Laura Hanft. 1996. "Narrative Battles in the Courtroom." In *Fieldwork: Sites in Literary and Cultural Studies*, edited by Marjorie Garber, Rebecca L. Walkowitz, and Paul Franklin. New York: Routledge.

Krauthammer, Charles. 1993. "Subsidized Illegitimacy . . ." *Washington Post* (November 19): Editorial page.

Ladd-Taylor, Molly, and Lauri Umansky, eds. 1998. *"Bad Mothers": The Politics of Blame in Twentieth-Century America.* New York: New York University Press.

Ladner, Joyce A. 1977. *Mixed Families: Adopting across Racial Boundaries.* Garden City, N.Y.: Doubleday.

Langness, L. L., and Gelya Frank. 1985. *Lives: An Anthropological Approach to Biography.* Novato: Chandler and Sharp.

Lauter, Paul. 1995. "Versions of Nashville, Visions of American Studies: Presidential Address to the American Studies Association, October 27, 1994." *American Quarterly* 47 (2) (June): 185–203.

Lewis, Oscar. 1966. "The Culture of Poverty." *Scientific American* 215 (October) (5): 19–25.

Lifton, Betty Jean. 1994. *Journey of the Adopted Self: A Quest for Wholeness.* New York: Basic Books.

———. 1988. *Lost and Found: The Adoption Experience.* 2d ed. New York: Harper and Row.

Lindsey, Duncan. 1994. *The Welfare of Children.* New York: Oxford University Press.

Livingston, Frank B. 1993. "On the Nonexistence of Human Races." In *The*

"Racial" Economy of Science: Toward a Democratic Future, edited by Sandra Harding. Bloomington: Indiana University Press.

Loux, Ann Kimble. 1997. *The Limits of Hope: An Adoptive Mother's Story*. Charlottesville: University Press of Virginia.

Lubiano, Wahneema. 1992. "Black Ladies, Welfare Queens, and State Minstrels: Ideological War by Narrative Means." In *Racing Justice, Engendering Power: Essays on Anita Hill, Clarence Thomas, and the Construction of Social Reality*, edited by Toni Morrison. New York: Pantheon Books.

———. 1996. "Like Being Mugged by a Metaphor: Multiculturalism and State Narratives." In *Mapping Multiculturalism*, edited by Avery F. Gordon and Christopher Newfield. Minneapolis: University of Minnesota Press.

———, ed. 1997. *The House That Race Built: Black Americans, U.S. Terrain*. New York: Pantheon Books.

Luker, Kristin. 1996. *Dubious Conceptions: The Politics of Teenage Pregnancy*. Cambridge: Harvard University Press.

McAdoo, Harriette Pipes. 1988. *Black Families*. 2d ed. Newbury Park, Calif.: Sage Publications.

McBride, James. 1996. *The Color of Water: A Black Man's Tribute to His White Mother*. New York: Riverhead Books.

McLanahan, Sara, and Gary Sandefur. 1994. *Growing Up with a Single Parent*. Cambridge: Harvard University Press.

McRoy, Ruth G., and Louis A. Zurcher. 1983. *Transracial and Inracial Adoptees: The Adolescent Years*. Springfield, Mass.: Charles C. Thomas.

McRoy, Ruth G., Louis A. Zurcher, Michael L. Lauderdale, and Rosalie N. Anderson. 1982. "Self-Esteem and Racial Identity in Transracial and Intraracial Adoptees." *Social Work* 27 (November): 522–26.

———. 1984. "The Identity of Transracial Adoptees." *Social Casework: The Journal of Contemporary Social Work*. 65(1) (January): 34–39.

———. 1989. "An Organizational Dilemma: The Case of Transracial Adoption." *Journal of Applied Behavioral Science* 25(2): 145–60.

Maharaj, Gitanjali. 1997. "Talking Trash: Late Capitalism, Black (Re)Productivity, and Professional Basketball." *Social Text* 50 (spring): 97–110.

Malinowski, Bronsilaw. 1954. *Magic, Science and Religion and Other Essays*. New York: Doubleday.

Mandell, Betty Reid. 1973. *Where Are the Children? A Class Analysis of Foster Care and Adoption*. Lexington, Mass.: D. C. Heath.

March, Karen. 1995. *The Stranger Who Bore Me: Adoptee-Birth Mother Relationships*. Toronto: University of Toronto Press.

Margolis, Seth J. 1993. *Losing Isaiah*. New York: Jove Books.

Marshall, Gloria A. 1993. "Racial Classifications: Popular and Scientific," In *The "Racial" Economy of Science: Toward a Democratic Future*, edited by Sandra Harding. Bloomington: Indiana University Press.

Mascia-Lees, Frances E., Patricia Sharpe, and Colleen Ballerino Cohen. 1989. "The Postmodernist Turn in Anthropology: Cautions from a Feminist Perspective." *Signs: Journal of Women in Culture and Society* 15(1): 7–34.

Massey, Douglas S., and Nancy A. Denton. 1993. *American Apartheid: Segregation and the Making of the Underclass*. Cambridge: Harvard University Press.

May, Elaine Tyler. 1988. *Homeward Bound: American Families in the Cold War Era*. New York: Basic Books.

Meigs, Anna. 1989. "The Cultural Construction of Reproduction and Its Relationship to Kinship and Gender (New Guinea Highlands)." In *Culture, Kin, and Cognition in Oceania: Essays in Honor of Ward H. Goodenough*, edited by Mac Marshall and John L. Caughey. Washington, D.C.: Special publication of the American Anthropological Association, 25.

Miller, Robin L., and Barbara Miller. 1990. "Mothering the Biracial Child: Bridging the Gaps between African-American and White Parenting Styles." *Women and Therapy* 10: 169–77.

Minerbrook, Scott. 1996. *Divided to the Vein: A Journey into Race and Family*. New York: Harcourt Brace.

Mishler, Elliot G. 1986. *Research Interviewing: Context and Narrative*. Cambridge: Harvard University Press.

Modell, Judith S. 1994. *Kinship with Strangers: Adoption and Interpretations of Kinship in American Culture*. Berkeley: University of California Press.

Morgenstern, Joseph. 1971. "The New Face of Adoption." *Newsweek* (September 13): 66–72.

Morrison, Toni. 1992. *Racing Justice, Engendering Power: Essays on Anita Hill, Clarence Thomas, and the Construction of Social Reality*. New York: Pantheon Books.

Morrison, Toni, and Claudia Brodsky Lacour. 1997. *Birth of a Nation 'hood: Gaze, Script, and Spectacle in the O. J. Simpson Case*. New York: Pantheon Books.

Moynihan, Daniel Patrick. 1965. *The Negro Family: The Case for National Action*. Washington, D.C.: U.S. Department of Labor.

Murray, Charles. 1993. "The Coming White Underclass." *Wall Street Journal* (November 17): Editorial page.

———. 1994. "Testimony July 29, 1994 Charles Murray, Ph.D. Bradley Fellow American Enterprise Institute, House Ways and Means/Human Resources,

Welfare Revisions." *Federal Document Clearinghouse Congressional Testimony.* Section: Capital Hill Hearing Testimony.

Murray, David W. 1994. "Poor Suffering Bastards: An Anthropologist Looks at Illegitimacy." *Policy Review* 68 (spring): 9–15.

Nash, Philip Tajitsu. 1992. "Multicultural Identity and the Death of Stereotypes." In *Racially Mixed People in America,* edited by Maria P. P. Root. Newbury Park, Calif.: Sage Publications.

National Adoption Information Clearinghouse. 1989. Information adapted from a report from the U.S. House Select Committee on Children, Youth, and Families (December 1989), and from a survey of selected states by the North American Council on Adoptable Children.

National Association of Black Social Workers. 1972. "Position Statement on Trans-Racial Adoptions." Unpublished position paper (September).

National Committee for Adoption. 1993. Statement by the Executive Committee of the National Committee for Adoption on the subject of transracial adoption, issued on August 14, 1984, submitted to Senator Howard Metzenbaum.

Nobles, Wade W. 1988. "African-American Family Life: An Instrument of Culture." In *Black Families,* edited by Harriette Pipes McAdoo. 2d ed. Newbury Park, Calif.: Sage Publications.

Obama, Barack. 1995. *Dreams from My Father: A Story of Race and Inheritance.* New York: Times Books.

Omi, Michael, and Howard Winant. 1986. *Racial Formation in the United States: From the 1960s to the 1980s.* New York: Routledge. Reprinted in 1994.

———. 1993. "On the Theoretical Status of the Concept of Race." In *Race, Identity, and Representation in Education,* edited by Cameron McCarthy and Warren Critchlow. New York: Routledge.

Parham, T. A. 1989. "Cycles of Psychological Nigrescence." *The Counseling Psychologist.* 17(2): 187–226.

Patton, Sandra. 1996. "Race/Identity/Culture/Kin: Constructions of African American Identity in Transracial Adoption." In *Getting a Life: Everyday Uses of Autobiography,* edited by Sidonie Smith and Julia Watson. Minneapolis: University of Minnesota Press.

———. 2001. "Routes of Identity: Dialogues on Race, Gender, and Adoption." In *Individuals and Cultures: A Life History Approach to the Study of American Identities,* edited by John L. Caughey. Wilmington: Scholarly Resources Press.

Perry, Twila L. 1993–94. "The Transracial Adoption Controversy: An Analysis of Discourse and Subordination." *New York University Review of Law and Social Change.* 21:33–80.

Petchesky, Rosalind Pollack. 1990. *Abortion and Woman's Choice: The State, Sexuality, and Reproductive Freedom.* Boston: Northeastern University Press.

Peters, Marie Ferguson. 1988. "Parenting in Black Families with Young Children: A Historical Perspective." In *Black Families,* edited by Harriette Pipes McAdoo. 2d ed. Newbury Park, Calif.: Sage Publications.

Peterson, Carla, and Rhonda M. Williams. 1997. "The Color of Memory: Interpreting Twentieth Century US Social Policy from a Nineteenth Century Perspective." *Intersections: A Series of Working Papers of the Consortium on Race, Gender and Ethnicity* 1 (April).

Pierce, William L. 1992. "Responses to Bartholet." *Reconstruction* 1(4): 53–54.

Popenoe, David. 1988. *Disturbing the Nest: Family Change and Decline in Modern Societies.* New York: Aldine de Gruyter.

Poster, Mark. 1993. "Foucault and the Problem of Self-Constitution." In *Foucault and the Critique of Institutions,* edited by John Caputo and Mark Yount. University Park, Pa: Pennsylvania State University Press.

Prater, Gwendolyn, and Lula T. King. 1988. "Experiences of Black Families as Adoptive Parents." *Social Work* 33(6) (November–December): 543–45.

Priddy, Drew, and Doris Kirgan. 1971. "Characteristics of White Couples Who Adopt Black/White Children." *Social Work* 16(3) (July): 105–7.

Rabinow, Paul, ed. 1984. *The Foucault Reader.* New York: Pantheon Books.

Rapp, Rayna. 1982. "Family and Class in Contemporary America: Notes toward an Understanding of Ideology." In *Rethinking the Family: Some Feminist Questions,* edited by Barrie Thorne and Marilyn Yalom. New York: Longman.

Reagon, Bernice Johnson. 1982. "My Black Mothers and Sisters or On Beginning a Cultural Autobiography." *Feminist Studies* 8(1) (spring): 81–96.

Reddy, Maureen T. 1994. *Crossing the Color Line: Race, Parenting, and Culture.* New Brunswick: Rutgers University Press.

Register, Cheri. 1991. *"Are Those Kids Yours?": American Families with Children Adopted from Other Countries.* New York: Free Press.

Riessman, Catherine Kohler. 1993. *Narrative Analysis: Qualitative Research Methods* 30. Newbury Park, Calif.: Sage Publications.

Roberts, Dorothy. 1997. *Killing the Black Body: Race, Reproduction, and the Meaning of Liberty.* New York: Pantheon Books.

Rodriguez, Pereta, and Alan S. Meyer. 1990. "Minority Adoptions and Agency Practices." *Social Work* 35(6) (November): 528–31.

Roman, Leslie G. 1997. "Denying (White) Racial Privilege: Redemption Discourses and the Uses of Fantasy." In *Off White: Readings on Race, Power, and Society,* edited by Michelle Fine, Lois Weis, Linda C. Powell, and L. Mun Wong. New York: Routledge.

Romano, Renee. 1998. "Immoral Conduct: White Women, Racial Transgressions, and Custody Disputes." In *"Bad Mothers": The Politics of Blame in Twentieth-Century America,* edited by Molly Ladd-Taylor and Lauri Umansky. New York: New York University Press.

Root, Maria P. P., ed. 1992. *Racially Mixed People in America.* Newbury Park, Calif.: Sage Publications.

———. 1996. "The Multiracial Experience: Racial Borders as a Significant Frontier in Race Relations." In *The Multiracial Experience: Racial Borders as the New Frontier,* edited by Maria P. P. Root. Thousand Oaks, Calif.: Sage Publications.

Rosaldo, Renato. 1993. *Culture and Truth: The Remaking of Social Analysis.* 2d ed. Boston: Beacon Press.

Rosenberg, Elinor B., and Thomas M. Horner. 1991. "Birthparent Romances and Identity Formation in Adopted Children." *American Journal of Orthopsychiatry* 61:1 (January): 48–53.

Rosenthal, James A., and Victor K. Groze. 1994. "A Longitudinal Study of Special-Needs Adoptive Families." *Child Welfare* 73(6) (November–December): 689–706.

Rosenthal, James A., Victor Groze, and Herman Curiel. 1990. "Race, Social Class, and Special Needs Adoption." *Social Work* 35(6): 532–39.

Ross, Andrew. 1989. *No Respect: Intellectuals and Popular Culture.* New York: Routledge.

Sacks, Karen Brodkin. 1996. "How Did Jews Become White Folks?" In *Race,* edited by Steven Gregory and Roger Sanjek. New Brunswick: Rutgers University Press.

Scales-Trent, Judy. 1995. *Notes of a White Black Woman: Race, Color, Community.* University Park, Pa.: Pennsylvania State University Press.

Schram, Sanford F. 1995. *Words of Welfare: The Poverty of Social Science and the Social Science of Poverty.* Minneapolis: University of Minnesota Press.

Sellers, Martha G. 1969. "Transracial Adoption." *Child Welfare.* 48: 6 (June): 355–56, 366.

Sen, Gita, and Rachel C. Snow, ed. 1994. *Power and Decision: The Social Control of Reproduction.* Boston: Harvard University Press.

Sharkey, Nora Clare. 1971. "White Parents, Black Children: Transracial Adoption." *Time* (August 16): 42.

Shepherd, Elizabeth. 1964. "Adopting Negro Children: White Families Find It Can Be Done." *New Republic* (June 20): 10–12.

Shireman, J. D., and P. R. Johnson. 1986. "A Longitudinal Study of Black Adoptions: Single Parent, Transracial, and Traditional." *Social Work* 31: 172–76.

Short, Carolyn R. 1972. "Letters: Biracial Adoption." *Social Work* 17(5) (September) 109–11.

Silverman, Arnold R., and William Feigelman. 1981. "The Adjustment of Black Children Adopted by White Families." *Social Casework* 62: 529–36.

———. 1990. "Adjustment in Interracial Adoptees: An Overview." In *The Psychology of Adoption*, edited by David M. Brodzinsky and Marshall D. Schechter. New York: Oxford University Press.

Silverman, Arnold R., and Dorothy E. Weitzman. 1986. "Nonrelative Adoption in the United States: A Brief Survey." In *Adoption in Worldwide Perspective: A Review of Programs, Policies, and Legislation in Fourteen Countries*, edited by R. A. C. Hoksbergen. Berwyn: Swets North America.

Simms, Margaret C., and Julianne M. Malveaux. 1986. *Slipping through the Cracks: The Status of Black Women*. New Brunswick: Transaction Books.

Simon, Rita. 1993. "Transracial Adoption: Highlights of a Twenty-Year Study." *Reconstruction* 2(2): 130–31.

Simon, Rita James, and Howard Altstein. 1977. *Transracial Adoption*. New York: John Wiley.

———. 1981. *Transracial Adoption: A Follow-Up*. Lexington, Mass.: D. C. Heath.

———. 1987. *Transracial Adoptees and Their Families: A Study of Identity and Commitment*. New York: Praeger.

———. 1992. *Adoption, Race, and Identity: From Infancy through Adolescence*. New York: Praeger.

Simon, Rita, Howard Altstein, and Maryann S. Melli. 1994. *The Case for Transracial Adoption*. Washington, D.C.: American University Press.

Smith, Lee. 1994. "The New Wave of Illegitimacy." *Fortune* (April 18): 81–87.

Smith, Sidonie, and Julia Watson. 1996. "Introduction." In *Getting a Life: Everyday Uses of Autobiography*, edited by Sidonie Smith and Julia Watson. Minneapolis: University of Minnesota Press.

Solinger, Rickie. 1992. *Wake Up Little Susie: Single Pregnancy and Race before Roe v. Wade*. New York: Routledge.

———. 1998. "Poisonous Choice." In *"Bad Mothers": The Politics of Blame in Twentieth-Century America*, edited by Molly Ladd-Taylor and Lauri Umansky. New York: New York University Press.

Spradley, James. 1979. *The Ethnographic Interview*. New York: Holt and Rinehart.

Stacey, Judith. 1996. *In the Name of the Family: Rethinking Family Values in the Postmodern Age*. Boston: Beacon Press.

Stack, Carol B. 1974. *All Our Kin: Strategies for Survival in a Black Community*. New York: Harper and Row.

Staples, Robert, ed. 1994. *The Black Family: Essays and Studies.* 5th ed. Belmont, Calif.: Wadsworth.

Steinberg, Stephen. 1989. *The Ethnic Myth: Race, Ethnicity, and Class in America.* 2d ed. Boston: Beacon Press.

———. 1995. *Turning Back: The Retreat from Racial Justice in American Thought and Policy.* Boston: Beacon Press.

Stephens, Sharon. 1995. "Children and the Politics of Culture in Late Capitalism." In *Children and the Politics of Culture*, edited by Sharon Stephens. Princeton: Princeton University Press.

Stoler, Ann Laura. 1995. *Race and the Education of Desire: Foucault's History of Sexuality and the Colonial Order of Things.* Durham: Duke University Press.

Thompson, Becky, and Sangeeta Tyagi, eds. 1996. *Names We Call Home: Autobiography on Racial Identity.* New York: Routledge.

Thompson, Vetta Sanders. 1990. "Factors Affecting the Level of African American Identification." *Journal of Black Psychology* 17(1) (fall): 19–35.

Thorne, Barrie. 1982. "Feminist Rethinking of the Family: An Overview." In *Rethinking the Family: Some Feminist Questions*, edited by Barrie Thorne and Marilyn Yalom. New York: Longman.

Thorne, Barrie, and Marilyn Yalom, eds. 1992. *Rethinking the Family: Some Feminist Questions.* 2d ed. Boston: Northeastern University Press.

Tisdale, Sally. 1991. "Adoption across Racial Lines: Is It Bad for Kids?" *Vogue* (December): 251.

Turner, Graeme. 1988. *Film as Social Practice.* London: Routledge.

Turner, Judy (as told to Barbara Bisantz Raymond). 1992. "The Color of Love." *Redbook* (August): 140–44.

United States Congress. 1996. Public Law 104-193, "Personal Responsibility and Work Opportunity Reconciliation Act of 1996."

———. 1996. Public Law 104-188, "Small Business Job Protection Act of 1996."

United States Senate. 1995. 141 *Congressional Record* S. 104th Congress., 13770, *S13777, September 5.

Van Dijk, Tuen. 1987. *Communicating Racism: Ethnic Prejudice in Thought and Talk.* Newbury Park, Calif.: Sage Publications.

Verniere, James. 1995. "Two Mothers and a Baby: Despite Jessica Lange's Efforts, Heartfelt 'Isaiah' Loses Its Way." *Boston Herald* (March 17): sec. SCE: S03.

Verrier, Nancy Newton. 1994. *The Primal Wound: Understanding the Adopted Child.* Baltimore: Gateway Press, Inc.

Vieni, Miriam. 1975. "Transracial Adoption Is a Solution Now." *Social Work* 20(5) (September): 419–21.

Vobejda, Barbara. 1994. "Legislation Fans Flames of Heated Interracial-Adoption Debate." *Washington Post* (March 19): A4.

Wallace, Anthony F. C. 1970. *Culture and Personality*. New York: Random House.

Wallerstein, Judith S. and Sandra Blakeslee. 1989. *Second Chances: Men, Women, and Children a Decade After Divorce*. New York: Tickner and Fields.

Washington, Mary Helen. 1998. "Disturbing the Peace: What Happens to American Studies If You Put African American Studies at the Center? Presidential Address to the American Studies Association, October 29, 1997." *American Quarterly* 50(1) (March): 1–23.

Wasson, Valentina P. 1950. *The Chosen Baby*. Philadelphia: J. B. Lippincott Company.

Watson, Julia. 1996. "Ordering the Family: Genealogy as Autobiographical Pedigree." In *Getting a Life: Everyday Uses of Autobiography*, edited by Sidonie Smith and Julia Watson. Minneapolis: University of Minnesota Press.

Watson, Lawrence C., and Maria-Barbara Watson-Franke. 1985. *Interpreting Life Histories: An Anthropological Inquiry*. New Brunswick: Rutgers University Press.

Wegar, Katarina. 1997. *Adoption, Identity, and Kinship: The Debate over Sealed Birth Records*. New Haven: Yale University Press.

Weiss, Michael J. 1994. "Love Conquers All." *Washingtonian* 30(1) (October): 98–107.

Welkos, Robert W. 1995. "Marketing the Movie through a Minefield." *Los Angeles Times* (March 17): sec. F(1).

Weston, Kath. 1995. "Forever Is a Long Time: Romancing the Real in Gay Kinship Ideologies." In *Naturalizing Power: Essays in Feminist Cultural Analysis*, edited by Sylvia Yanagisako and Carol Delaney. New York: Routledge.

Wheeler, David L. 1993. "Black Children, White Parents: The Difficult Issue of Transracial Adoption." *Chronicle of Higher Education* (15 September): A8–10.

Will, George. 1993. "Underwriting Family Breakdown." *Washington Post* (November 18): Editorial page.

Williams, Gregory Howard. 1995. *Life on the Color Line: The True Story of a White Boy Who Discovered He Was Black*. New York: Dutton.

Williams, Lucy A. 1995. "Race, Rat Bites, and Unfit Mothers: How Media Discourse Informs Welfare Legislation Debate." *Fordham Urban Law Journal* 22 (summer): 1159, 1164–66.

Williams, Patricia. 1991. *The Alchemy of Race and Rights: Diary of a Law Professor*. Cambridge: Harvard University Press.

Wilson, William Julius. 1996. *When Work Disappears: The World of the New Urban Poor.* New York: Alfred A. Knopf.

Winant, Howard. 1993. "Amazing Race: Recent Writing on Racial Politics and Theory." *Socialist Review* 23(2): 161–83.

———. 1994. *Racial Conditions: Politics, Theory, Comparisons.* Minneapolis: University of Minnesota Press.

Wing, Adrien Katherine. 1997. *Critical Race Feminism: A Reader.* New York: New York University Press.

Wong, Sau-ling C. 1994. "Diverted Mothering: Representations of Caregivers of Color in the Age of 'Multiculturalism.'" In *Mothering: Ideology, Experience, and Agency,* edited by Evelyn Nakano Glenn, Grace Change, and Linda Rennie Forcey. New York: Routledge.

Yanagisako, Sylvia, and Carol Delaney, ed. 1995a. *Naturalizing Power: Essays in Feminist Cultural Analysis.* New York: Routledge.

———. 1995b. "Naturalizing Power." In *Naturalizing Power: Essays in Feminist Cultural Analysis,* edited by Sylvia Yanagisako and Carol Delaney. New York: Routledge.

Zack, Naomi. 1993. *Race and Mixed Race.* Philadelphia: Temple University Press.

———., ed. 1995. *American Mixed Race: The Culture of Microdiversity.* Lanham: Rowman and Littlefield.

Zastrow, Charles H. 1979. *Outcome of Black Children-White Parents Transracial Adoptions.* San Francisco: R & E Research.

Zelizer, Viviana A. 1985. *Pricing the Priceless Child: The Changing Social Value of Children.* Princeton: Princeton University Press.

INDEX

McRoy, Ruth, 52–53
Malinowski, Bronislaw, 30
Mandela, Nelson, 94
Margolis, Seth J., 136
Marked, 38, 48
Matching: in adoption, 20, 32, 35, 41, 56
"Matriarchal" culture, 163
May, Elaine Tyler, 34
Media, 68, 71, 74; and family, 162; and
  politics, 158; representations of adoptees'
  identities, 32; representations of race, 91;
  109; representations of searches and re-
  unions, 100–101, 109, 113; representa-
  tions of transracial adoption, 139
Medical history, 99
Meigs, Anna, 31
MEPA (Multiethnic Placement Act),
  22–24
"Mestizo," 78
Metalanguage of race, 90
Metzenbaum, Senator Howard, 22, 142
Mexican, 38, 54–56, 59, 76, 107, 145,
  168, 186, 187
Minstrelsy, 72
"Mixed-race" children: in adoption system
  in 1950s, 35
"Mixed-race" couples, children of, 14
Modell, Judith, 114
Morrison, Toni, 178, 181
Moynihan, Daniel Patrick, 162, 173–174
Multicultural identity, 11, 14, 64, 77, 84
Multiethnic Placement Act (MEPA): con-
  gressional consideration of, 142; intro-
  duction and passage, 22; premise of, 152;
  public debate about 133, 140
Multiple consciousness, 75
Multiracial: adoptees, 2, 78, 64; communi-
  ties 96, 156; families, 156
Murray, Charles, 160, 162, 164–167, 174,
  180

National Association of Black Social Workers (NABSW), 3, 50, 140–141, 147; and
  adoption legislation, 156; and existing
  research on transracial adoption, 5; 1972
  statement against transracial adoption,
  153, 155
National Urban League, 156
Native American children, 46
Native ethnographers, adoptees as, 8
Nature-nurture: definitions of kinship, 32;

explanations for identity, 15, 25, 39, 127,
  171–172
Non-identifying information, 36, 38, 42,
  59–60, 168, 185
Nu, 31–32

Omi, Michael, 54, 179
"One drop rule," 37
Oppression, 64, 101; racial, 165, 179
Orphanage, 81, 166–167
Otherness, 90
"Out of wedlock births," concern in wel-
  fare legislation, 23, 160, 162, 164–165,
  178

Parental rights, 114
Parham, T. A., 76
"Pass," 41, 45, 155, 172
Personal Responsibility Act: and adoption,
  138; and block grants, 22; and "illegiti-
  macy," 22–24, 133, 160–161
Peters, Marie Ferguson, 66
Peterson, Carla, 174, 176, 180
"Political correctness," 5
Politics of identity, 54
Poster, Mark, 142
Poverty: cycle of, 146; and foster care, 149,
  190; and "illegitimacy," 162, 170; inter-
  generational, 145, 180; regulating repro-
  ductive behavior as means to reduce,
  17,72, 123; and women, 137–138; and
  work and family, 167
Pregnant teenagers, 46
"Primal wounds," 109, 112
Procreation, idealization of, 34
"Productive citizens": and socialization, 24,
  134, 158, 164–165, 167, 169, 178, 180
Public policy: adoption and welfare, 63,
  134; and American studies, 188; and
  child welfare, 2 169; and "culture of
  poverty," 145; and families, 146; identity,
  15, 100, 112, 169, 172, 187; and narrative, 133; and transracial adoption, 171

Racial categories, 79, 92, 191
Racial difference, salience of, 25, 49, 60,
  91, 92, 105, 147, 176, 179
Racial equality, 157
Racial–ethnic identity, 57, 75, 187
Racial gaze, 90
Racial identity, 3, 26, 37, 53, 142, 185,

ABOUT THE AUTHOR

Sandra Patton is Visiting Assistant Professor of Women's Studies at the University of Minnesota.